Wrestling

with the

Angel

Books by David Patterson

Open Wounds
Hebrew Language and Jewish Thought
Along the Edge of Annihilation
Sun Turned To Darkness
The Greatest Jewish Stories Ever Told
When Learned Men Murder
Pilgrimage of a Proselyte
Exile
The Shriek of Silence
In Dialogue and Dilemma with Elie Wiesel
Literature and Spirit
The Affirming Flame
Faith and Philosophy

Wrestling

with the

Angel

Toward a Jewish Understanding of the Nazi
Assault on the Name

by David Patterson

First Edition 2006

Published in the United States by
Paragon House
1925 Oakcrest Aveune
Suite 7
St. Paul, MN 55113

Cover image: Jacob Wrestling with the Angel by Gustave Doré (1832-83).

Library of Congress Cataloging-in-Publication Data

Patterson, David, 1948-
  Wrestling with the angel : toward a Jewish understanding of the Nazi assault on the Name / by David Patterson.-- 1st ed.
    p. cm.
  Includes bibliographical references.
  ISBN 1-55778-845-6 (pbk. : alk. paper) 1. Holocaust, Jewish (1939-1945) 2. God (Judaism)--Name. 3. Names, Personal--Psychological aspects. 4. Jews--Identity. 5. Antisemitism--History. I. Title.
  D804.3.P3777 2006
  940.53'18--dc22
                                              2005037742

Manufactured in the United States of America
10 9 8 7 6 5 4 3 2 1

The paper used in this publication meets the minimum requirements of American National Standard for Information Sciences—Permanence of Paper for Printed Library Materials, ANSIZ39.48-1984.

For current information about all releases from Paragon House,
visit the web site at http://www.paragonhouse.com

For Gerri

Acknowledgement

I would like to express my gratitude to Paragon House editor Rosemary Yokoi for her good work and valuable assistance in the publication of this volume.

CONTENTS

INTRODUCTION

WRESTLING WITH THE ANGEL

They will even take away our name: and if we want to keep it,
we will have to find in ourselves the strength to do so.

—Primo Levi, *Survival in Auschwitz*

ॐ

ON THE NIGHT BEFORE JACOB WAS TO RECONCILE with his brother Esau and return to the land of his birth, the Angel of Death fell upon him, and the two of them wrestled until dawn. Jacob overcame the Angel and would not release him until he obtained a blessing from the unearthly being. The blessing began with a question: "What is your name?"

And the man answered, "Jacob."

To which the Angel of Death replied, "No longer will you be called Jacob. Henceforth you will be called Israel, for you have struggled against G-d and humanity, and you have prevailed" (see Genesis 32:25–31).

What can it mean for Jacob to have "struggled against G-d *[Elokim]* and humanity?" The Lubavitcher Rebbe Menachem Mendel Schneerson, z"l, offers the following insight: "'Elokim' in this context means 'angels' [cf. *Chullin* 92a], and generally connotes the 'seventy heavenly princes' through whom flow the Divine emanations which sustain physical existence, and who thereby act to conceal G-dliness. 'Men' ['humanity'] signifies a still greater concealment, for men are capable of denigrating the Jew for performing G-d's will, and this is a harder concealment to bear. For this reason, the first paragraph of the entire Shulchan Aruch warns us 'not to be ashamed of men who ridicule.' And this is the basis of the whole of a Jew's service—to break down the concealment of G-d."[1] No place was the denigration of the Jew by men more pronounced than in the time of the Shoah. And at no time was the concealment of G-d greater. How does a Jew in the post-Holocaust era break down the concealment of G-d, of the One whom we call "the Name"? By assuming his own name, the name of Israel. That is why the Jew—then as now—is faced with wrestling from the angel the name of Israel.

There is, however, another question that arises in the account of Jacob's wrestling with the angel, especially in the post-Holocaust era: What does it mean to say he "prevailed"? The word translated as "prevailed" is *vatukhal,* a cognate of *takhlit,* meaning "aim" or "purpose." Which is to say: He received a renewed meaning and mission, a renewed soul, by wrestling a new name from the Angel. What, then, is the difference between Jacob and Israel? The psalmist states it this way: "He [G-d] has established a testimony in Jacob and placed a teaching [Torah] in Israel" (Psalms 78:5). In the wrestling we have the testimony; in the name we have the teaching. And the teaching is both a summons and a blessing. Wrestling a blessing from the Angel, Jacob attained meaning and purpose—attained a teaching, a Torah—by attaining a name, the name *Yisrael,* or Israel. Thus receiving that name, Jacob received a summons. For the name Yisrael, Rashi points out, is a cognate of *serarah,* which denotes a blessing received through "noble and open conduct" (see Rashi's commentary on Genesis 32:29). Which means: In order to attain the name of Israel, the Jew must live according to the teaching of the Name. Thus the name and the Name, with the *N* writ large, are interconnected. Especially in the post-Holocaust era.

In the time of the Shoah the Jewish people wrestled incessantly with the Angel of Death. It was an age of assault not only upon the body but also upon the soul of Israel, the soul attained as a blessing and a name. Therefore the Nazi affliction of the Jewish soul entailed an assault against the blessing and the name, both human and divine, an assault against understanding and origin, against meaning and redemption. The Rabbi of Shilev understood this point even as he and his fellow Jews awaited their turn in the gas chambers of Birkenau. "Can't you see," he addressed a man named Ferber, "G-d's spirit hovering here now above this Destruction and Creation? Can't you feel that Jacob—in our bones—now wrestles with the

Angel? We are the sinew of his thigh vein in this struggle!"

And Ferber asked him, "Rabbi of Shilev, for whose sake does Jacob wrestle with the Angel, if his children did not cross the river, but stayed here in the blackness of the night?"

And the Rabbi answered, "From the very blackness of this night Jacob will bring forth the name 'Israel!'"[2]

And from the blackness of those ashes. For the *Zohar* tells us that the dust raised when Jacob wrestled the name "Israel" from the Angel "was not ordinary dust, but ashes, the residue of fire" (*Zohar* I, 170a).

The camps and ghettos of the concentrationary universe have been dismantled, but it remains to be seen whether Jacob will indeed wrestle a blessing and a name from the Angel of Death: The wrestling for a blessing and a name—for a remembrance and a name, a *yad vashem*—continues. This unprecedented affliction of the soul has led to an unprecedented confusion among the Jews over who they are and what they mean. Perhaps at no other time in our millennial history has a Jew made a statement like the one made in the Israeli documentary on Zionism *Pillar of Fire*. In that film a Holocaust survivor introduces himself by saying, "My name, when I can remember it, is…" *When I can remember it…!* We are not speaking here of a victim of amnesia or senility; this is not a case of absentmindedness. Therefore one might wonder: How is it that a person can forget his name? And yet that was precisely what the Nazis contrived in their obliteration of the soul of the Jewish people: the obliteration of the name and the memory of the Name in a tearing of the name from the soul.

This tearing of the name from the soul took its first concrete form in 1938, when the Nazis added the name *Israel* to every Jewish male and the name *Sarah* to every Jewish female in Germany. In the former we have the obliteration of the name of a people, in the latter the obliteration of the origin. In both we have an assault not only on the Jews of Germany but also on the Name Himself. For, according to a Jewish tradition, mothers and fathers do not make up names for their children; rather, they are granted a moment of prophetic insight, when it is revealed to them what G-d has named the soul. Thus, presuming to name the Jews of Germany, the Nazis take their first step toward the usurpation of the Name, as if to say, "You think the G-d of Israel has named you? You are wrong: *We* have named you and thus have chosen you after the image and likeness of our choosing."

In the camps, of course, the obliteration of the Name of the Holy One through an erasure of the names of His chosen ones assumed dimensions that only evil could conceive.

Indeed, the memory of the assault on the soul through the assault on the name is central to the testimony of many camp survivors. Germaine Tillion, for example, remembers being stripped of her name upon her arrival at Ravensbrück: "All we had now were a few filthy rags which didn't belong to us—and a number."[3] Jewish tradition teaches that the name and the soul, the name and the person, are of a piece.[4] The substance of the name of the human being, her very I, derives from the One known as *HaShem,* "the Name," who alone can say "I."[5] When the number takes over the name, it is not just the word but also the *holiness* and the *humanity* attached to the word that is assailed. Inscribing the number on the body— no, forcing it *into* the body, *under* the skin, and indelibly into the core of the body—is the first step toward draining the body of its soul, which is the divine image of the Name. In her memoir Sara Nomberg-Przytyk says as much: "In Auschwitz we were just numbers, without faces or souls."[6] And so through the number the Nazis made the Jew into a *Stück,* that is, a "piece" or a "unit."[7] In the parlance of the Party, not a single human being was murdered at Auschwitz—"units" were merely "processed."

Reducing the person to nothing more than an object to be disposed of, the number is the first weapon drawn in the ontological war to slay the human being by slaying all blessing that derives from beyond being. As it is taught in the Talmud: "Blessing is not found in something weighed, nor in something measured, nor in something counted" (*Bava Metzia* 42a). And numbers are precisely the language—or the antilanguage—of weight, measurement, and enumeration. Robbed of his name and marked with a number, the human being is robbed of his life and his humanity. "A serial number," Sim Kessel states in his memoir, "dispenses you from having had a name, having had a soul, having had a life."[8] Thus, seeking the recovery of their humanity, the authors of numerous memoirs set out to recover a name by remembering a number. For example:

Elie Wiesel: I became A-7713. After that I had no other name.[9]

Miklos Nyiszli: Henceforth I would be, merely, KZ prisoner Number A 8450.[10]

Sara Zyskind:	Mine was 55091—my new name from now on.[11]
Alexander Donat:	I looked at my number: 7,115. From that moment I ceased to be a man.[12]
Rudolf Vrba:	That, indeed, was the last time I used my name…for now I was prisoner number 44070.[13]
Nathan Shapell:	A filthy needle…erased Natan Schapelski from the human race and brought into being *Häftling* 134138.[14]
Olga Lengyel:	I was number "25,403." I still have it on my right arm and shall carry it with me to the grave.[15]
Moshe Sandberg:	We ceased to be human beings with family names…. In my metamorphosis I was No. 124753.[16]

"Ceased to be a man," "erased from the human race," "ceased to be human beings": Memory clutches at such phrases in an attempt to articulate the death that the survivor survives but never lives through, for it follows him from the massive grave that was Planet Auschwitz to his own grave. Inscribed with the number, the human being does not merely experience the Shoah; rather, the Shoah "experiences" the human being to become part of his essence and his experience ever after. He leaves Auschwitz, but he does not leave it behind: The prisoner is not in Auschwitz—Auschwitz is in the prisoner. "This is an indelible mark," the tattoo declares, "you will never leave here."[17] In her memoir Judith Dribben explains: "Once the number was there, there was no chance to escape. It bound us more strongly than any chain. It was something that could only be removed together with a piece of flesh."[18] Through the needle Auschwitz invades the flesh and stains the image of the human being; through the flesh it enters his soul and substance.

In *Survival in Auschwitz*, Primo Levi dwells at length on the significance of the number in the antiworld, describing the details of the tattooing process as well as the aftermath of the process. Prisoners would not be fed, for example, without first showing their numbers and repeating them in German: Not only was the name effaced, but the Jew is himself effaced in this recitation in a tongue alien to his essence. Not only is the number alien to the man, but the German language in which the number is spoken adds to the Jew's alienation from himself by removing his new "name" from his native tongue.

Levi reveals much in his remarks about the imposition of the number and the loss of the name, and how they are tied to the assault on the soul. First of all, the eclipse of the name is tied to the breakdown of the body: Showing the number in exchange for food, the prisoner declares his name-lessness and his nothingness as he wastes away on the meager ration. "You must watch over your name and your soul," says Rabbi Nachman of Bres-lov.[19] Sensing this, the Nazis assailed the Jewish soul by forcing these men and women to watch over a number rather than a name.

Living in Auschwitz, then, is precisely like "living" in a grave. And it continues to cast its shadow over us—indeed, its shadow is within us, cast to the inside, despite all appearances. Remember the disaster that occurred in Chernobyl on 26 April 1986, when a cloud of radioactive material was released into the air from one of the chimneys at a nuclear power plant? Two weeks later radiation levels in Montana were up. In fact, one can determine air pollution levels for any given year by taking a plug of snow and ice from Antarctica. In the time of the Shoah the smoke of human remains—of the Jewish dead—bellowed into the air not for one day but for a thousand days, not from one chimney but from dozens. The winds have spread the ashes of those 6 million Jews over the face of the earth, east to west, pole to pole. They inhabit the soil from which we harvest our bread. They abide in the bread we put into our mouths. In a grim eucharistic union we bind ourselves to those ashes each time we place a piece of bread in our mouths. As we are made of that bread, so are we—all of humanity—made of those ashes: We are the grave to those denied a grave. The ashes nag. And in their nagging abides a nagging question: What is your name?[20]

Having become a vessel of the dead, we find that the Angel of Death has become our constant companion. And so we wrestle with the Angel with a Thousand Eyes, the Angel as yellow as the star that Nazis stamped on the Jews.[21] Only this time the Angel comes not to take us but to leave us with new eyes, through which we may gaze into the mirror of our soul. And through which the Angel puts to us a question, in keeping with the ancient Jewish legend. According to the legend, when we die and lie in the grave, the Angel of Death comes to us so that he might bring us into the presence of the Holy One. But in order to draw nigh unto the Divine Presence, we must correctly answer a certain question. The question is the same for all, but for each the answer is different. And so, with all of his eyes gazing upon us, the Angel poses the fearsome question, the very question he put to Jacob when they wrestled till dawn: "What is your name?"[22] But what, indeed, do we know when we know our name? To know our name is to know the names of those who confer a name upon us, the names of our mother and father. It means knowing a tradition borne by those who have borne our names before us; it means knowing a teaching that harbors our future and our mission in life, as inscribed in our name; it means recognizing that we are called by name and must answer to our name. Hence Rabbi Chayim ben Attar teaches that one who knowingly violates G-d's commandment forfeits his original name (*Or HaChayim* on Genesis 3:30). Asking our name, the Angel tries to establish something about our being that is intimately tied to our doing: Knowing our name, like knowing G-d,[23] means knowing what must be done.

There, however, lies the problem: What must be done? For in order to answer this question, we must first answer another question: What has been done? The purpose of this book is to respond to these questions.

Examining the "Modern and Postmodern Dimensions of the Holocaust," chapter 1 argues that, in accordance with the modern and postmodern impetus to rid our thinking of all transcendent absolutes, the assault on the Name in the person of the Jews has its seeds in what is often glorified as "the Enlightenment." Making the Holocaust thinkable begins with thinking G-d—and, by association, the Jews—out of the picture, a process that is traceable to the European Enlightenment in general and to the German Enlightenment in particular. Once G-d is eliminated and thought is equated with being, the name of the human being, which emanates from G-d, is also eliminated, so that the individual becomes a specimen evolved from other species—a member of this race or that culture, as postmodern thought would have it—and not a unique child of the unique G-d.[24] To be sure, in the postmodern era, a human being is not even a "higher life form" but is merely another life form, without any claim to any particular sanctity. Instead of the Creation that Creator pronounces to be "very good" (Genesis 1:31), we have a merely accidental Being, which has no inherent value. Learning becomes scientific, and learned men become murderers.

This process, I argue, not only contributed to the Holocaust but also continues in the post-Holocaust age, dominating more and more the study of the Holocaust itself. As postmodernist approaches to the Shoah proliferate, so does the thinking that would think the Jew out of the event, so that he is nothing more than one victim among many, faceless and nameless. The assault on the name, then, is an anti-Judaic, postmodern phenomenon with roots in modern thought. The Nazis did not invent it; they simply pursued such thinking to its logical end, with many, if not most, of the great intellects of Germany talking the lead. In the post-Holocaust age we find an implicit complicity with the Nazi agenda, inasmuch as the Jew and what the Jewish people signify by their presence in the world have been removed from the scholars' response to the Holocaust. Wrestling a name from the Angel, then, would entail wrestling the Jew back into that response.

Because the core of this anti-Judaic thinking lies in the effort to get rid of G-d by getting rid of His Chosen, chapter 2, "The Harrowing of the Holy One," begins with a consideration of the assault on the Divine image within the human being, which is an assault on *HaShem,* the Name. For just as human sanctity is derived from the Divine image, so is the human name an emanation of the Divine Name: According to Jewish teaching, the soul comes into being as the Name utters its name. It is written in the *Zohar,* for example, that the soul originates "in fire, being an emanation from the Divine Throne" (*Zohar* II, 211b), and that fire is the fire of Torah, which is itself the Name of G-d, as the great sage Nachmanides has taught: "The entire Torah is composed of Names of the Holy One blessed be He."[25] Because, according to the commandments of Torah, our most direct relation to the Holy One is through the embrace of our fellow human beings, the assault on G-d takes the form not just of killing people but also of killing the *humanity* of people. Hence the subtitle of Levi's *Survival in Auschwitz:* "The Nazi Assault on Humanity." A key point in this connection is the calculated first-targeting of children and the elderly, the living vessels of the Jewish future and the Jewish past, of Jewish meaning and Jewish memory.

Since the sanctity of life unfolds in the life *time* of our future and our past, chapter 2 goes on to consider the Nazi assault on time itself. This assault comes in an attempt to slay the eternal in time by removing the holy days from human time, those days when the Divine Presence grows more intense, as we summon the memory of the past for the sake of the future. Particularly important to this portion of the chapter is the witness of the Holocaust diaries that measured those holy days. Next, moving from the diaries to the memoirs, we have the struggle of the survivors to recover time and the holy in time through what I call "the memory of G-d." Central to this memory is the memory of one's own name, which in turn is connected to the return of meaning to the word; if words have no meaning, as it happened in the concentrationary universe, then people have no names—and vice versa. And a key to returning meaning to the word, it is argued, is returning prayer to the soul. For prayer is about the memory of G-d, taken both as His memory of us and our memory of Him. The pivotal figure in the transmission of that memory is the child, who in Jewish tradition is the most immediate vessel of holiness, memory, name, and time. Therefore this chapter concludes with an examination of the Nazi murder of the Jewish child.

Wherever there is a child, of course, there is a mother. To be sure, according to the mystical tradition, G-d the Creator is best understood as the Supernal Mother (see, for example, *Zohar* III, 65b); indeed, in our prayers we often use the feminine form of the Hebrew "you" when addressing G-d.[26] Chapter 3, "The Desecration of the Origin," then, determines what the calculated obliteration of the Jewish mother has to do with the assault on the Name. Because, for the Nazis, there is no crime greater than the *being* of the Jew, there is no criminal greater than the one who brings the Jew into being, the first to utter the name of the Jew with the love that only a mother can offer. After a consideration of some fundamental Jewish teachings concerning woman and mother, the chapter examines a key text, *Shivitti: A Vision* by Ka-tzetnik 135633, in which the author discovers what he calls the "key" to Auschwitz: It is a memory—or a vision—of his mother going to be gassed. Proceeding from Ka-tzetnik's vision, the chapter then explores in detail the Nazi assault on the mothers of Israel in order to explain why this dimension of the Shoah is so crucial to an understanding of the distinctively Nazi assault on *HaShem*. I draw both from diaries and from memoirs in this portion of chapter 3.

The last section of the chapter, however, draws only on memoirs, as it must, in order to get that core of the horror perpetrated upon the mothers of Israel. This horror lies not in the gassing of Jewish mothers but rather in their forced transformation into antimothers fashioned after the image of the Nazis themselves: In order to save the lives of their fellow Jews, women in the camps were forced to kill newborns so as to save the babies' mothers. Here we see the Nazi assault on the souls not only of the mothers of Israel but of any Jew who tried to save those mothers. What we have in this instance is a desecration of the very origin of the Jewish people as an origin of what is ethical and moral. Therefore this chapter closes with an investigation into the intractable moral dilemma of whether such killing of infants to save mothers can have any justification.

Just as the Shoah is distinguished by the obliteration of life before it is life, so do we find in this event the obliteration of death before it is death. The Nazis did not want the Jews to be dead; they did not want them to *be* anything. Setting out to kill the soul before they killed the body of Israel, they set out to erase every predicate from the Jew. Thus the concentrationary universe became a realm in which even death was denied the Jew in the erasure of his name, a realm with "The Death of the Angel of Death," as chapter 4 is called. I have already noted the Jewish teaching that when we lie in the grave, the Angel of Death comes to us in order to ask us our name. During the Shoah, however, the Jews were deprived of their graves. Some lost the graves they had had for centuries; others were transformed into columns of smoke and ash that transformed the sky into a mass grave in an overturning of heaven and earth. As Miklos Nyiszli stated it, Auschwitz was a "cemetery of millions, a cemetery without a single grave."[27] That is why, unlike death, we cannot situate Auschwitz within life. And so the question arises: If we must wrestle a name and a blessing from the Angel of Death, with whom do we wrestle when the Angel is no more?

But there is more. In order to understand how death can be obliterated, this chapter explores the implications of Primo Levi's remark on the *Muselmänner,* saying, "One hesitates to call them living: one hesitates to call their death death."[28] A man's death is not death when, having been rendered utterly nameless and thus removed from the Name, a man is not a man. Simply stated, death is no longer death when a name is no longer a name. This horror of the Shoah is the horror of no exit; it is the horror of what Lévinas calls the "there is" that will not go away, an insomnia that will not be overcome. This horror, he says, "is a participation in the *there is,* in the *there is* which returns in the heart of every negation, in the *there is* that has 'no exit.' It is, if we may say so, the impossibility of death, the universality of existence even in its annihilation."[29] Like the "there is" that is merely there, the man with no name is merely there, without exit because he has no name, nothing to be inscribed on a memorial stone, no marker or sign. Not even martyrdom is available to him. Therefore chapter 4 addresses the problem of martyrdom.

Finally, chapter 4 explains why the deprivation of death that comes with the annihilation of the name renders any return from the Kingdom of Night at best problematic. If there is no dying, there is no getting it over with or putting it behind us, no cemetery where we may pay our respects and then go our way. The term *liberation,* then, is not only misleading; it is yet another example of a word stripped of its meaning.

Having made the argument concerning what has been done, the investigation comes to chapter 5, "Word and Meaning: A Memory and a Name," which addresses the matter of what it all means and therefore what must be done about it. Many scholars, both Jewish and Christian, call for a *tikkun olam,* a "mending of the world," but most who issue this call either know or say nothing about the origins of the term and what it means; this chapter explains what this distinctively Jewish notion has to do with what must be done. Among other things, it entails a *teshuvah*—not a "repentance," as the word is often mistranslated, but a "return" and a "response" in the wake of what Alvin Rosenfeld calls "the emptiness and silence of an imposed Absence."[30] Therefore, after a brief consideration of the modern and postmodern interest in language, this chapter discusses the problem of silence and the return of meaning to the word. It examines how those who were in the eye of the whirlwind sought to retrieve a word and a name from the abyss of wordlessness and thereby restore a memory and a name.

Moving from the time within the event to the time after, the chapter examines ways in which the imposed silence of the Shoah becomes a speaking silence, so that the Jew may once again wrestle his name from the Angel—whether the Angel of Death or the Angel of Murder—and become Israel, "one who struggles with G-d." A key to this portion of the investigation is an analysis of how silence might "speak" from within the word and from beyond memory. The matter addressed here, in other words, is this: How can the word restore a memory and a name to the one for whom neither is ever settled? Responding to this question, the chapter closes with a reflection on the late-life memories of the last of the survivors and a consideration of the future of memory, which is a future of meaning—and the future of a name—for post-Holocaust Jewry.

The book concludes its wrestling with the Angel by returning once more to the Angel's question: What is your name? To be sure, it is the question that guides this entire inquiry. The aim here is not so much to answer the question as to ask it and to ask further. It is an effort to remember to ask. Therefore this investigation ends more with a reminder than with an answer.

Just one more point: Because the one wrestling with the Angel is the Jew, we seek a *Jewish* understanding of the Nazi assault on the Name (of the Holy One) and on the name (of the human being). "Jewish understanding" here is not to be taken to mean any view that any Jew may hold. Rather, Jewish understanding pertains to an outlook informed by Jewish teachings and traditions and in some sense devoted to Torah. Therefore, in addition to drawing upon the testimony of Jews who were there, the inquiry is guided by the holy texts and holy tongue of the Jewish people. For in those texts and in that tongue lies the root of who the Jews are. As Rabbi Adin Steinsaltz has said, "The soul of a [person] is the Divine speech that speaks the [person],"[31] and that speech unfolds in the holy texts and holy tongue. In this introduction, references to the Torah, *Zohar,* and midrashic texts as well to sages such as the Ramban (Nachmanides), Chayim ben Attar, and Nachman of Breslov provide an example of how the *sifrei kodesh,* or "holy books," will be incorporated into the investigation.

With regard to the *lashon hakodesh,* or holy tongue, a glance at two Hebrew words for the event will serve as an introductory example of what the language may reveal about the Holocaust. The first is a Hebrew word that in fact has a Yiddish usage: It is *Churban.* In ancient times the most traumatizing events to plunge the Jews into the abyss of exile were the destructions of the two Temples, first in 586 B.C.E. and then in 70 C.E. In the holy tongue this "destruction" is known as the *Churban,* which is a cognate of *cherev,* the word for "sword." Both words are from the verb *charav,* which means to "destroy" or to "lay waste." Referring to the devastation wrought by the destruction of the Temple, *Churban* pertains to the loss of the Divine Presence, a loss of the Name, in the world. It signifies a radical assault on *HaShem* through a radical assault on His Chosen. Therefore, drawing on the Hebrew, the Yiddish language uses this same word to refer to history's most devastating assault on G-d through the extermination of the Jews: the Holocaust.

In Hebrew usage there is another word that refers to the abyss that since 1945 characterizes the exile of world and humanity: It is Shoah. To be sure, Shoah means "abyss." It also means "pit," "destruction," and "ruin." And it means "Holocaust." Connected to this horrendous noun is another noun, *shav*, which translates as "lie" or "nothingness." And the verb *shaah* means to "become desolate," to "be devastated"; in its *hitpael* or reflexive form, *hishtaah*, it means to "wonder," to "be astonished," or to "gaze in wonder or awe." What is the Holocaust? Exceeding the parameters of genocide, it is the calculated, carefully implemented imposition of the abyss that is *Shoah* upon the world. It is a spiritual devastation and desolation that follows us into our affluence. It is the lie made truth, the unreal made real, the return of the world to the nothingness, to the *shav*, that the Jews now struggle to overcome in a recovery of the Name. It is the astonishment not over what is unimaginable but over everything imaginable, and that is exactly what the Nazis did in the process of undoing the image of the human being: not the unimaginable but everything imaginable. For there was no limiting principle at work in their actions, hence no possibility of going too far. On the contrary, they could never go far enough—there lay the dimension of the infinite in their assault on the Infinite One, on *HaShem*, the G-d of Abraham, Isaac, and Jacob, whom the Angel blessed and named Israel.

As the Angel wrestled with Jacob, it is related in the Midrash, "He put his finger to the earth, whereupon the earth began spurting fire. Said Jacob to him: 'Would you terrify me with that! Why, I am altogether of that stuff.' Thus it is written, *And the house of Jacob shall be a fire* (Obadiah 1:18)" (*Bereshit Rabbah* 77:2). To be sure, the children of Jacob are made of that stuff. Just as the Torah is made of black fire on white fire (*Tanchuma Bereshit* 1; *Devarim Rabbah* 3:12; *Shir HaShirim Rabbah* 5:11:6; *Zohar* II, 226b), so does fire "form the basis of the soul," as Rabbi Chayim ben Attar states it (*Or HaChayim* on Genesis 23:2). After Auschwitz that fire takes on a new dimension. In the post-Holocaust wrestling with the Angel, the earth erupts in a strange fire, a fire of which we now are made and a fire from which me must now be delivered. Just as Jacob wrestled a name from the Angel, we must now wrestle a name from the fire that would consume the Name. Thus we may better understand at least one implication of Elie

Wiesel's insight that fire was the dominant image of the Event.[32] It is a dominant image because it lies at the core of the task that confronts us as we continue to wrestle with the Angel at Peniel. And, as the Rashbam, Rabbi Shmuel ben Meir, notes in his commentary on Genesis 32, to know that our name is Israel is to know not just our identity but also its inescapability, which is the inescapability of wrestling with G-d and humanity.[33] When the dawn will come no one knows. But it is clear that we must wrestle until it does and thereby merit the blessing and the name of Israel.

Notes

1. Menachem M. Schneerson, *Torah Studies,* adapted by Jonathan Sacks, 2nd ed. (London: Lubavitch Foundation, 1986), 45.

2. Ka-tzetnik 135633, *Kaddish,* trans. Nina De-Nur (New York: Algemeiner Associates, 1998), 97–98.

3. Germaine Tillion, *Ravensbrück,* trans. Gerald Satterwhite (Garden City: Doubleday, 1975), 6.

4. See, for example, the *Sefer Chasidim* (244) of the medieval sage Rabbi Yehuda HeChasid; see also Nachman of Breslov, *Tikkun,* trans. Avraham Greenbaum (Jerusalem: Breslov Research Institute, 1984), 103.

5. As the Zlotzover Maggid, Rabbi Yechiel Mikhal, taught, "The word *I* only G-d can utter." See Louis I. Newman, ed., *The Hasidic Anthology* (New York: Schocken Books, 1963), 423.

6. Sara Nomberg-Przytyk, *Auschwitz: True Tales from a Grotesque Land,* trans. Roslyn Hirsch (Chapel Hill: University of North Carolina Press, 1985), 15.

7. See, for example, Primo Levi, *Survival in Auschwitz: The Nazi Assault on Humanity,* trans. Stuart Woolf (New York: Simon & Schuster, 1996), 16.

8. Sim Kessel, *Hanged at Auschwitz,* trans. Melville and Delight Wallace (New York: Stein and Day, 1972), 169.

9. Elie Wiesel, *Night,* trans. Stella Rodway (New York: Hill & Wang, 1960), 51.

10. Miklos Nyiszli, *Auschwitz: A Doctor's Eyewitness Account,* trans. Tibere Kremer and Richard Seaver (New York: Fawcett Crest, 1960), 26.

11. Sara Zyskind, *Stolen Years,* trans. Margarit Inbar (Minneapolis: Lerner, 1981), 211.

12. Alexander Donat, *The Holocaust Kingdom* (New York: Holocaust Library, 1978), 168.

13. Rudolf Vrba and Alan Bestic, *I Cannot Forgive* (New York: Bantam, 1964), 78–79.

14. Nathan Shapell, *Witness To the Truth* (New York: David McKay, 1974), 116.

15. Olga Lengyel, *Five Chimneys* (London: Granada, 1972), 116.

16. Moshe Sandberg, *My Longest Year,* trans. S. C. Hyman (Jerusalem: Yad Vashem, 1968), 55.

17. Primo Levi, *The Drowned and the Saved*, trans. Raymond Rosenthal (New York: Vintage Books, 1988), 119.

18. Judith Dribben, *And Some Shall Live* (Jerusalem: Keter, 1969), 185.

19. Nachman of Breslov, *Advice*, trans. Avraham Greenbaum (Brooklyn: Breslov Research Institute, 1983), 301.

20. Arnošt Lustig states it more eloquently than I: "These ashes would be indestructible and immutable, they would not burn up into nothingness because they themselves were remnants of fire…. No one living would ever be able to escape them; these ashes would be contained in the milk that will be drunk by babies yet unborn and in the breasts their mothers offer them…. These ashes will be contained in the breath and expression of every one of us and the next time anybody asks what the air he breathes is made of, he will have to think about these ashes; they will be contained in books which haven't been written and will be found in the remotest regions of the earth where no human foot has ever trod; no one will be able to get rid of them, for they will be the fond, nagging ashes of the dead who died in innocence." See Arnošt Lustig, *A Prayer for Katerina Horovitzova*, trans. Jeanne Nemcova (New York: Harper & Row, 1973), 50–51.

21. See Saadia Gaon, *The Book of Belief and Opinions*, trans. Samuel Rosenblatt (New Haven: Yale University Press, 1976), 255–56. See also Talmud tractate *Avodah Zarah*, 20b.

22. Says Nachman of Breslov, "All a person's deeds are inscribed in his soul. That is why after death a person is asked if he remembers his name." See Nachman of Breslov, *Tikkun*, 102; see also Rabbi Nathan of Nemirov, *Rabbi Nachman's Wisdom: Shevachay HaRan and Sichos HaRan*, trans. Aryeh Kaplan, ed. Aryeh Rosenfeld (New York: A. Kaplan, 1973), 148.

23. Cf. Emmanuel Lévinas, *Difficult Freedom: Essays on Judaism*, trans. Sean Hand (Baltimore: Johns Hopkins University Press, 1990), 17. It is also edifying to note that in the Talmud the rabbis refer to the teaching of the truth about G-d from one generation to another as a "handing down of names" (see *Kiddushin* 71a).

24. As Franz Rosenzweig states it, "Evolution takes the place of man." See Franz Rosenzweig, *Understanding the Sick and the Healthy*, trans. Nahum Glatzer (Cambridge: Harvard University Press, 1999), 89.

25. Nachmanides, *Writings and Discourses*, vol. 1, trans. Charles B. Chavel (New York: Shilo, 1978), 112.

26. We open the *Kiddushah*, for example, with the words *nakedishakh venaaritsakh*, "We hallow and adore You," using the feminine endings for "You."

27. Nyiszli, *Auschwitz*, 151.

28. Levi, *Survival in Auschwitz,* 90.

29. Emmanuel Lévinas, *Existence and Existents,* trans. Alphonso Lingis (The Hague: Marinus Nijhoff, 1978), 61.

30. Alvin Rosenfeld, *A Double Dying: Reflections on Holocaust Literature* (Bloomington: Indiana University Press, 1980), 14–15.

31. Adin Steinsaltz, *The Sustaining Utterance: Discourses on Chasidic Thought,* trans. and ed. Yehuda Hanegbi (Northvale, NJ: Jason Aronson, 1989), 32.

32. See Elie Wiesel, *Evil and Exile,* trans. Jon Rothschild (Notre Dame: University of Notre Dame Press, 1990), 39.

33. See Jonathan Sacks, *Crisis and Covenant: Jewish Thought after the Holocaust* (Manchester, England: Manchester University Press, 1992), 274.

CHAPTER ONE

MODERN AND POSTMODERN DIMENSIONS OF THE HOLOCAUST

To think for oneself is a matter of seeking the highest touchstone
of truth in oneself (that is, in one's own reason); and the maxim
of thinking for oneself at all times constitutes *enlightenment.*
—Immanuel Kant, *What Is Orientation in Thinking?*

❧

"*COGITO, ERGO SUM,*" DECLARED RENÉ DESCARTES, "I
think, therefore I am" (*Meditationes de Prima Philosophia* 27). Thus
equating thinking with being, the man known as the father of modern Philosophy ushered in a new understanding of the human being, one
that equates the being of the human being with thought, and not with the
holy likeness of the Holy One. Since that time there has developed a certain philosophical stance that is hostile toward revealed religion in general
and toward Judaism in particular. But why Judaism?

For one thing, fundamental to Jewish teaching is that, in the words of
Rabbi Yechiel Mikhal, the Zlotzover Maggid, only G-d can say the word
I,[1] which is the first word in the first utterance at Mount Sinai. If at Mount
Sinai we have the Revelation of G-d as *Anokhi* or "I," then what sort of revelation do we have about the thinking human being? Rabbi Adin Steinsaltz
offers a helpful insight: "When a person contemplates this truth that He is
our very life [cf. Deuteronomy 30:20], then the thought takes us beyond

1

the fact of His greatness to the core of one's own self.... Thus, when we say, 'He is our life,' the intention here is not that He is the giver of life, but that He Himself is our life. When I search for the I in the body, I find the I of the soul; when I search for the I of the soul, I find the I of the Divine."[2] The premise for such thinking is that G-d is not the projection of my ego or my I-saying; rather I am a projection of the Divine I-saying. G-d says, "I," therefore I am. Which is to say: G-d commands me, therefore I am. While it is true that in his *Meditations on First Philosophy* Descartes "proves" the existence of G-d and the soul, his god is a philosophically determined "supreme being," and not the Creator of all being, who is otherwise than being. It is the god of the philosophers that Pascal invoked when he cried, "The G-d of Abraham, the G-d of Isaac, the G-d of Jacob, not the god of the philosophers."[3] It is much like the god that Spinoza identified with nature and that Newton relegated to the status of a cosmic maintenance man who made adjustments in nature when the Newtonian laws of motion did not quite fit.

Ushering in the Enlightenment, this line of thinking views the Torah not as the Word of G-d revealed to humanity through the Israelites but as another quaint and curious volume of forgotten lore. Any embrace of the G-d of Moses and His commandments is taken to be not only superstitious but also dangerous, since, it is supposed, the Scriptures can be used to justify all sorts of crimes that are unjustifiable before the high court of reason. Yes, many thousands of people have been murdered in the name of religion, but this prejudice derives from a distinctively modern myopia: We are so hostile toward the G-d of Abraham and those who embrace revealed biblical monotheism, that when we ask how the genocidal horror could happen, we immediately go looking for its "theological warrants."[4] Indeed, seeking to justify Enlightenment thinking, many people continue to espouse the cliché that "institutionalized" religion is responsible for more deaths than any other institution, agency, or ideology. Religion, we assume, is the cause of genocide. Religion, we assume, is the cause of war and murder. More often than not, we assume, it is in the name of G-d that people engage in mass murder and megamurder, genocide and democide. Therefore, says Leo Kuper, "A common characteristic of genocide is the presence of religious difference between perpetrators and victims,"[5] as if this difference were a necessary if not a sufficient cause of genocide.

As R. J. Rummel has demonstrated in *Death by Government,* however, this is simply not the case. Not a single pope or ayatollah can compete with Stalin, Mao, or Hitler. Of course, as we shall see, it may be argued that the likes of Hitler may tap into a religious fervor, but it is the fervor of a false religion. It has its myth, but it is empty of any theology of the commanding G-d of Abraham. While power and technology may be part of the reason why the pope cannot compete with Hitler, these differences are not definitive. Even Kuper concludes that "the role of sacred texts in genocidal conflict is variable and appreciably indeterminate."[6] And, coming to this conclusion, he demonstrates that he is an honest scholar: It is indeterminate because it does not hold up even under a cursory examination. The question is not whether there are religious differences between the two parties; the question, rather, is whether among the perpetrators there is a Divine, absolute prohibition against murder that would limit their actions even if they would like to kill more people. And neither modern nor postmodern thought can determine such an absolute.

By itself, hatred for another religious group is not enough to justify mass murder; it must be coupled with an ideology or worldview that places no limit on the extent of murder. Faulting biblical religion for mass murder, people often bring up the example of what Joshua did in Jericho. But if the killing in the Book of Joshua is problematic, it is the Divine prohibition against murder from Mount Sinai, and not our reason or sensitivity, that makes it so. Where, then, might one find a relation between "sacred" texts and genocide? *Mein Kampf* is an obvious example. And what is full-blown in *Mein Kampf* has its unwitting seeds in the seemingly innocuous philosophical texts that shape modern thinking. It is no coincidence that genocide is a distinctly modern phenomenon. And it is distinctively modern due as much to modern philosophy as to modern technology, as philosophical outlook determines the direction of scientific technology. Stalin, Mao, and Hitler—the twentieth century's top three megamurderers—do not come from nowhere. Steeped in certain ways of viewing the world and humanity, they emerge from a process of thinking G-d out of the picture, a process that is traceable to the European Enlightenment.

Seeds Planted in the Enlightenment

When struggling to identify the elements of Western civilization and German culture that contributed to the Holocaust, often the last place we look
is the philosophical tradition of the Enlightenment. After all, from the Enlightenment we have the principles of democratic government, civil rights,
scientific inquiry, organized education, technological advancement, and so
on. And it is true: without the Enlightenment we would have neither research hospitals nor human rights, neither high-tech computers nor space
flight. How then could such a movement, a movement that seems to have
glorified "man" and brought about so much good, have anything at all to
do with the Holocaust?

And yet, as Rabbi Jonathan Sacks has rightly pointed out,

> It is no accident that almost all the great continental phi-
> losophers of the eighteenth and nineteenth centuries—Vol-
> taire, Kant, Hegel, Schopenhauer and Nietzsche—deliv-
> ered sharp attacks on Judaism as an anachronism. Voltaire
> described it as a "detestable superstition." Kant called for
> its euthanasia. Hegel took Judaism as his model of a slave
> morality. Nietzsche fulminated against it as the "falsifica-
> tion" of all natural values. In the twentieth century, Sartre
> could see no content to Jewish existence other than the
> defiance of anti-Semitism. Martin Heidegger, the greatest
> German philosopher of his time, became an active Nazi.
> Modern Western philosophy, promising a new era of tol-
> erance, manifestly failed to extend that tolerance to Juda-
> ism and the Jews. Against this background, the transition
> from Enlightenment to Holocaust is less paradoxical than
> it might otherwise seem.[7]

Berel Lang adds this point: "There are few figures of the Enlightenment in
fact who in their common defense of toleration do not qualify that principle where the Jews are concerned. This fact alone would be significant for
assessing the Enlightenment in relation to its ideals; it becomes still more
significant in the light of evidence that this attitude toward the Jews was

not accidental or simply the recrudescence of earlier prejudices, but was engendered by the doctrines of the Enlightenment itself."[8]

To be sure, the lie of the thinking that promised tolerance to all was declared long before Rabbi Sacks and Berel Lang arrived at their insights. With the same clarity of vision that led him to declare that those who burn books will end by burning people, in 1834 Heinrich Heine, himself a child of the Enlightenment, wrote:

> The German revolution will not be milder and gentler because it was preceded by Kant's *Critique,* by Fichte's transcendental idealism, and even by the philosophy of nature. These doctrines have developed revolutionary forces that wait only for the day when they can erupt and fill the world with terror and admiration. There will be Kantians forthcoming who will hear nothing of piety in the visible world, and with sword and axe will mercilessly churn the soil of our European life, to exterminate the very last roots of the past. Armed Fichteans will enter the lists, whose fanaticism of will can be curbed neither by fear nor by self-interest.... But the most terrible of all would be natural philosophers..., [who] can call up the demoniac energies of ancient Germanic pantheism.... A play will be performed in Germany that will make the French Revolution seem like a harmless idyll in comparison.[9]

It turns out that, *in part,* the Holocaust happened not due to any breaking away from "these doctrines" of the Enlightenment, as Heine calls them, but precisely because the Nazis' chief instigators were so thoroughly versed in the German intellectual and cultural history that emerges from the Enlightenment. To be sure, Hans Sluga calls Johann Gottlieb Fichte "the first National Socialist philosopher."[10] One reason why he says this may be Fichte's famous comment on whether or not Jews should be given citizenship: "The only way to give them citizenship would be to cut off their heads in the same night in order to replace them with those containing no Jewish ideas."[11] The Fichteans to whom Heine refers are armed with Fichte's notion that "the real destiny of the human race...is *in freedom to make itself* what it really is originally."[12] No creation of the human being in the Divine image here. Rather, what we have is the free resolve of the human being to forge his or her own essence, after the image of a primal *Volk*—and later in the name of the Nazi *Führer.*

Emphasizing the self's autonomy, authenticity, and resolve, the thinking that arose in the Enlightenment and contributed to the Holocaust follows a clear line of development from Immanuel Kant onward. For Kant is the giant upon whose shoulders Fichte stood, whatever the differences between them. If the Cartesian *cogito* situates being within the thinking ego, the Kantian critique deduces everything from the thinking ego and thus, as Franz Rosenzweig astutely points out, "reduces the world to the perceiving self."[13] Far from glorifying the human being, however, the reduction of the world to the perceiving self is radically dehumanizing. "Corresponding to the Copernican turn of Copernicus which made man a speck of dust in the whole," says Rosenzweig, "is the Copernican turn of Kant, which, by way of compensation, placed him upon the throne of the world, much more precisely than Kant thought. To that monstrous degradation of man, costing him his humanity, this correction without measure was, likewise, at the cost of his humanity."[14] Insisting upon the creation of himself after his own image (as if he were there before he was there), the human being loses his human image. In the end he attempts to reshape and thus dehumanizes the *other* human being.

With the advent of German Enlightenment thinking, all values, moral and otherwise, are soon viewed as a product of either natural accident or human will, and nothing outside the self has any inherent or absolute value. Kant himself sets the example not only in his *Grounding for the Metaphysics of Morals*, where he understands autonomy to be the key to freedom,[15] but also in his *Anthropology from a Pragmatic Point of View*, where he ascribes certain inherent characteristics to various peoples of the world according the accidents of nature. Jews and people of color, of course, do not fare very well here.[16] One soon recognizes in this thinking the rudimentary ingredients of what is now termed "postmodernism," namely the idea that the "nature" of a human being is determined by race, gender, culture, and other accidents and that neither world nor humanity has any absolute meaning. And one soon realizes that the "postmodern period" does not arise in the "post-Holocaust period"; rather, it begins with a mode of thinking that contributed to the Holocaust and that led to the thinking of Germany's greatest thinker, the one who bridges modernism with postmodernism: the unrepentant, card-carrying Nazi, Martin Heidegger. With the emergence of Heidegger—who is more concerned with authenticity, mortality, and freedom than with responsibility, morality, or justice—thinking is already postmodern because the holy has already been thought out of the picture. And with Heidegger's entry into the Nazi Party, postmodernism and Nazism become bedfellows.

I want to be clear about one thing, however, before continuing: I do *not* maintain that either German Idealism or postmodernism is the same as Nazism. But I do maintain that Nazism has its connections with both.

It is no accident, for instance, that many of the postmodern thinkers have responded to the scandal of Heidegger by rushing to the defense of the Nazi philosopher. In *De l'esprit,* for instance, Jacques Derrida suggests that Heidegger's turning to Nazism in the early 1930s was a sign of his involvement not with that incarnation of evil but with metaphysics; once Heidegger renounced metaphysics, argues Derrida, he renounced Nazism and moved beyond philosophy.[17] Although Heidegger never uttered a word of regret or retraction, Derrida views his silence as a form of recantation and repentance; thus the German philosopher's saying nothing gets deconstructed into confession and expiation. Derrida adds his own silence to the silence of Heidegger, moreover, for he never mentions Heidegger's comment on "the inner truth and greatness" of Nazism, which appears at the end of the 1953 edition of the *Introduction To Metaphysics.*[18] It seems that such a statement may be beyond deconstruction.

What Heidegger refers to as "the inner truth and greatness" of Nazism is an outlook traceable to Kant's notion of the autonomous will. This accent on the will finds expression in Nietzsche's insistence on the will to power and is exemplified in Heidegger's emphasis on resolve as the mark of human authenticity. "Dasein *is its own self,*" he maintains, "in the original isolation of silent resolve."[19] Here, as Hans Jonas points out, "decision in itself is the greatest virtue.... [Heidegger] identified the decisiveness (of the *Führer* and the Party) with the principle of decisiveness and resoluteness as such. When I realized, appalled, this was not only Heidegger's personal error but also somehow set up in his thinking, the questionability of existentialism as such became apparent to me."[20] A key category in existentialism is autonomous freedom, which is derived from German Idealism. In existentialism, as in German Idealism, freedom lies in doing anything one can find the resolve to do within the contexts of a self-legislating autonomy—and not in the adherence to a divinely given law, as Jewish teaching maintains.

The thinking that began with Kantian Idealism and culminated in Heideggerian postmodernism *has to* seek the elimination of heteronomous Jewish thought, since Jewish thought embraces the absolute authority of the Holy One, who is known only through His uncompromising commandment. That embrace is what Heidegger complained of when he complained about the "Jewification" of the German mind.[21] And so the philosopher joined the party that would see to a final solution to the Jewification problem. Like everyone else, he saw the solution to the problem to lie in education and became rector of the University of Freiburg in April 1933. By then, of course, the final solution to the Jewification problem was well under way in the universities of Germany. For Hitler knew he could count on the professors.

Seeds Sprouted in the Twentieth Century

Yes, the *universities,* not only of Germany but throughout the Western world, are those centers of learning where our most enlightened minds are entrusted with what Ka-tzetnik 135633 refers to in his first novel as "all humanity's teachings." In 1946 his novel *Salamandrah* was the first Holocaust novel to be published in Israel (its English title is *Sunrise over Hell*). And yet, it is hardly a novel at all but rather is one survivor's artistic attempt to relate what happened to him, body and soul, "over there." In this shattering account, Harry Preleshnik, an inmate of Auschwitz modeled after the author, discovers the corpse of his friend Marcel Safran. "Prone before his eyes," writes Ka-tzetnik, "he saw the value of all humanity's teachings, ethics and beliefs, from the dawn of mankind to this day…. He bent, stretched out his hand and caressed the head of the Twentieth Century."[22] Yes, the head of the *twentieth century,* the culmination of all the centuries of human moral and philosophical sophistication. The value of humanity's teachings and of the human image itself meet this fate at the hands not of ignorant brutes but of highly educated people who acted in a meticulous, calculated, and systematic manner. It is well known, for example, that three of the four commanders of the *Einsatzgruppen* killing units had doctorate degrees, as did eight of the thirteen men whom Reinhard Heydrich summoned to the Wannsee Conference on 20 January 1942. The purpose of this meeting of great German minds? To discuss the logistics of murdering all the Jews of Europe. There, indeed, we see what had become of "higher learning" in Germany.

The meeting that took place at Number 56–58 Am Grossen Wannsee had originally been scheduled for 9 December 1941, but it was postponed due to the bombing of Pearl Harbor and America's entry into the war. The ninety-minute session was held in a large home once owned by a Jew. In attendance were *Gauleiter Doktor* Alfred Meyer of the East Ministry, *Staatssekretär Doktor* Wilhelm Stuckart of the Interior Ministry, *Reichsamtleiter Doktor* Georg Leibbrandt of the East Ministry, Staatssekretär *Doktor* Roland Freisler of the Justice Ministry, *Staatssekretär Doktor* Josef Bühler of the Government-General, *SS-Oberführer Doktor* Karl Schöngarth of the Government-General, *SS-Sturmbannführer Doktor* Rudolf Lange, *Unterstaatssekretär Doktor* Martin Luther of the Foreign Office, and five other less highly educated men, including the infamous murderer and expert on Jewish affairs, Adolf Eichmann. It is evident that most of the men who gathered around the table to plot mass murder and sip brandy were laden with credentials. Graduates of the finest universities of Central Europe, they were highly intelligent and quite successful pillars of their German communities. But the universities of Europe, then as now, were guided by a modern principle of *Voraussetzunglose Wissenschaft,* learning that is free of value-laden assumptions and that already articulates a postmodern outlook. Among the principles that guided them, there was no principle that did not pose a contradiction to the premise of postmodern thought, namely that there are no absolute values—the will alone determines value.

At the conference, in fact, Heydrich made a point of noting that the meeting had been called "in order to obtain clarity on questions of principle" and to galvanize the will.[23] Among the first principles that ruled the Wannsee Conference were the postmodern axioms that there is no higher truth at work in the world, but only a struggle for power; that human beings bear no spiritual or Divine aspect, but rather are products of their biological origin and cultural environment; and that, with enough resolve, one group of people may justify its extermination of another people.[24] In a word, the principle at work at Wannsee was a principle of idolatry, opposed neither to religion nor to "spirituality." On the contrary, it insists religiously upon a "spirit" and a blind devotion to the sovereignty of the self that has enough will to justify itself. Thus one sees a massive exploitation of religious fervor, so that millions surrender their souls to *Volk* and *Führer* for the purpose of exterminating the Jews.[25]

Here we see the deadly nature of idolatry. And here we may clear up a certain confusion. On the one hand we have the thinking that would produce a man-god or an *Übermensch*, a thinking that rests on concepts of autonomous self-legislation, self-determination, a will to power, authenticity rooted in resolve, and other such categories from German philosophy. On the other had we have the complete surrender of the "self" to *Volk* and *Führer*. How can we clear up this apparent contradiction? The answer lies in a distinction between self and soul.

If the self as a *res cogitans* (the Cartesian "thinking thing") is at the center of the philosophical thinking that contributed to the Holocaust, the soul is at the center of the Jewish thinking that the Nazis tried to obliterate. In the introduction to this volume it was noted that, from a Jewish perspective, "the soul of a [person] is the Divine speech that speaks the [person]."[26] And what is Divine speech? It is Torah, which, therefore, is both the origin and the substance of the soul. When the soul burns with the fire of Torah, the Light of G-d that is called Torah emanates into the world through that soul. Two key verses in the Book of Proverbs make this point clear and open up some of its ramifications: "The commandment is the lamp and the Torah the light" (6:23), and "The soul of the human being is the lamp of *HaShem*" (20:27). The commandment is called a lamp, because, says the Midrash, when we perform a *mitsvah* or commandment, it is as if we had kindled a light before G-d and have thus revived our soul (*Shemot Rabbah* 36:3). For the soul is made of the commandments or *mitsvot* of Torah. And, as the lamp of G-d, the soul's task is to transform darkness into the light of Torah.

The light of Torah, which is the light of the soul, moreover, reveals the face of our neighbor. Revealing the face of our neighbor, the soul announces our definitive tie to one another: Like a beam of light connected to the sun—and, through the sun, to every other beam of light—the soul is linked to G-d and, through G-d, to every other soul. The soul *is* that linkage. Whatever the soul is, then, unfolds in the midst of a relation *to* another, *for the sake of* another. Understanding that the substance of the soul lies in a relation to the other human being, we see more clearly the truth of Abraham Joshua Heschel's statement that the ego or self is a self-deception.[27] The deception inheres in the illusion of the self's autonomy, which in turn lies at the core of its will to power. Thus understood, *the self is just the opposite of the soul.* What we might take to be a surrender of the self to *Volk* and *Führer,* then, is in fact the surrender of the soul in a waxing of the self. For the Nazis' devotion to *Volk* and *Führer* required the abandonment of the *other* human being.

Realizing this, we realize that if the Nazis set out to murder souls before they murdered bodies, they set out to murder the Divine image—the Torah, the commandment, and the being-for-the-other—of which the soul is made. The Nazi idolatry cannot be established without the murder of G-d, and the murder of G-d requires the elimination of G-d's commandment, which is Torah. Because the soul is made of Torah, souls must be murdered—*both in the German and in the Jew.* How do the Nazis murder their own souls? First through a surrender to *Volk* and *Führer,* and then through the extermination of the Jews, whose very presence represents the Torah's prohibition against murder. And one who murders the other human being—precisely in order to eliminate the Divine prohibition against murder—murders his own soul by radically severing all that ties him to his fellow human being, the one whom the Jew regards as brother. That is why, according to Torah, the first murder is a fratricide: It is to teach that every murder is a murder of one's brother—and of one's own soul.[28]

This murder, of brother and of soul, was the defining feature of National Socialism, so that in Fackenheim's words, "the murder camp was not an accidental by-product of the Nazi empire. It was its pure essence."[29] For murder is ultimately the essence of the self that would be as god—not the G-d of Torah, who is loving and long-suffering, but the self-styled god of terror, who insists upon the death of the soul. Thus the death's head insignia of the SS. There is no loss of self in obedience to Hitler, as it may seem to some; there is, rather, a rapid rising of the self at the expense of the soul. Here we see a movement from the autonomy of the self to a devotion to *Volk* and *Führer,* who now constitute the self: In *Volk* and *Führer* the self-made god now finds its voice and its justification. The Jew, by contrast, represents the anti-*Volk* and the anti-*Führer:* Whereas King David must answer to the Prophet Nathan, the *Führer* answers to no one. The *Führer is* the answer, for he has the *final* solution. The Final Solution to what? To the Jewification Problem, the problem posed by the Torah's teaching on the value of the human being as one who is created in the Divine image.

The Jewification Problem

The Nazis' annihilation of the Judaism that defines the Jews is not so much about Judaism's understanding of G-d as it is about G-d's understanding of the human being as a soul who is forever implicated in his relation to his neighbor. Consider the famous injunction in Leviticus 19:18: *V'ahavta l'reekha kamokha,* "and you shall love your neighbor as yourself." Contrary to the assumptions of egocentric speculative thought, this commandment does not mean, "I know how much you love yourself, and that is how much I want you to love your neighbor." No, given the possibilities of meaning for the word *kamokha,* "as yourself," a better translation would be: "You shall love your neighbor, for that loving is your self," the soul and substance of who you are. Therefore, who you are is always in question. And it relies not on a capacity for thought but on a capacity for an embrace of the other human being: I love my neighbor, therefore I am.

Related to this Jewish teaching is the view that, contrary to modern and postmodern thought, the human being is an insertion of something greater than the all into the midst of the all. Therefore a human being is not reducible to a product of race, gender, culture, or environment; nor is the human being justified by an inner reason, resolve, or power or even by morality. Created in the image and likeness of the Holy One, the human being harbors the presence of what sanctifies all of being from beyond being. In a word, the human being is a breach of being, commanded from beyond being, both morally and liturgically. The function of the liturgy of prayer, which is alien to the modern and postmodern outlook, is to affirm the absolute, transcendent nature of the moral commandment. Once the liturgy is lost, so is the morality that implicates me *prior* to my having reached any understanding or any decision. According to Jewish understanding, then, prayer is essential to the life of the human being; from the standpoint of modern and postmodern thought it is superfluous. Indeed, Kant held prayer in contempt,[30] and the Nazis viewed it as an act of sabotage.[31]

If, as Judaism maintains, prayer is essential to our moral life, it is because the ethical demand placed upon me arises not from the dictates of reason or from the will to power but from the cry of my neighbor, from the widow and the orphan, from the stranger and the beggar. These are the ones who are closest to G-d and through whom I receive the commandment of G-d, who even as He commands me to look out for my fellow human being repeatedly declares, "*Ani HaShem,* I am the Lord!" And *every* human being is my fellow human being—indeed, is my relative, descended as we are from a single human being. There are no races, and we are all "blood." To be sure, Rabbi Shimon ben Azzai teaches that the single origin of all humanity from one human being is among the most fundamental of all Jewish teachings (see *Sifra* 7:4; *Yerushalmi Nedarim* 9:4). Why does G-d begin humanity with just one human being, and not two? According to Jewish tradition, it is to teach us that no one may say to another, "My father is better than your father." Or: "My side of the family is better than your side of the family" (see, for example, *Tosefta Sanhedrin* 8:4). There is only one side of the family: Each one, beginning with the first one, comes from the hand and the mouth of *HaShem.* Which means: Each one is *created for a purpose,* and not evolved by chance. Neither modern nor postmodern philosophy can determine such a relation to the Creator or to one another.

From what has been said with regard to Jewish thinking about G-d and humanity, "the adjective *Jewish,*" as Henri Crétella correctly states it, "does not designate an ethnic group. On the contrary, it signifies that there is no true humanity without being related to divinity—as the Jews have shown us. In other words, it is not blood and soil *[Blut und Boden]* which properly define us, but rather the possibility of emancipating ourselves from this very blood and soil."[32] This freedom from the accidents of nature is attained not through the autonomy of a self-legislating ego but through a devotion to the commanding G-d. It lies in the heteronomous "responsibility" expressed by the Hebrew word *acharayut,* whose root is *acher,* meaning "other," indicating orientation toward and care for the other person. To be created in the Divine image is to be summoned to this very care for the other human being. There lies the liberation from *Blut und Boden,* from "blood and soil," a liberation that is alien to modern and postmodern thought. That Divine summons to the care for the other human being is precisely the Jewification problem that the Nazis set out to solve. And they had the worldview that would dictate the solution.

The Nazi Weltanschauung

Opposite the Jewish outlook outlined above we have an assertion from the notorious Nazi philosopher Alfred Rosenberg: "This heroic attitude [of National Socialism], to begin with, departs from the *single* but *completely* decisive avowal, *namely from the avowal that blood and character, race and soul are merely different designations for the same entity.*"[33] Hence, Rosenberg insisted, "our race has been poisoned by Judaism,"[34] and not merely by Jewish blood, for the -ism is *in* the blood. National Socialism, therefore, is not an instance of racism, as the term is generally understood in the American context, where "race" is nearly always associated with color. Here the churches that tried to educate the Native Americans in the 1880s could adopt the slogan "Kill the Indian, Save the Man." No Nazi could ever conceive of a slogan like "Kill the Jew, Save the Man." It was utterly beyond the categories of Nazi thinking.

Here we realize that National Socialism is more than a political or ideological stance: It is a complete Weltanschauung that professes a total and totalizing view of world, humanity, and reality. Therefore "race" in this context is not about color or physiognomy or anything else that meets the eye. Quite unlike what Americans understand to be a "race issue," it is a *metaphysical* category: *Race* means *soul*. In keeping with Kant's *Anthropology* and Rosenberg's *Race and Race History,* in the Nazi discourse race determines the nature of thought, which, in accordance with the modern and postmodern philosophical outlook, determines the substance of one's being. Every Jew must be eliminated because every Jew is *inclined* to think Talmudically, whether this one or that one now thinks that way or not.

"It must be emphasized," wrote Rosenberg, "that the situation would not be altered if the Jew denied the Talmud, because the national character...remains the same."[35] Any Jew, therefore, can contaminate the very substance of humanity, because every Jew is a "carrier" of the "disease" of Jewish thinking. "Just as fleas and elephants have different spiritual constitutions," wrote Nazi Nobel laureate Philipp Lenard in 1936, "so the spirits of different human races and ethnic groups are totally different from each other."[36] Hence "Nordic man," writes the Nazi scholar Ludwig Clauss, "can overcome almost anything in the world save the distance separating man from man."[37] How does bridging this gap lie outside the power of even the Master Race? Because, from a Nazi standpoint, the distance separating man from man is infinite, because neither this man nor that contains the Divine spark as Judaism understands that notion. And that distance ultimately justifies murder.

Taking the Divine spark within every human to be derived from one G-d, Judaism represents a view of G-d, world, and humanity that is diametrically opposed to the Nazi Weltanschauung. Hence the Nazi economist Peter Heinz Seraphim insisted that National Socialism was indeed a Weltanschauung that was based on much more than prejudice or racial hatred; the racial foundations, he maintained, were based on an all-encompassing philosophical outlook, not on something so banal or vulgar as ethnic or religious difference.[38] Which is to say: The Jew is not the "other"—the Jew is the *evil*. Hence, as Fackenheim has argued, the Nazis are not anti-Semitic because they are racists. It is just the reverse: They are racists because they are anti-Semitic.[39] The Nazi philosopher Max Wundt is quite right then when he asserts that the Jewish view of the world and humanity "stands opposed to the folkish worldview as its total antithesis."[40] If the Nazis are to be Nazis, then they *have to* eliminate the notion of a higher, Divine image within the human being that places upon each of us an infinite responsibility for the *other* human being. In order to eliminate this Hebrew sense of responsibility, the *acharayut* that binds each of us to the other, the Nazis must eliminate the Hebrew people, whose very presence in the world signifies this responsibility that derives from the Divine spark.

Emil Fackenheim observes that, once they took the word of the *Führer* to be law, the Nazis made the rejection of the Divine image a matter of law. "The law itself," he writes, "came closest to the self-fulfilling prophecy aimed at in the murder camp. The murder camp was not an accidental by-product of the Nazi empire. It was its pure essence. The Divine image in man *can* be destroyed. No more threatening proof to this effect can be found than the so-called *Muselmann* in the Nazi death camp.... The *Muselmaenner* are a new way of human being in history, the living dead."[41] It is a Nazi way derived from the way that would make the human being the measure of himself, something as impossible as a man picking himself up by his own hair. The *Muselmann* is the incarnation of the human being who has no trace of a Divine image. As Primo Levi says, "the Divine spark" is "dead within them."[42] The *Muselmann* is the human being who is simply and indifferently there, reduced to the most stark manifestation of being. This assault on the Divine image of the human being was conceived by philosophers and carried out by the SS. First conceptual and then actual, it is an assault on divinity and humanity implemented through the extermination of the people chosen to attest to the Divine chosenness of every human being.

In this extermination project the "thinking for oneself" that characterizes much of Enlightenment philosophy comes into a radical opposition to thinking for the sake of G-d and neighbor. Thus, in its philosophical implications, the Nazis' annihilation of the Jews and Judaism was not simply a case of scapegoating or racism run amok. In keeping with a major line of philosophical development from Kant onward, the Nazis sought the destruction of the G-d of Abraham and everything He signifies through the destruction of G-d's chosen. Above all, the intellectual elites of Germany sought to redefine the human being in such a way as to eliminate every Jewish definition of the human being. As Yehuda Bauer has rightly observed, "If there was a uniquely German phenomenon that prepared the ground for Nazism, it was not the spread of anti-Semitism among the population in general *but its spread among the intellectual elites.*"[43] And, beginning with Heidegger—that philosophical giant from whom, along with Nietzsche, the postmodern movement draws its inspiration—Germany's intellectuals were generally with the program.

From the Idealist Kant To the Nazi Heidegger

At the June 1939 meeting of the National Socialist Association of University Lecturers, its head Walter Schultze declared before the assembly, "What the great thinkers of German Idealism dreamed of, and what was ultimately the kernel of their longing for liberty, finally comes alive, assumes reality....Never has the German idea of freedom been conceived with greater life and greater vigor than in our day."[44] A respected and leading intellectual in Nazi Germany, Schultze saw as clearly as any of Nazi

Germany's philosophers the link between the German philosophical tradition and National Socialism. And he articulated the general German intellectual thinking of his day.

Given the history of the philosophers' involvement in the party, it is perhaps startling but certainly not surprising to discover that by 1940 nearly half of the philosophers of Germany were members of the Nazi Party.[45] In 1923, Hermann Schwarz, a "prominent" German thinker influenced by Meister Eckhart and Jacob Boehme, distinguished himself by becoming the first philosopher to publicly support the Nazis. He was followed by Bruno Bauch, Max Wundt, Hans Heyse, and Nicolai Hartmann, all of whom were Kantian Idealists; then there was the noted Hegelian Theodor Haerung and the Nietzscheans Alfred Bäumler and Ernst Krieck. The most renowned of them all, of course, was Martin Heidegger. What these thinkers have in common is their embrace of a philosophical tradition that is fundamentally hostile toward Judaic theism and that takes individual autonomy to be the measure of human freedom and authenticity. To be sure, in 1922, Heidegger proclaimed that what attracted him to philosophy was "the full-blown anti-religious attitude of the German *Geist* ripened from German Idealism."[46] And in the *Introduction To Metaphysics* he maintains that "it was not German Idealism that collapsed; it was the era that was not strong enough to match the stature, the breadth, and the originality of that spiritual world."[47] In the Nazis he saw the strength necessary to match the stature, the breadth, and the originality of the original idea. That is why, as rector of the University of Freiburg, he embraced National Socialism so wholeheartedly.

The "ripening" of the antireligious stance from German Idealism begins with Kant. And Heidegger had a profound appreciation for that fact. Paul Guyer has rightly said (but perhaps without realizing the ramifications of what he was saying) that "at the philosophical level of the transformation of the Western concept of a human being from a mere spectator of the natural world and a mere subject in the moral world to an active agent in the creation of both, no one played a larger role than Immanuel Kant."[48] Once the human being is the active agent in the creation of nature and morality, G-d becomes all but superfluous, as Kant himself understood: "All that does depend upon the direct will of G-d," he writes in his *Universal Natural History,* "is the creation of matter."[49] Insisting, then, that religion and G-d derive from morality, and not the other way around,[50] Kant embraces a rationalist theology that is opposed to anything resembling a revealed religion such as Judaism. Contrary to being defined according to his embrace of the Divine commandment, the human being is "determinable," says Kant, "only by laws which he gives to himself through reason."[51] Judaism is the opposite of Kantian Idealism—that is why Kant wanted to see it eliminated.

Indeed, in *The Conflict of the Faculties,* Kant declares, "The euthanasia of Judaism is the pure moral religion."[52] And the euthanasia of Judaism *must* entail the elimination of the G-d of Abraham, Isaac, and Jacob. Kant takes a step in that direction when he relegates G-d to the status of creator of matter, and removes from Him the status of the G-d of the Covenant who gives to us commandments that are both rational (*mishpatim* in Hebrew) and beyond the rational *(chukim)*. Here we would do well to recall that the Hebrew word for "commandment," *mitzvah,* derives from the Aramaic word *tsavta,* which means "connection." Therefore the abrogation of the commandment from *HaShem* is an abrogation of the connection to *HaShem:* Once matter is the only thing that comes from G-d, G-d soon becomes meaningless not only as Lawgiver and Redeemer but also as Teacher and Father. Losing the fatherhood of G-d, then, we lose the brotherhood of humanity.

After Kant we have Hegel. His writings, as Paul Lawrence Rose has noted, "conform to the basic Kantian idealist and moralist critique of Judaism. Judaism is seen as the epitome of an unfree psyche."[53] Although, like Kant, Hegel understands freedom in terms of autonomy, unlike Kant, he takes revealed religion to be the highest form of religious consciousness; still, similar to Kant and in keeping with the spirit of Idealism, Hegel maintains that revealed religion is superseded by the absolute knowledge of reason.[54] Drawing on the Christian notion of the Christ as the Incarnation, Hegel develops a view of G-d that ultimately denies the otherness of the divinity. In Hegel, Fackenheim explains, "divinity comes to dwell, as it were, in the same inner space as the human self."[55] Which in the end means: The ego is divine.

Resisting this apotheosis of the ego, Jews live an "animal existence" in Hegel's words; they are in a "state of total passivity, of total ugliness" and are to blame for refusing to "die as Jews."[56] With Hegel the perceiving self that had appropriated the world now appropriates the divinity. And so the sequence of thought that situates the self at the center marginalizes both G-d and neighbor. By the time the neo-Hegelian Ludwig Feuerbach comes on the scene, G-d is nothing more than a projection of one's own psyche,[57] so that the other human being does not summon who I am in my responsibility for another, but rather threatens who I am in my being-for-myself. For here the other human being is a threat to my freedom. Once we get to Nietzsche, the intermediary between German Idealism and Heideggerian ontology, G-d is what one aspires to become in a self-apotheosis,[58] and other human beings are mere *Untermenschen*.

The philosophical result of this incarnation of G-d in the self and the subsequent relegation of other people to the status of "the crowd" demands the deprecation of the Jews. Why? Because the Jews pose the most direct threat to the atheistic thinking of neo-Hegelians such as Feuerbach and Marx, where, says Fackenheim, "divinity vanishes in the process of internalization, to be replaced by a humanity potentially infinite in its modern 'freedom.'"[59] Christians do not pose the same threat that the Jews do because Christians introduce the confluence of G-d and humanity in the Incarnation in such a way as to free humanity from the commandments of Torah (see, for example, Galatians 3:13). Therefore, as history has shown, Christians could accommodate this modern freedom, which is an absolute freedom determined by an absolute autonomy of the self, without becoming a counterculture. In the end, however, this modern "freedom" represents the compete surrender to the temptation of the serpent, but with a more radical difference: Not only will you be like god, knowing good and evil, but you will be the self-legislating god of your own good and evil,[60] as one sees in Nietzsche's assertion that "German philosophers" are "*commanders and legislators:* They say, '*Thus* it *shall* be!'...their will to truth is—*will to power.*"[61] Because it is infinite, the "modern freedom" eliminates the Infinite One, so that human beings now may do whatever they have the will to do. Indeed, they are justified by will alone. The G-d of Abraham, then, is dead, as per Nietzsche.[62]

Here Edith Wyschogrod offers a telling insight that establishes a telling connection between Hegel and Nietzsche, despite the differences that separate the two thinkers: "The intellectual implications of Hegel's radical vision [of the internalized god] are first realized in Nietzsche's depiction of the madman who not only declares the death of G-d, but makes the equally important and unthinkable claim that man is the killer."[63] "Man" here is first the modern, Enlightened man, who engineers the killing of G-d, only to shrink in terror at the abyss that remains; later he is the postmodern man, who glorifies and wallows in the nothingness that yawns with the elimination of absolutes. With Nietzsche, power is the only reality, and weakness is the only sin. Which means: The "oppressor" can never be in the wrong. The will to power is a will to freedom, where freedom is understood as an autonomy beyond any law, resolute and decisive. Indeed, "the expression 'will to power,'" says Heidegger in his study on Nietzsche, "designates the basic character of beings; any being which is, insofar as it is, is will to power. The expression stipulates the character that beings have as beings."[64] And so, after Nietzsche's will to power defines the *character* of beings, Heidegger's resolve defines the *authenticity* of beings. For resolve is the height of autonomy, freedom, and authenticity. It means that what is mine is mine not by right but by determination. It means that what is mine is mine, and what is yours is mine, which, says the Talmud, is a manifestation of *evil* (see *Pirke Avot* 5:10). It is indeed the manifestation of the Nazi evil. It is the Heideggerian evil. It is the postmodern evil.

The Postmodern, Heideggerian Evil

Emmanuel Lévinas accurately states the implications of this ontological thinking that begins in Kant and culminates in Heidegger: "A philosophy of power, ontology is, as first philosophy which does not call into question the same, a philosophy of injustice.... Heideggerian ontology, which subordinates the relationship with the Other to the relation with Being in general, remains under obedience to the anonymous and leads inevitably to another power,[65] to imperialist domination, to tyranny."[66] Grounding freedom in autonomy and authenticity in resolve, this strain of German philosophy situates freedom beyond the Law and is therefore lawless. It is, as Lévinas rightly argues, "the outcome of a long tradition of pride, heroism, domination, and cruelty" that "continues to exalt the will to power." Such is the philosophy of *Volk* and *Führer,* which insists, as Heidegger did, that "the *Führer* himself and he alone is the present and future German reality and its law."[67] There could be no more blatant statement of sheer idolatry.

It articulates a theme that runs throughout a pamphlet published by the National Socialist German Teachers Union in 1933; the pamphlet contains various affirmations of the "new order," such as this one: "To know means to us: to have power over things in reason and to be ready to act…. The National Socialist movement is not merely the taking over of an already existing power…, but this revolution means a *complete* revolution of our German existence."[68] This and other such assertions in the pamphlet bore the signatures of nine prominent university professors, including Heidegger's.

Where did Heidegger see the emergence of the new gods who would return authenticity to humanity in a "new unconcealment of Being?"[69] In National Socialism and the *Führerprinzip,* that is, the "Führer principle," which makes the Hitlerian, exterminationist hatred of the Jews not just a policy of state (although that too was a *novum* in history), but *German reality and its law.*

On 27 May 1933—by which time Hitler had assumed dictatorial powers, Jews were being removed from civil service jobs, Dachau was in operation, and Jewish businesses had been boycotted—Heidegger delivered the infamous Rectorial Address at the University of Freiburg. Extolling the "magnificence and greatness" of Nazism,[70] he declared that "all abilities of will and thought, all strengths of the heart, and all capabilities of the body must unfold *through* battle, heightened *in* battle, and presented *as* battle"[71] —where any contemporary German listener would immediately associate the word *battle,* or *Kampf,* with Hitler's manifesto *Mein Kampf,* the "sacred text" that provided the ideological warrant for the Nazi genocide, which, indeed, was more than genocide: it was deicide, as we shall show in chapter 2. Thus the philosopher joins his discourse to the discourse of the *Führer.* Indeed, from the Rectorial Address it is evident that Heidegger considered himself "the born philosopher and spiritual leader of the new movement."[72] This view of himself was not merely a matter of intellectual conceit. More than that, Heidegger believed he was addressing a philosophical vacuum that threatened the new movement and the German *Volk.*

What was to fill that vacuum? Not, according to Heidegger, a "Jewified" philosophy of values. Opposing himself to the "misguided" Nazi philosophers of values—such as Bauch, who sought to ground "values" in race—Heidegger understood the Nazi order to be one that "would find secure grounding not in values but in a new unconcealment of Being, a new truth of Being."[73] In keeping with what he had understood of Nietzsche, Heidegger knew that the new man would emerge not through the embrace of values but only through the will to power exemplified by the Nazi movement. Thus Heidegger saw in Nazism the "new unconcealment of Being" that finally frees itself from the appeal to an infinite or Divine being, from all revelation of values, both above and below, from every remnant of "ontotheology."[74]

Over against the "inauthentic" ontotheology stands the authentic "existential ontology." "Existential ontology," Heidegger declared in his book on Kant, "has as its sole objective the explication of the primordial transcendental structure of the *Dasein* in man," which in turn "manifests itself as need of the comprehension of Being,"[75] and not as, say, the need for the embrace of the other person or of G-d, the responsibility for the life of one's neighbor, prayer, or the like. *Comprehension* is here to be taken literally: It is the "grasping" or "seizure" of being exemplified, for instance in the notion of *Lebensraum,* which provided the justification for Germany's program of expansion. Here the self, or the *Volk,* appropriates the other, both politically and philosophically, as it always happens—at least since the advent of modernism and postmodernism.

To be sure, one of the central features of Heideggerian thinking that characterizes both Nazi ideology and postmodern thought is the elimination of the other human being from its concern. *"Das Dasein existiert umwillen seiner,"* Heidegger declares: *"Dasein* exists for the sake of itself."[76] Which means, as Jacques Taminiaux rightly points out, "that Dasein is always engaged in the care of itself, and of itself alone, and that Dasein wills itself alone."[77] Thus we have the empty postmodern platitude that there is no such thing as an altruistic act: Even the ostensible being-for-the-other, the equation goes, is in fact a being-for-the-self. Indeed, there can be no other *Dasein.* Whereas for the Jewish thought, other people are children of G-d who are placed in my care, for Heidegger and the postmodernists, other people are the "They," who threaten my authenticity. Ideologically extended, this existence for the sake of oneself alone becomes an existence for the sake of the *Volk;* one can be only with others who are like oneself, that is, who are German.

Neither the new unconcealment of Being nor the comprehension of Being has anything to do with relation; hence it has nothing to do with either a moral or a religious good. As Wyschogrod has rightly pointed out, "such realism as love…and friendship…play no part in Heidegger's analysis."[78] That is why Heidegger wrote no treatise on ethics or morality; to him such matters were either irrelevant or harmful. Hence neither Heidegger nor his Nazi colleagues thought they were doing a moral good by pursuing the Nazi agenda. On the contrary, they believed they were doing an ontological good beyond moral good and evil, with its corollary *social, political,* and *cultural* good—all of which are among the shibboleths of postmodernism.

Diametrically opposed to this being-for-oneself that characterizes the postmodern, Heideggerian evil is the being-for-the-other represented by Jewish teaching and tradition—what Heidegger deprecated as "Jewified" thought and Hegel regarded as a slave mentality.[79] The *Sein-zum-Tod,* or "being-toward-death," that Heidegger takes to be so central to authentic existence is a concern for *my* death.[80] The death that concerns the Jews, on the other hand, is the death of the *other* human being, the widow, the orphan, and the stranger, who are of no concern to Heidegger. Kant's "moral philosophy," moreover, cannot be held up as a response to Heidegger because, as we have seen, it led to Heidegger. What is the mark of contradiction, for example, that guides the categorical imperative? It is a contradiction of *self-interest.*[81] Indeed, once the world is reduced to the perceiving self; once thinking for oneself is a matter of seeking the truth in oneself; once authenticity is reduced to the appropriation of the other by the same—the only contradiction left is a contradiction of self-interest. Which is no *transgression.* What must be opposed to the evil of Heidegger's postmodern ontology is precisely the Jewish metaphysics that the Nazis opposed: not the autonomy of the self but the sanctity of the other, not the universal maxims of reason but the uncompromising commandments of G-d, not freedom but justice, without which freedom itself is reduced to sheer but ephemeral power.

Of course, what I refer to as "the evil of Heidegger's ontology" cannot be seen as evil from within the framework of that ontology. It certainly cannot be seen as evil from the standpoint of postmodernism, since such a category implies an appeal to a Holy One, who, like the very notion of evil, has no place or significance in postmodern thought. Here we see one of Heidegger's chief contributions to postmodernism: It is the erasure of vertical, "logocentric" categories that would enable us to speak of anything holy or evil, so that we are left with what is merely "there" or what is simply "at hand." Once the dimension of height is lost, we are left only with the power struggles of culture and politics that have come to determine who and what we are and that have left the soul utterly alienated. One of the greatest challenges to Jewish identity in a postmodern age, then, is to refuse to allow the power struggle to determine identity. Jewish identity must derive from the dimension of height that, with Heidegger, postmodernism would obliterate. Which is to say: It must derive from the wrestling that characterizes the name *Yisrael,* which postmodernism would erase.

Inasmuch as Judaism insists upon a dimension of height and holiness and therefore upon the evil of Heideggerian Nazism—inasmuch as a Jew seeks his or her identity in the Commanding Voice—postmodern thought *has to be* anti-Semitic, anti-Judaic, and anti-Zionist. For opposed to postmodernism's erasure of absolutes is the Jewish insistence on absolutes that are neither culturally nor politically determined but are given from *on high.* This height, and not our resolve or our power, is what opens up truth, meaning, and the good in life. In the words of Lévinas, "Height introduces a sense into being. It is already lived across the experience of the human body. It leads human societies to raise up altars. It is not because men, through their bodies, have an experience of the vertical that the human is placed under the sign of height; because being is ordained to height the human body is placed in a space in which the high and the low are distinguished and the sky is discovered."[82] To be sure, in Jewish thought the capacity to make such distinctions—between high and low, G-d and humanity, good and evil, sacred and profane—forms the basis of every notion of the Holy, from which the sanctity of human life is derived.

As Heidegger ushers in postmodernism, however, being is emptied of the dimension of height that imparts meaning to it, to be leveled into a flatland of neutrality. This leveling of all into the same is characteristic of the postmodern thinking that went into the making of the concentrationary universe, where the living were ultimately indistinguishable from the dead.[83] Heidegger himself illustrates this postmodern leveling of life into death by equating technologically driven agriculture with the technologically driven murder of the Jews.[84] Commenting on Heidegger's view in this regard, Jürgen Habermas wrote, "Under the leveling glance of the philosopher of Being, the extermination of the Jews, too, appears as a happening, where everything can be replaced as one likes with anything else."[85] Thus we have the postmodern systems of signs, in which anything can be replaced with anything else. Since everything is all the same, anyone can take the place of another, and everyone is expendable. Thus the human being is rendered faceless. And since, in the words of Lévinas, "the face is what forbids us to kill,"[86] with the postmodern loss of the dimension of height, we also lose the absolute nature of the prohibition against murder. That is why Fackenheim declared the murder camp to be the essence of National Socialism. That is why the murder camp is a logical outcome of a line of German thought traceable from Kant's Idealism to Heidegger's postmodernism.

In 1936, Karl Löwith expressed his concern to Heidegger that there was an essential "partnership" between National Socialism and Heidegger's philosophy. "Heidegger agreed with me [about this]," says Löwith, "without reservation and elucidated that his concept of 'historicity' was the basis of his political 'engagement.' He also left no doubt about his belief in Hitler."[87] You see, Heidegger himself understood that he was not a philosopher who happened to be a Nazi; no, he was a Nazi who happened to be a philosopher. His Nazism was not a personal shortcoming or a character flaw but a central feature of his ontological thinking, a thinking influenced by a line of philosophical inquiry that runs from Kant to Nietzsche to Heidegger himself. And the line continues to run.

Responding To Heidegger after the Holocaust

We now see the truth of Lévinas's insight and better understand its implications, when he asserts, "Heideggerian philosophy precisely marks the apogee of a thought in which the finite does not refer to the infinite (prolonging certain tendencies of Kantian philosophy: the separation between the understanding and reason, diverse themes of transcendental dialectics), in which every deficiency is but weakness and every fault committed against oneself…. Heideggerian ontology subordinates the relation with the other to the relation with the neuter, Being, and it thus continues to exalt the will to power, whose legitimacy the other alone can unsettle, troubling good conscience."[88] In the case of Holocaust studies in the postmodern era, the other who unsettles and troubles good conscience is the Jew. That is why many of us seek to eliminate the Jew from our thinking about the Holocaust; that is why many of us, including Jews, follow the postmodern fashions and fads spawned by Heidegger. We do not deal with the Jews because we do not want to deal with the flesh and blood of Jewish life, which is rooted in Judaism. We do not want to look into the faces that put to us the question of what is ultimate in life, from beyond life. Instead, we prefer to level the Jew annihilated before and after his death into the sameness of just another victim. And so the study of the Holocaust becomes increasingly *Judenrein*. Rather than speak of Jews and Judaism, we speak of coping and trauma, dialogue and healing, representation and remembrance, textual analysis and ethical implications—everything except the singular assault on Jews and Judaism. Thus we have Holocaust studies without the Holocaust.

A detailed look at just a couple of examples will illustrate this point. One is *Words and Witness: Narrative and Aesthetic Strategies in the Representation of the Holocaust* by Lea Wernick Fridman, whom I would place in the category of modern thought, since she subscribes to a view that allows room for evil. The other is *Writing History, Writing Trauma* by Dominick LaCapra, whom I would place in the category of postmodern thought, since he is more concerned with personal trauma than with a metaphysically determined evil. Therefore, while LaCapra is the more thoroughgoing postmodern of the two, both are instances of the elimination of the Holocaust from the response to the Holocaust.

In her book Fridman explores "an existential connection between the experience of historical trauma and its utterance in poetic and literary form."[89] She opens her volume by contrasting Edgar Allen Poe's psychological horror with Joseph Conrad's "historical horror" to show, quite rightly, that in *Heart of Darkness* Conrad opens a realm of horror previously unrepresented in literature. In her analysis of Conrad's novel, however, she mistakenly views Kurtz's famous dying words, "The horror, the horror," as an "insight into the human capacity for and complicity with evil,"[90] a view that is perfectly in keeping with modern sensibilities on evil but that misses Conrad's all-but-postmodern point. In other words, what Fridman fails to understand—and what feeds the forces that led to the Holocaust—is this: The horror that Kurtz collides with lies not in an insight into evil but in the realization that there is no evil. Nor is there any good; hence there is no meaning. There is simply what is "there," neutral and void of any value except the value we impose through our will. It is the horror of what Lévinas describes as the "there is," from which emerges nothing but the anonymous rumble of silent emptiness.[91]

Moving then to Aharon Appelfeld's *Badenheim 1939,* Fridman offers an excellent observation on the function of silence when she notes that "the words have died…the way the Jews of Badenheim will die."[92] In the Holocaust the tearing of word from meaning indeed parallels the tearing of the soul from the Jew, the Divine spark from the human being, before murdering him. But Fridman does not address this connection between the assault on the word and the assault on the human being. Similarly, she cites Dr. Pappenheim's comment in the novel on the Jews' need to return to their origins,[93] but she addresses neither Jewish origins nor Jewish identity. And here lies much of the horror of Badenheim: The Jews here had lost their Jewish souls long before they were murdered for being Jewish. They had ceased their wrestling with the Angel, even as the Angel of Death descended upon them. Hence, in a tragic effort to fit into the world that murdered them, they had lost their identities as adherents of the Torah that forbids murder.

Continuing with the theme of word torn from meaning, in her third chapter Fridman examines the works of Claude Lanzmann, André Schwarz-Bart, Jerzy Kosinski, Tadeus Borowski, Paul Celan, and Dan Pagis. Here she argues that the "rupture of language" running through these artists' "representations of the Holocaust" indicates "a breakdown of a poetic process and of a speech process."[94] While her claim may be true, it misses the *Holocaust* in this Holocaust art. For the rupture of language that distinguishes the Holocaust belongs to the rupture of the Divine image in which the human being is created.[95] It is a rupture not only of a speech process but also of a Divine commandment, not only of an aesthetic endeavor but also of an ethical absolute. Therefore the rupture of *this* narrative and *these* aesthetic norms results in a breach in the identity of the Jew. As a collapse of the "representation of the Holocaust," it is significant not merely because the conventions of art have been undermined, but because the value of the other human being has been obliterated—a point ignored in Fridman's study yet powerfully conveyed in the works she examines.

When in chapter 4 she goes on to discuss Elie Wiesel's *Night,* Fridman elaborates further on the "shattered expectations" and the wrenching apart of "a world of words" from "a world of experience" that one certainly finds in this memoir.[96] But the assault on G-d in the hanging of the child, the overturning of prayer, the collapse of the relation to G-d and the parallel loss of the father, the Nazis' exploitation of the holy days to plan their measures against the Jews—all of this is not only obvious in the text but is crucial to what characterizes *Night* as a "representation of the Holocaust." And Fridman has little to say about any of it; therefore she has little to say about the Jews. Indeed, it is as though Wiesel's being a Jew, who was sent to Auschwitz because he was a Jew, were a superfluous detail. It is, therefore, as if Eliezer ben Shlomo were nameless—as if there were merely the text, only the text, and nothing but the text.

In her fifth chapter Fridman makes a comparison between Wiesel and Conrad, who both, as she rightly observes, "call attention to the chasm that the traumatic historical experience opens up between words and fact, symbol and history, language and experience."[97] But what is decisive to Wiesel—what is definitive for the Holocaust as the annihilation of the Jews—is the "trauma" that transpires in Jewish *sacred* history. That history is the history of a certain teaching on G-d and humanity, and the remembrance of that history lies in the remembrance of the truth of the tradition that the Nazis set out to destroy. The Holocaust, as both Elie Wiesel and Primo Levi have pointed out, was a war against memory, that is, against the memory of the Jews, in both a subjective and an objective sense.[98] Hence it was a war against the ethical injunction that enters the world through the Jews. Such concerns lie quite outside Fridman's interest in "how to use form in such a way as to enact a breakdown of form."[99] In her examination of the aesthetic and formal aspects of the "representation of the Holocaust"—for all its acumen and insight—Fridman has forgotten what is crucial to the Holocaust: Like all thinkers who are truly "modern," she has forgotten the Jews.

One thing that Dominick LaCapra has in common with Lea Wernick Fridman is that he too has written a book that only ostensibly deals with the Holocaust; for, like Fridman, he leaves the Jews out of his investigation. However, whereas in her modern approach, Fridman is merely indifferent toward the Jews, in his postmodern approach LaCapra is offensive toward the Jews. In *Writing History, Writing Trauma,* LaCapra explores ways of "working through" the Holocaust so as to avoid the pitfalls of "acting out." Proceeding from a Freudian position, moreover, he begins by adopting some of the views of a Jew who repudiated Judaism. In his introduction LaCapra says his intention is to provide a "critical perspective on the problems of trauma, notably with respect to major historical events."[100] To this end he adapts "psychoanalytical concepts to historical analysis as well as sociocultural and political critique in elucidating trauma and its aftereffects in culture and in people."[101] No mention of evil here; indeed, there is no evil. And there are no Jews. There is only me and my trauma.[102]

Adopting such a method to achieve such an end, in the book's title chapter LaCapra makes some very good points with respect to distinctions between the positivist and constructionist approaches to historiography. He is equally wary of certain deconstructionist theories, but what he offers as an alternative is no more illuminating and no less postmodern. Although he understands that the "absence of a radically transcendent divinity" transforms existence into "a fundamentally traumatic scene,"[103] he treats such an absence as a psychological phenomenon, as if it were a failed projection of the psyche and not a discreet reality. Nor does he explain what such a loss has to do with the Holocaust, since he does not connect the Holocaust to Jews or to Judaism or to G-d as Creator of heaven and earth or to human beings as His children. My complaint is not that LaCapra is not "Jewish" enough; rather, it is that, if he wants to address the trauma of the *Jewish* victims, he might consider religious elements that were significant to the Jews. But that's just the problem: To LaCapra, that they were Jews is merely incidental.

Similarly, he sees history as "a dialogic exchange" with the past, where "knowledge involves not only the processing of information but also affect, empathy, and questions of value."[104] Is that what Elie Wiesel, Isabella Leitner, Primo Levi, and other survivors are doing? Having a dialogic exchange with the past? Is their anguished outcry reducible to processing information? The idea, moreover, that some of those who were slaughtered and tortured might have seen history as an avenue of revelation—or as the eclipse of revelation—does not even occur to him. Therefore he does not say *in the name of what* questions of affect, empathy, and value might be raised. Here too LaCapra follows the general postmodern academic line that erases Jews and Judaism from the response to the Shoah.

In his subsequent examination of South Africa and Germany, LaCapra makes the valid point that absence converted into loss leads to a quest for a united community, while loss converted into absence leads to endless mourning and despair.[105] Making such distinctions, he says, is part of "a complex process of working through."[106] Yet LaCapra avoids any definition of community based on ethical and testimonial absolutes, such as the covenantal *Am Yisrael*. To be sure, psychoanalytic and postmodern assessments of trauma avoid such absolutes. One gets the impression that LaCapra is trying to avoid postmodern moral relativism—since, he says, moral relativism "need not be inevitable on a normative level"—but he carefully avoids appealing to what he calls a "superordinate master language,"[107] such as one finds in Torah. Facts, for LaCapra, remain hard facts, and that is where relativism ends. Therefore he does not altogether play into the hands of a relativist postmodernism that in turn plays into the hands of Holocaust revisionism. There is nothing, however, in LaCapra's position that would lead to any *moral* hard facts. And in that respect he is quite postmodern.

One thing that LaCapra wants to avoid in any approach to the Holocaust is what he calls a "sacralization of the event,"[108] which would include any attempt to situate the Shoah within Jewish sacred history. In other words, he wants to keep the Name out of the picture. Here too, then, LaCapra writes the Jews out of history and denies them any attempt to see the Shoah in terms of Divine revelation or of the withdrawal of the Divine Presence. Fackenheim's Commanding Voice of Auschwitz,[109] for example, or Rabbi Kalonymos Kalmish Shapira's invocation of the suffering G-d[110] is irrelevant to the event, as LaCapra represents it. From LaCapra one gets the impression that if Jews want to see the event in such religious terms, it is merely an indication of a neurosis that they have yet to "work through."

Equally dangerous, he maintains, is the "negative sublime," or "the Nazi quest for redemption and regeneration" through a "violent, distorted sacrificial process involving quasi-ritual anxiety about contamination and the quest for purification of the *Volksgemeinschaft* from putatively contaminating presences."[111] These lines are a good example of how a postmodern, academic jargon eludes rather than elucidates the Holocaust. Instead of Nazis who are bent on the extermination of the Jews and the Divine Presence they signify, we have "the Nazi quest for redemption." Instead of murder we have a "distorted sacrificial process." Instead of Jews and their

Torah we have "contaminating presences." There is also the dubious contention that the Nazis were offering up a sacrifice rather than conducting a purge. In order to serve as a sacrifice, the offering must be unblemished; if it is a contaminating presence and therefore a distorted sacrifice, then what we have is not a sacrificial process at all. What we have is murder. But, of course, "murder" is one of those absolute categories, an act prohibited *by G-d,* that falls outside the realm of postmodern reality.

LaCapra argues, moreover, for an "empathetic unsettlement" that avoids "full identification" with the victims.[112] At first glance it seems that he has a very good point: Coming to sense "how it must have felt," an absurd approach that is increasingly popular in "Holocaust education," brings one no closer to understanding what took place. Still, he tries to have it both ways when he invokes "empathetic unsettlement," which is just as vacuous when it comes to any insight or reflection on the event. Yet, with its egocentric orientation, a postmodern response to the Holocaust cannot go any farther than "empathetic unsettlement." Even this call for empathy is ultimately empty, since there is nothing in LaCapra's position that is inconsistent with indifference. Indeed, indifference toward the victims might be psychologically healthier, since empathy, he points out, is "bound up with a transferential relation to the past" that could pose problems for the psyche.[113] What reason is there, then, not to become an accomplice of the Nazis and just forget the whole thing, including one's covenantal Jewish identity? True to form, LaCapra never answers such a question; he never explains what it means to experience "empathetic unsettlement" toward the Jews *as* Jews. Such a criticism, however, may be unfair, since LaCapra is not interested in who the Jews are or in what was annihilated in the murder of the Jewish people. In a word, he is not interested in the Holocaust.

Perhaps that is why LaCapra complains about Daniel Goldhagen's excessive identification with the Jews in *Hitler's Willing Executioners.*[114] De-emphasizing the Jews and Jewish teaching, LaCapra analyzes how anti-Semitism is related "to other forms of racism and victimization."[115] He has no idea of the metaphysical dimensions of anti-Semitism that would remove it from the categories of "other forms of racism and victimization." He ignores, in other words, any view of anti-Semitism as an opposition to the Divine Law revealed through the Torah that forms the basis of Jewish identity. Rather, he psychoanalyzes anti-Semitism into a case of "quasi-sacrificial acting out," which also describes the victimization of Gypsies, Bolsheviks, Slavs, and homosexuals.[116] In this way LaCapra levels the millennial hatred of Jews and the centuries of testimony that underlie their significance into just another case of prejudice.

True to his postmodern form, LaCapra collapses defining distinctions even further by questioning the "binary opposition" between Nazi and Jew, which he regards as "actually a way of concealing anxiety."[117] Of course, he never comments on the radical difference between Nazi and Jew with regard to how they understand the foundations for the value of the other human being. As we have seen, the former sees the value of the other human being in terms of race and power, the latter in terms of the Divine image. To be sure, LaCapra himself opposes the Jewish testimony to a common humanity, insisting that the Holocaust "shatters the assumption"—and is not just an assault on the teaching—"that there's something like a common humanity binding people together."[118] In this statement he plays into the hands of the postmodern Nazi teaching that nothing links the "Aryan" with the non-Aryan. Our task, according to LaCapra, is not to incorporate a Divinely commanded morality into our lives but to cultivate healthy empathy and to work through our trauma. And that means something other than working our way back to Torah. There is no room here for the most fundamental category of Jewish thought and Jewish identity: *teshuvah* or "return." For "working trough trauma" appears to amount to little more than finding ways to "get over it" and becoming "sensitive" to others, including Nazis.

As LaCapra indicates in his concluding chapter, this "working through" might entail trying to understand how Hitler and Himmler read the world.[119] Indeed, from a postmodern standpoint, their reading of the "text" of the world is just as legitimate as any other—except a Jewish reading. But LaCapra says nothing on this point. What he does say is hard to say. With regard to his critical distinction between absence and loss, for example, LaCapra explains, "Absence applies transhistorically to absolute foundations; loss applies to historical phenomena. The conflation of absence and loss induces either a metametaphysical etherealization, even obfuscation, of historical problems or a historicist, reductive localization of transhistorical, recurrently displaced problems—or perhaps a confusingly hybridized, extremely labile discourse that seems to derive critical analyses of historical phenomena directly from the deconstruction of metaphysics and metam-etaphysical, at times freely associative (or disseminatory), glosses of specific historical dynamics."[120] The obscurity of what he is saying here is typical of postmodern discourse, which is calculated to be obscure because it actually says next to nothing. Once we decipher this postmodern, LaCapraesque sentence, we discover that we have been overcharged. It amounts to this: Confusing absence and loss, we slip either into absolute meaning or into absolute meaninglessness when our genuine interest lies not in having meaning but in feeling better. Here too, then, one discovers the egocentric outlook that undermines any true sense of post-Holocaust identity.

This undermining of any foundation for Jewish identity is directly tied to LaCapra's attack on "contentless utopianism" or "messianicity": Contrary to the testimony of the Jewish people, LaCapra suggests, G-d has no place in history, and the Messiah is not coming.[121] Like other postmodern thinkers, LaCapra's thinking is clearly anti-Judaic; and, inasmuch as it is anti-Judaic, it is latently anti-Semitic. One implication of LaCapra's approach to the Holocaust is that, basically, what the Jews have to do is "put it behind them"—"it" being not just the Holocaust but, more important, the Judaism marked for annihilation. In this way he joins the Nazi war against memory, which is a war against Jewish identity. Since it was "contentless," the messianic hope of the Jews was never legitimate anyway; therefore losing it is no loss. Hence the absence of the Jews from LaCapra's approach to the Holocaust is an absence that he does not regard as a loss.

If we view the Holocaust in terms of the murder of the Jews, then in order to understand the Holocaust, we must address the question of what the Jews signify *by their very presence in the world,* so that we may have some inkling of what was targeted for destruction. And whatever the Jews may signify, it has been shaped by the Torah and Talmud of Judaism. There can be no understanding of the Holocaust, even if one wants to speak of "trauma," without an understanding of the Judaism that defines the identity of the Jew, before and after; that the Nazis marked for extinction upon the extermination of the Jews; and that Western ontological thought, from German Idealism to postmodernism, has sought to eliminate. Making these connections is nothing less than a matter of life and death. For making these connections is a matter of arriving at the talmudic insistence that I must sanctify G-d's Name in a *Kiddush HaShem* rather than commit murder (*Sanhedrin* 74a). Unless we can come to *this* absolute, we shall be left either with the egocentric idealism or with the relativistic postmodernism that have proven to be equally incapable of achieving anything more than the position of bystander. Here we see a deeper dimension of the Nazis' assault not only on the Jews but on anyone who would be a Jew in the post-Holocaust era. Like the assault on the Jews, this assault on post-Holocaust Jewish identity is an assault on G-d. For, from a Jewish religious standpoint, the one who determines Jewish identity is G-d.

In the next chapter, then, we shall consider how the Nazi assault on the Holy One is tied to the assault on what it means to be a Jew.

Notes

1. See Louis I. Newman, ed., *The Hasidic Anthology* (New York: Schocken Books, 1963), 423.

2. Adin Steinsaltz, *The Sustaining Utterance: Discourses on Chasidic Thought,* trans. and ed. Yehuda Hanegbi (Northvale, NJ: Jason Aronson, 1989), 6.

3. Blaise Pascal, *Pensées* (Paris: Club des Libraires de France, 1961), 19. Unless noted otherwise, all translations in this volume are my own. –D.P.

4. See, for example, Omer Bartov and Phyllis Macks, eds., *Genocide and Religion in the 20th Century* (New York: Berghahn Books, 2001); see also Marc H. Ellis, *Unholy Alliance: Religion and Atrocity in Our Time* (Minneapolis: Fortress Press, 1997).

5. Leo Kuper, "Theological Warrants for Genocide: Judaism, Islam and Christianity," *Terrorism and Political Violence* 2 (1990): 351. In defending my position that the absence of G-d in one's thinking makes for a greater potential for murder than the presence of G-d, I am speaking only of the Jewish and Christian traditions in the West; I do not have in mind the murderous agendas of certain Arab versions of Islam.

6. Ibid., 372.

7. Jonathan Sacks, *Crisis and Covenant: Jewish Thought after the Holocaust* (Manchester, England: Manchester University Press, 1992), 268–69.

8. Berel Lang, *Act and Idea in the Nazi Genocide* (Syracuse: Syracuse University Press, 2003), 185.

9. Heinrich Heine, "The German Revolution," in *Words of Prose,* trans. E. B. Ashton (New York: L. B. Fischer, 1943), 51–53.

10. Hans Sluga, *Heidegger's Crisis: Philosophy and Politics in Nazi Germany* (Cambridge: Harvard University Press, 1993), 29.

11. From "Beitrag zur Berichtung der Urteils des Publikums über die französischen Revolution" (1793); cited in Lang, *Act and Idea,*169.

12. Johann Gottlieb Fichte, *Addresses To the German Nation,* ed. George Armstrong Kelly (New York: Harper & Row, 1968), 40; emphasis added.

13. See Nahum Glatzer's introduction to Franz Rosenzweig, *Understanding the Sick and the Healthy,* trans. Nahum Glatzer (Cambridge: Harvard University Press, 1999), 24.

14. Franz Rosenzweig, *Franz Rosenzweig's 'The New Thinking,'* trans. and ed. Alan Udoff and Barbara Galli (Syracuse: Syracuse University Press, 1999), 96.

15. See Immanuel Kant, *Grounding for the Metaphysics of Morals,* trans. James W. Ellington, 3rd ed. (Indianapolis: Hackett, 1993).

16. See Immanuel Kant, *Anthropology from a Pragmatic Point of View,* trans. Victor Lyle Dowdell, ed. Hans H. Rudnick (Carbondale: Southern Illinois University Press, 1978).

17. See Jacques Derrida, *De l'esprit* (Paris: Éditions Galilee, 1987), 11, 12, 64, 65, 155, 156.

18. Martin Heidegger, *Introduction To Metaphysics,* trans. Ralph Mannheim (New York: Doubleday, 1961), 199.

19. Martin Heidegger, *Sein und Zeit* (Tübingen: Max Niemeyer, 1963), 322.

20. Hans Jonas, "Heidegger's Resoluteness and Resolve," in Guenther Neske and Emil Kettering, eds., *Martin Heidegger and National Socialism,* trans. Lisa Harries (New York: Paragon, 1990), 202–3.

21. Reported in *Die Zeit,* 29 December 1989; see Theodore Kisiel, "Heidegger's Apology: Biography and Philosophy and Ideology," in Tom Rockmore and Joseph Margolis, eds., *The Heidegger Case: On Philosophy and Politics* (Philadelphia: Temple University Press, 1992), 12.

22. Ka-tzetnik 135633, *Sunrise over Hell,* trans. Nina De-Nur (London: W. H. Allen, 1977), 111. For a more thorough discussion of Ka-tzetnik, see chapter 3.

23. See "Protocol of the Wannsee Conference, January 20, 1942," in Yitzhak Arad, Yisrael Gutman, and Abraham Margolit, eds., *Documents on the Holocaust* (Jerusalem: Yad Vashem, 1981), 250.

24. Many postmodernists would presumably object to this last of the first principles, but in the name of what do they raise their objection?

25. For an excellent discussion of this point, see Margaret Brearley, "Fire and Ashes: The 'Tempter-god', Evil, and the Shoah," in John K. Roth and David Patterson, eds., *Fire in the Ashes: God, Evil, and the Holocaust* (Seattle: University of Washington Press, 2005), 7-20.

26. Steinsaltz, *Sustaining Utterance,* 32.

27. Abraham Joshua Heschel, *Man Is Not Alone* (New York: Farrar, Straus and Giroux, 1951), 47.

28. Recall here an incident that Emmanuel Ringelblum relates: "A police chief came to the apartment of a Jewish family, wanted to take some things away. The woman cried out that she was a widow with a child. The chief said he'd take nothing if she could guess which of his eyes was the artificial one. She guessed the left eye. She was asked how she knew. 'Because that one,' she answered, 'has a human look.'" See Emmanuel Ringelblum, *Notes from*

the Warsaw Ghetto, trans. and ed. Jacob Sloan (New York: Schocken Books, 1974), 84.

29.   Emil L. Fackenheim, *The Jewish Return into History* (New York: Schocken Books, 1978), 246.

30.   In a letter to Johann Caspar dated 28 April 1775, Kant refers to prayer as "the so-called worshipful supplications which have perennially constituted the religious delusion." See Ernst Cassirer, *Kant's Life and Thought,* trans. James Haden (New Haven: Yale University Press, 1981), 377.

31.   On the eve of Tisha B'Av 5700 (1940), for example, Chaim Kaplan writes in his Warsaw Ghetto diary, "Public prayer in these dangerous times is a forbidden act. Anyone caught in this crime is doomed to severe punishment. If you will, it is even sabotage, and anyone engaging in sabotage is subject to execution." See Chaim A. Kaplan, *Scroll of Agony: The Warsaw Diary of Chaim A. Kaplan,* trans. and ed. Abraham I. Katsh (Bloomington: Indiana University Press, 1999), 179. For a more detailed discussion of Jewish thinking about prayer, see chapter 2.

32.   Henri Crétella, "Self-Destruction," in Alan Milchman and Alan Rosenberg, eds., *Martin Heidegger and the Holocaust* (Atlantic Highlands, N.J.: Humanities Press, 1996), 159.

33.   Quoted in Max Weinreich, *Hitler's Professors: The Part of Scholarship in Germany's Crimes against the Jewish People* (New Haven: Yale University Press, 1999), 26.

34.   Alfred Rosenberg, *Race and Race History and Other Essays,* ed. Robert Pais (New York: Harper & Row, 1974), 131–32.

35.   Ibid., 183.

36.   Quoted in George L. Mosse, *Nazi Culture* (New York: Grosset & Dunlop, 1966), 202.

37.   Quoted in ibid., 70.

38.   See Weinreich, *Hitler's Professors,* 78.

39.   See Emil L. Fackenheim, "The Holocaust and the State of Israel," in Michael L. Morgan, ed., *A Holocaust Reader: Responses To the Nazi Extermination* (New York: Oxford University Press, 2001), 132.

40.   Max Wundt, *Deutsche Weltanschauung* (Munich: J. F. Lehmans, 1928), 75; see also Sluga, *Heidegger's Crisis,* 113.

41.   Fackenheim, *The Jewish Return into History,* 246.

42.   Primo Levi, *Survival in Auschwitz: The Nazi Assault on Humanity,* trans. Stuart Woolf (New York: Simon & Schuster, 1996), 90.

43.   Yehuda Bauer, "Is the Holocaust Explicable?" in Joseph R. Mitchell and Helen Buss Mitchell, eds., *The Holocaust: Readings and Interpretations* (New York: McGraw-Hill, 2001), 28; emphasis added.

44.   Quoted in Mosse, *Nazi Culture,* 316.

45.   See Sluga, *Heidegger's Crisis,* 7.

46.   See Kisiel, 34.

47.   Quoted in Victor Farías, *Heidegger and Nazism,* trans. Paul Burrell (Philadelphia: Temple University Press, 1989), 219.

48.   Paul Guyer, Introduction to *The Cambridge Companion to Kant,* ed. Paul Guyer (Cambridge: Cambridge University Press, 1992), 3.

49.   Cited by Frederick C. Beiser, "Kant's Intellectual Development, 1746–1781," in Guyer, *Cambridge Companion,* 39.

50.   For a good discussion of Kant's views in this regard, particularly as related in his *Religion within the Limits of Reason Alone,* see Allen W. Wood, "Rational Theology, Moral Faith, and Religion" in Guyer, *Cambridge Companion,* 394–416.

51.   Immanuel Kant, *The Critique of Practical Reason,* trans. Lewis White Beck (New York: Macmillan, 1985), 101.

52.   Immanuel Kant, *Conflict of the Faculties,* trans. Mary J. Gregor (New York: Abaris, 1979), 95.

53.   Paul Lawrence Rose, *German Question/Jewish Question* (Princeton: Princeton University Press, 1990), 109.

54.   For a good discussion of this point, see Edith Wyschogrod, *Spirit in Ashes: Hegel, Heidegger, and Man-Made Death* (New Haven: Yale University Press, 1985), 69–72.

55.   Emil L. Fackenheim, *Encounters between Judaism and Modern Philosophy* (New York: Basic Books, 1993), 190–91.

56.   See G. W. F. Hegel, "The Spirit of Christianity and Its Fate" in *Early Theological Writings,* trans. T. M. Knox (Chicago: University of Chicago Press, 1948), 201–5. See also Jean-François Lyotard, *Heidegger and "The Jews,"* trans. Andreas Michael and Mark S. Roberts (Minneapolis: University of Minnesota Press, 1990), 87.

57.   See Ludwig Feuerbach, *The Essence of Christianity,* trans. George Eliot (New York: Harper & Row, 1957), 12–13. Recall, also Fackenheim's insight: "The G-d of traditional Judaism can be present to man. If man is autonomous, then G-d can be present only *in* man, as 'conscience' or 'insight' or 'creative genius.' But to accept this is in the end to fall prey to idolatry."

See Emil L. Fackenheim, *Quest for Past and Future: Essays in Jewish Theology* (Bloomington: Indiana University Press, 1968), 139.

58. This is the meaning of Nietzsche's statement that "in man creature and creator are united," in Friedrich Nietzsche, *Beyond Good and Evil,* trans. Walter Kaufmann (New York: Vintage Books, 1966), 154.

59. Fackenheim, *Encounters,* 191.

60. I write "god" here, and not "G-d," because the god one would be like is not the G-d of Abraham, Isaac, and Jacob, who is the G-d of love and patience, longsuffering, and quick to forgive. No, it is the god for whom power is the only reality.

61. Nietzsche, *Beyond Good and Evil,* 136.

62. Nietzsche's most famous pronouncement on the death of G-d appears in Section 125 of *The Gay Science.* See Friedrich Nietzsche, *The Gay Science,* trans. Walter Kaufmann (New York: Vintage Books, 1974).

63. Wyschogrod, *Spirit in Ashes,* 146.

64. Martin Heidegger, "Will To Power as Art," in *Nietzsche,* vol. 1, trans D. Krell (San Francisco: Harper & Row, 1979), 18.

65. Emmanuel Lévinas, *Totality and Infinity,* trans. Alphonso Lingis (Pittsburgh: Duquesne University Press, 1969), 46–47.

66. Emmanuel Lévinas, *Collected Philosophical Papers,* trans. Alphonso Lingis (Dordrecht: Martinus Nijhoff, 1987), 52.

67. From the *Freiburger Studentenzeitung* 3 (November 1933); see Neske and Kettering, *Martin Heidegger,* 45.

68. Quoted in Weinreich, *Hitler's Professors,* 14.

69. See Martin Heidegger, "Martin Heidegger: A Philosopher and Politics: A Conversation" in Neske and Kettering, *Martin Heidegger,* 217.

70. Quoted in ibid., 13.

71. Ibid., 12.

72. Sluga, *Heidegger's Crisis,* 4.

73. Heidegger, "Martin Heidegger: A Philosopher and Politics," 217.

74. "Ontotheology" refers to an inauthentic appeal to a god outside of being to justify being, when our own being, our *Dasein,* can be justified only by our own will to power, and not by the will of any god.

75. Martin Heidegger, *Kant and the Problem of Metaphysics,* trans. J. S. Churchill (Bloomington: Indiana University Press, 1962), 244.

76. Martin Heidegger, *Vom Wesen des Grundes*, 5th ed. (Frankfurt am Main: Klostermann, 1965), 38.

77. Jacques Taminiaux, *Heidegger and the Project of Fundamental Ontology*, trans. and ed. Michael Gendre (Albany: SUNY Press, 1991), xxi.

78. Wyschogrod, *Spirit in Ashes*, 166.

79. In his commentary on the human being created in the image of the Divine being, for example, the great sage Rabbi Ovadiah ben Yaakov Sforno teaches that only through a life devoted to one's fellow human beings can the meaning of being created in the Divine image be realized. See Sforno, *Commentary on the Torah*, vol. 1, trans. Raphael Pelcovitz (Brooklyn: Mesorah, 1987), 25.

80. Heidegger, *Sein*, 118.

81. See, for example, Kant, *Grounding*, 30–32.

82. Lévinas, *Collected Philosophical Papers*, 100.

83. Recall Primo Levi's statement about the *Muselmänner:* "One hesitates to call them living: one hesitates to call their death death." See *Survival in Auschwitz*, 90. In chapter 4 we shall examine this point in detail.

84. See John D. Caputo, "Heidegger's Scandal: Thinking and the Essence of the Victim," in Rockmore and Margolis, *The Heidegger Case*, 265.

85. Quoted by Neske and Kettering, *Martin Heidegger*, xxxi.

86. Emmanuel Lévinas, *Ethics and Infinity*, trans. Richard Cohen (Pittsburgh: Duquesne University Press, 1985), 86.

87. Karl Löwith, "Last Meeting with Heidegger," in Neske and Kettering, *Martin Heidegger*, 158.

88. Lévinas, *Collected Philosophical Papers*, 52.

89. Lea Wernick Fridman, *Words and Witness: Narrative and Aesthetic Strategies in the Representation of the Holocaust* (Albany: State University of New York Press, 2000), 3.

90. Ibid., 28.

91. See, for example, Emmanuel Lévinas, *Existence and Existents*, trans. Alphonso Lingis (The Hague: Martinus Nijhoff, 1978), 57-61.

92. Fridman, *Words and Witness*, 39.

93. Ibid., 42.

94. Ibid., 72.

95. Recall, for example, Maimonides' argument, based on the Targum, that the creation of the human being in the image of the Holy One lies in the

human being's capacity for speech. See Maimonides, *The Guide for the Perplexed,* trans. M. Friedlaender (New York: Dover, 1956), 68.

96. Fridman, *Words and Witness,* 90, 93.

97. Ibid., 99.

98. See Elie Wiesel, *Evil and Exile,* trans. Jon Rothschild (Notre Dame: University of Notre Dame Press, 1990), 155, and Primo Levi, *The Drowned and the Saved,* trans. Raymond Rosenthal (New York: Vintage Books, 1989), 31.

99. Fridman, *Words and Witness,* 132.

100. Dominick LaCapra, *Writing History, Writing Trauma* (Baltimore: Johns Hopkins University Press, 2001), ix.

101. Ibid.

102. This egocentric outlook shows up perhaps most blatantly in LaCapra's index, where the longest entry is: LaCapra, Dominick.

103. Ibid., 23.

104. Ibid., 35.

105. Ibid., 46.

106. Ibid., 47.

107. Ibid.. 62.

108. Ibid., 92–93.

109. See, for example, Fackenheim, *Jewish Return into History,* 251.

110. See Kalonymos Kalmish Shapira, *Sacred Fire: Torah from the Years of Fury, 1939–1942,* trans. J. Hershy Worch, ed. Deborah Miller (Northvale, NJ: Jason Aronson, 2000), 61.

111. LaCapra, *Writing History,* 94.

112. Ibid., 102.

113. Ibid.

114. Ibid., 121–22.

115. Ibid., 129.

116. Ibid., 132.

117. Ibid., 149. Here too we see LaCapra's egocentrism in his inclusion of an interview with himself in a book that is ostensibly—but only ostensibly—about the victims of the Holocaust.

118. Ibid., 177. Recall the statement from the Nazi Ludwig Clauss cited above: "Nordic man can overcome almost anything in the world save the distance separating man from man." Here LaCapra proves himself to be a Claussian.

119. Ibid., 204.
120. Ibid., 195.
121. Ibid., 198.

CHAPTER TWO

THE HARROWING OF THE HOLY ONE

One morning some Germans saw me on the stairs. Richard, a
blond and fresh young man who spoke Ukrainian, stopped me.

"Last night we set your synagogue afire!
Didn't it burn wonderfully, Hans?"

"The Jewish G-d is burnt to ashes."

—Judith Dribben, *And Some Shall Live*

CB

THE NATURE OF HOW ONE THINKS ABOUT THE HOLY
is perhaps the most crucial distinction between the Western ontological tradition and Jewish thought in their understanding of G-d
and humanity. While the two traditions have their variations on certain
themes, and each has its exceptions, there are some general differences.
Western philosophy sees G-d as a first principle of Being; Jewish thought
sees G-d as the Holy One beyond Being, the Creator, *not* the Cause, of all
things. Western philosophy takes the human being to be a "highly evolved"
animal among many animals in the natural world; Jewish thought sees the
human being not as an animal but as the bearer of the image and likeness
of the Holy One, what I referred to in the last chapter as a "breach of
being." Hence the holy is most immediately manifest in the human being—and the Holy Name in the name of the human being.

Because the holy is a category that lies outside of speculative thought—
a kind of noncategory or anticategory—the value of a human being lies

outside of anything that speculative thought can conceive. We can esteem, honor, and admire moral integrity, intellectual acumen, athletic ability, professional accomplishment, courage in the face of danger, and simple loving kindness. But the notion of holiness tells us that the value of a human being is determined by none of these things of the world, by nothing that can be weighed, measured, counted, or otherwise determined by circumstance. Holiness circumvents circumstance. And yet it is precisely what makes circumstance intelligible as circumstance.

Hence, from the standpoint of Jewish teaching, a human being has infinite value—or rather a human being is *holy*—outside of any context, whether he or she is moral or immoral, intelligent or stupid, strong or frail, a success or a failure, brave or cowardly, nice or mean. That is why Torah and Talmud teach that we must come to the aid of an enemy before we come to the aid of a friend, lest we forget that our enemy, too, is a child of G-d (see Exodus 23:4-5; *Bava Metzia* 32b).[1] That is why Ben Zoma teaches, "Who is wise? He who learns from every person" (*Pirke Avot* 4:1)—*every* person, from autistic infant to Alzheimer's patient. For the wisdom that we receive from *every* human being lies in a realization of the exigency of the holy.[2] Such a view of a human being can be derived only from the notion of the holy that is couched in the holy tongue. Why? Because such a view of the human being must come from beyond being—not like the Cartesian concept of the infinite, but like the revelation of a Divine commandment.

Contrary to most speculative thinking on the topic, the holy is not what is very, very, very, very good. It is not an extreme degree of goodness, a moral ideal, a principle of reason, or any other facet of being. As expressed in the *lashon hakodesh*, "the holy tongue," the holy is what is *kadosh*. It is a word that implies setting something apart and making it distinct from everything else in the world, not as a "special thing" among things in the world but as a vessel of what is beyond the world. And only the Holy One can effect this setting apart. Just so, the word for "holiness," *kodesh*, also refers to the "Holy Temple," the site where being finds it tangent with what transcends being. Further, the verb *kidesh* translates as to "hallow" or to "sanctify"; it also means to "betroth," as in the phrase *kidesh ishah*, to "betroth a woman," which is also a setting apart, for the consecration of the life that may be borne of that union. Hence the word for "marriage," *kidushin*, is a cognate of *kadosh*, the word for "holiness." The categories that shape Western ontological thinking cannot accommodate these interconnections that are rooted in the distinctively Jewish "category" of the holy.

In the days of destruction called Shoah all of these dimensions of *kadosh* came under assault. As we shall see, the Nazis set out both to obliterate the holy in the extermination of the Jews and to exterminate the Jews in the obliteration of the holy. For the Jews are known as the *am kedoshim,* the "nation of holy ones," whom G-d set apart from all other nations, in an act of betrothal. Assailing and usurping G-d, the Nazis too would set the Jews apart—not only from every category of humanity and from all human memory, but from all such betrothal. Thus they created ghettos, camps, and cemeteries like Auschwitz, cemeteries with neither graves nor memorial stones. Thus they transformed the very heavens, the very dimension of height that sanctifies every human life, into a cemetery.

What makes Israel a chosen people—what makes them an *am kedoshim*—has nothing to do with their merit or anything intrinsic to their "race" (a completely meaningless term from a Jewish point of view). Rather, it is the holiness of the Holy One, who chose to separate the Jews from all other nations, as it is written: "You shall be holy, for I HaShem am holy, and I have separated you from the nations" (Leviticus 20:26). "You shall be holy" means "you shall be a people apart." And what is the distinction that separates them? It is their mission: The Jews are chosen to attest to the chosenness of every human being. All nations are a people apart, each with its own place in Creation. But separate does not mean isolated: As children of G-d, the nations are not isolated from each other but intimately tied to each other—a notion utterly alien to Nazi thinking about the distinction of the "Aryan race." Since we all derive from a single human being, each of us is bound to the other, body and soul—that, too, is part of the message that the Jews are chosen to deliver. All nations are a people apart in that every person is a being who is distinct from and hence not reducible to the categories of being. In a word, every human being is holy—that is the testimony that the Chosen People are chosen to bear. That is what makes Israel an *am kedoshim.* And that is why the master race had to see to their extermination.

The scholar and archivist Herman Kruk leaves no doubt as to whether the Nazis actually understood the religious and metaphysical implications of their actions against the Jews. In his diary from the Vilna Ghetto, he often refers to the Gestapo's "Jew Specialists" such as the infamous Dr. Pohl, director of a department known as Judenforschung ohne Juden, that is, "Research on Jews without Jews."[3] It was the responsibility of some of the Nazis to thoroughly know the Jews and Judaism, Jewish texts and teachings, and to use their information to destroy Jewish teaching. He points out, in fact, that under Nazi occupation the Polish and German press referred to the war as the "Jew War" or the "War against the Jews," demonstrating that the *complete* annihilation of the Jewish people and Jewish testimony was not a mere side agenda in the war but was Germany's prime directive in waging its war against the Chosen of G-d.

Why did the Nazis target the Jews? According to Ignaz Maybaum, it was because Hitler "knew that the Jew, historically and existentially, even without any choice, stands for justice, mercy and truth. He stood for everything which made every word of Hitler a lie. The Jew, without opening his mouth to utter a single word, condemned Hitler."[4] While Maybaum was certainly wrong in his conclusion that the *Churban* was "progress through sacrifice," he was right on this point. The Nazis targeted the Jews not because some Jews may have prospered during an economic depression; otherwise it would have been enough to impoverish them. Nor was it because they were an easy scapegoat for social problems; otherwise it would have been enough to rid only Germany of its Jews. No, it was because the Jewish presence in the world contains a testimony to the sanctity of every human being, and that testimony cannot exist in the same universe with Nazi ideology. The Jews, then, were not an economic or political or social evil, but a cosmic, *ontological* evil that had to be eradicated, a point that Oskar Rosenfeld makes very clear in his diary from the Łódź Ghetto.[5] The Nazis fought the Jews because, as Julius Streicher asserted in 1936, whoever fights the Jew fights the devil, and whoever masters the devil conquers heaven: To get rid of the Jews, in other words, is to get rid of the Holy One, which was the Nazis' ultimate aim.[6] Seeing the existence of the Jew as an ontological "crime," the Nazis assailed the Holy One by assailing the Jews and, through the Jews, all of humanity. For it was the Jewish testimony concerning the holiness of humanity that had to be eliminated *at all costs*.

The Assault on the Holiness of Humanity

In order to remove the notion of holiness and the Holy One from the realm of abstraction, we must turn to the flesh-and-blood human beings who were targeted for destruction. One way to approach that concrete reality is to examine some of the diaries that the Jews wrote along the edge of their annihilation. In those texts we discover the question that belongs both to the singularity and to the universality of the Holocaust, a question that is central to the matter of Jewish identity after the Holocaust: What is a human being? "At Auschwitz, not only man died, but also the idea of man," Elie Wiesel has said.[7] But what exactly is the idea of man? And how does it die? Or better: How does it come to be murdered in the murder that is the defining feature of the Holocaust?

Most fundamental to "the idea of man" is the idea of the sanctity of the human being. That is why the human being, in his image, can be not only murdered—he can be *desecrated*. The calculated desecration of the divine spark within the human being is part of the singularity of the Holocaust; it is a distinctive aspect of the Nazis' singular assault on the essence of the Jews and Judaism. As we have noted, Judaism maintains that all of humanity stems from a single human being, so that no one can take either himself or his people to be better than another.[8] Leo Baeck states it by saying, "The most important thing which Judaism gave to man—the contribution which enables man to feel the ethical consciousness of his dignity as an individual human being—is the idea of his likeness to G-d."[9] The Koretzer Rebbe, a disciple of the Baal Shem Tov, makes precisely this point in his commentary on the Hebrew word for "man," *ish,* spelled *alef-yud-shin.* "'Alef,'" he explains, "means the 'Source, the Leader.' The word *Ish* (Man) is composed of the 'Alef' and the word *Yesh* (There Is). This signifies that there is in Man the Source, that Divinity abides in Man."[10] Not just in the Jew, be it noted, but in Man, in every human being—that is the idea of the human being that comes to the world through the Jews. And that is what the Nazis set out to destroy.

Undertaking the extermination not only of the Jews but of every idea that arises from them, the Nazis set out to destroy this very notion of a trace of something holy, of something beyond both personal will and natural accident, that abides at the core of humanity. In a word, they undertook an assault on the holy within the human, beginning with the Jew. Emil Fackenheim makes the connection between the annihilation of the Jew and the assault on the idea of humanity as clear as it is incontrovertible. "Never was a more exalted view of man conceived than that of the divine image, and never one more radically antiracist," he writes. "It was therefore grimly logical—if to be sure uniquely horrifying—that the most radical racists of all time decreed a unique fate for the Jewish people."[11] To harbor the image of the divine is to seek the presence of the divine through a relation to our fellow human being that is expressive of a higher relation. For the Divine Presence abides in that seeking. Hence the teaching from the sacred tradition: "Only when you are My witnesses, am I G-d, but when you are not My witnesses, I—if one dare speak thus—am not G-d" (*Pesikta de-Rab Kahana* 12:6; see also *Sifre* on Deuteronomy 33:5). Thus, according to their grim and horrifying logic, the Nazis understood that both the Source and its seekers, both G-d and His witnesses, had to be destroyed.

Perhaps even more horrifying than the Nazis' logic was their exploitation of the Jews' humanity as a weapon against them; this point comes out in the diarists' accounts of the disbelief that plagued the Jewish communities. Hillel Seidman, for example, makes it clear that the victims' incredulity cannot be attributed to stubbornness, blindness, stupidity, or naive optimism. No, they disbelieved in the Nazi horrors because they continued to believe in the idea of the human being that was given to the world through the Torah.[12] "Blessed are we that we could not believe it!" Yitzhak Katznelson cries out from the pages of his *Vittel Diary.* "We could not believe it because of the Image of G-d that is in us…. We did not believe it could happen because we are human beings."[13] For to be a human being is to affirm the holiness and the humanity of our fellow human beings—even German human beings. In Katznelson's outcry we see the struggle to sustain the idea of the human being in the midst of the slaughter of humanity and the assault on the holy within the human. Which is to say: The diarist struggles to maintain his face in the midst of a radical assault upon the face.

The Mystery, Meaning, and Obliteration of the Face

In his *Notes from the Warsaw Ghetto,* historian Emmanuel Ringelblum records a statement made by a Nazi to his friend Rabbi Velvele: "You're not human, you're not animal, you're Jew,"[14] suggesting that the Jew is in a category outside the realm of living things. Just so, Josef Katz relates a conversation that he had with a German guard at Kaiserwald. After reporting to the guard that he had brought thirty men to be washed, the guard looked puzzled and asked, "What men? What do you mean?" And Katz corrected himself, saying, "Thirty Jews for washing." To which the guard replied, "Oh, okay."[15] How is the Jew, then, transformed into something other than human in the eyes of the Nazi? By replacing the human face with a racial physiognomy.

The great sage of the Talmud, Rabbi Akiba, maintains that the humanity and the dignity of the human being are revealed in the face; in the face, he held, lies the image of the Holy One.[16] This way of thinking about the face is distinctively Jewish, as a brief consideration of the Hebrew word for "face," *panim*, suggests. *Panim* is plural because, according to one tradition, each of us has two faces: the face of Adam and our own individual face. The face, therefore, is both universal and particular, harboring both a human and a divine presence. Announcing a fundamental difference *between* one another, the face reveals a fundamental link *to* one another, which is a fundamental responsibility *for* one another. To be an individual is to have one's own unique face, and this is what it means to be irreplaceable: Only I can meet this responsibility here and now for this human being. Definitively tied to one another, we live in community with one another, that is, in a oneness that inheres in the Oneness of G-d, each sharing the sanctity that attests to the absolute dearness of *every* human being. To encounter the face, in other words, is to encounter Torah. Through the face Torah enters this world. Through the face, Torah commands us to be there for the sake of another.[17] Through the face G-d "placed Torah in Israel" (cf. Psalms 78:5).

Emmanuel Lévinas rightly sees that the most fundamental commandment to arise from the face is the prohibition against murder, which issues from *on high*.[18] That is why the Nazi *must* obliterate the face of the Jew: The Nazi's aim is to eliminate the *absolute* nature of the prohibition against murder. The face, however, not only forbids us to kill—it commands us to open the door, offer a word of encouragement, and do any number of small, mundane things for the sake of another. And yet, like every act of kindness, the face is laden with mystery. As it is written in the Mekilta, "When one welcomes his fellow man, it is considered as if he had welcomed the Divine Presence" (*Mekilta, Amalek* 3). For to welcome another is precisely to greet the face with a face. Anything less than a welcome, anything less than kindness shown toward another, is not only to mistreat another—it means we have failed to fathom the holiness that the face signifies.

When the holy within the human is assaulted, as in the Nazi assault against the Jew, the mystery and the meaning of the face are obliterated in a twisting and torturing of the face itself.[19] One means of attaining this twisting was to render the Jew *shamefaced,* both in the eyes of others and in his own eyes. This point becomes evident when we consider an observation from Auschwitz *Sonderkommando* diarist Salmen Lewental. "We were ashamed of one another," he writes, "and dared not look one another in the face. Our eyes swollen with pain, shame, tears and lamentations, each of us burrowed into a hole to avoid meeting one another."[20] And so we see yet another dimension of the Nazi perversion of the Good:[21] It is not the perpetrator, not the murderer, who is ashamed, but his victim. The hole these Jews burrow into swallows up their humanity, because what is buried in this hole that resembles a grave is the human face. This distance between one human being and another creates a void into which every trace of humanity disappears. For the human image belongs not just to this person or that but rises up where two come together face-to-face.

Lewental's remark suggests, moreover, that the imposition of shame is not the only thing that characterizes the twisting of the face of humanity. Along with shame are tears and lamentations, sorrow and terror, which become not just the transitory emotions that may pass over any face but the *defining* features of the Jewish face. As the Jews are plunged more and more into the definitive sorrow and terror that the Nazis impose on them, they are less and less able to retain a trace of the human image. Thus it happened that Jews could be recognized not only by the insignia on their sleeves, as Chaim Kaplan points out, but "by the sorrow implanted on their faces"—*implanted,* mind you, as if the face would not be a Jewish face without this sorrow that is rooted in it.[22] The human face is lined with the life that the human being has lived; the Jewish face is harrowed by the erasure of the human image that might distinguish a human life. For the fear that marks these faces signifies an assault on the face of humanity to the point where human being dissipates into sheer terror.

But terror is not the last stage in the attempt to render the Jew faceless. As the assault on the face of the Jew runs its course, his face is gradually emptied of every expression of life that would animate the face. Commenting on Jews awaiting deportation from the Lvov Ghetto, for example, David Kahane describes them by saying, "Their faces bespoke quiet, meditative resignation, devoid of fear and theatrics. They had come to the simple conclusion: 'We are Jews and therefore we must die. There is no alternative.'"[23] Drained of life, these faces lose their animation to a death that has disfigured them before they are dead, making the Jewish face into nothing more than a breathing death mask. And so we begin to see a progression in this mutilation of the face, from shame to sorrow to terror to emptiness. And from there the Jew would often descend into self-hatred.

This self-hatred is, indeed, the ultimate aim of the assault on the face of humanity. As Fackenheim has noted, "Nazism can seek nothing higher from the 'non-Aryan' 'race'-enemy than self-destruction, preceded by self-transformation into the loathsome creature which, according to Nazi doctrine, he has been since birth."[24] A passage from Katznelson's diary illustrates Fackenheim's point. "Instead of loathing and despising those foulest dregs of humanity, the accursed German nation," writes Katznelson, "we have begun to hate ourselves."[25] As Fackenheim suggests, this self-hatred is more than the hatred of oneself as a person; it is a hatred of oneself as a *Jew*. This, then, is the height of the Nazis' extermination of the human image within the Jew: They engender among the Chosen a longing to be unchosen—which would mean abandoning the sacred task of attesting to the sanctity of each human being.

"When you remove from a child his 'Jewish gene,'"[26] Katznelson states it, "you remove from him the 'human gene.'" When the assault on the face of humanity is successful, it results in a longing on the part of the Jew to be rid of his Jewish face. When it works most nefariously, it works on a child. Ringelblum, for example, relates, "In a refugee center an eight-year-old child went mad. Screamed, 'I want to steal, I want to rob. I want to eat, I want to be a German.'"[27] Since it was impossible for a Jew to become a German, some did the next best thing—or the next worst thing—as Ringelblum indicates. "A great many cases of conversion," he laments. "At Hoshana Raba time more than fifty Jews were converted (data from the Council). The reason being that the Catholics look after their converts.... This is a pathological phenomenon."[28] This last phrase is crucial: *a pathological phenomenon.* For even more than Ringelblum's previous remark about the madness of the eight-year-old child, it points up a fragmentation of identity indicative of the assault on the holy within the human. Instead of the image of man, what the Nazis imposed on the Jew was the image of the madman. A consideration of that madness will help us avoid another madness, the post-Holocaust madness of forgetting who we are by trying to resemble those who have murdered us.

Of Madness and Monstrosity

From the testimony of Jews who were there, we find that during the Holocaust a certain madness, a madness that threatened the very substance of the Jew, unfolded on a massive scale. "The popular unrest is dreadful," says Ringelblum in October 1941. "The populace has lost its head."[29] Why? Because the erasure of the reference points by which these people make sense of the world, as well as their own identity, leads to a loss of the senses. Madness, then, is something that Ringelblum addresses in one of the first entries of his diary. On 24 March 1940, for instance, he notes, "Mietek Zucker from Łódź, who defended his father from an attack by soldiers, is in the madhouse."[30] Then there is the woman who tried to save her three-year-old child after a guard had thrown him out of a truck headed for Warsaw. As she was about to jump off the truck and go to her child, the Nazi threatened to shoot all the Jews on the truck if she should make a move. "The mother arrived in Warsaw," Ringelblum finishes this terrible tale, "and here went out of her mind."[31] What these examples have in common is the struggle to keep hold on one's human image by attending to the need of a loved one. Those who are sane derive their sanity from their relation to the humanity closest to them. When that relation—which is a relation to the holy—is lost, they are plunged into the absolute isolation of madness.

Buried in the solitude of insanity, the madman rapidly loses all ties with a life that might sustain the human image. The engineered isolation of Jewish humanity into ghettos and camps is calculated to create this absolute isolation of the human being from life, which often culminates in the isolation of madness. Indeed, in an entry from Josef Katz's diary we see a madness that manifests itself as a severing from the very wellspring of life. "A young Jew from Łódź," he relates, "goes insane. 'Mama,' he screams incessantly, 'Mama!'"[32] Katz takes this scream of "Mama!" to signify madness, because it invokes the signifier of life—the mother—from which the young Jew has been torn; torn from the source of his human being, he is twisted into madness. As though falling into a black hole, the man recedes from the one who first uttered his name with love and in that utterance announced his humanity.[33] When his humanity is undone, he cries out for the one who first affirmed his humanity, but he receives no response. Receiving no response from his human origin, he slips away from all humanity; receding from the source of his humanity, he recedes into insanity.

The metaphor of the black hole has other implications. It suggests, for example, a field of gravity surrounding the madman that draws others into its depths; just as a black hole swallows up all light, madness can swallow up the light of reason in all who are near it. In this connection Katz describes a scene from a barge floating down the Vistula on its way to Danzig in the fall of 1944: "I don't know whether from hunger or pain, but crying women are dangerous because their crying is contagious and can cause a panic. We try to comfort them as best we can and apply improvised bandages, but the prolonged hardships of the voyage without sleep or food have found their ultimate expression in this one hysterical scream."[34] Thus, like the human image lost in the abyss of madness, madness too is a condition that arises *between* people. That is what makes the isolation of madness an isolation *from* others.

Within the realm of human being, reality is a human reality that rests upon the sanctity and the meaning of the human image as it is revealed in human relation. The defilement of that image is accompanied by a collapse of humanity into a void where the real and the unreal exchange places; instead of arms open to relation we find arms folded in isolation, as though constrained by a straitjacket. Struggling to survive in the midst of a rising tide of madness, both within them and around them, the Jews had to labor to hold on to their own humanity. This struggle comes out when Moshe Flinker, for instance, writes, "My sister told me that Mrs. Keller, who was taken away with her whole family, has gone mad! I never before imagined that from the immensity of one's troubles one can go mad, but now I have found that even this affliction has not been spared us. Madness, too, is among us. When I heard that this good woman had gone mad I suddenly understood what I had been fearing until now."[35] Yes, even without knowing that it was madness he feared, young Moshe feared madness. What appears before his eyes is a darkness gathering within his eyes. Like many others, in the faces of the Jews who surround him, oozing with madness, young Moshe beholds his own face. It is a face that he is less and less able to recognize. It is a face defiled in the harrowing of the Holy One.

As for the Nazi who locks the Jew into the torment of madness, he suffers from a different kind of madness. Or better: He is not precisely mad—he is monstrous. Representing the essence of idolatry, wantonness, and murder, the Nazi embodies the evil that is not only the contrary of good—it is the contrary of humanity, "a counter-nature," as Lévinas expresses it, "a monstrosity, what is disturbing and foreign of itself."[36] Here it may be helpful to briefly consider the Hebrew word for "monster": *mifletset*. It is a cognate of the verb *hitpalets*, which means to "shudder in horror." From the standpoint of Jewish thinking, the monstrous is not the same as the bestial; it is, rather, what sends a shudder of horror through the soul—indeed, through thought itself. What, then, is a monstrosity? It is not the animal in the animal kingdom, but is rather the joining of the animal to the image of the human, where the face becomes a snout and hands turn into claws.[37] A huge and grotesque animal is not a monster; it is a huge and grotesque animal. Only a human being can become monstrous, because a human being is required for the unholy blending of the human and the inhuman. Therefore, to deem the Nazis monstrous is not to demonize them or to rob them of their humanity, but just the opposite: It is to affirm their humanity turned inhuman and to hold them responsible for the transformation.

The horror with which we shudder is that the other man, the man at war with the Holy One, has lost his human image, that this other who resembles a man is in fact inhuman: The killer may have facial features, but he does not have a face—that is the horror. He does not have a face, despite his appearance, because he is deaf to the prohibition against killing that comes to us in the face-to-face encounter and that exemplifies the holy within the human. One cannot undertake a harrowing of the Holy One without undoing his own humanity. There lies the horror. And yet behind this horror there lurks a greater horror: This monstrous other looks very much like everyone else, very much like *me*. Once again we realize that the image of the divine is implicated in the human image.[38]

The monstrosity of the Nazis who would render the Jews shamefaced, moreover, is that they are as shameless as they are faceless. Realizing in this connection that what the Jews suffer in the ghetto is unlike any other instance of brutality, Kaplan points out what distinguishes the Nazis from others who have reveled in torturing the Jews. "Even the sadists," he says, "used to be tempered with a sense of shame; their cruelty was perpetrated in secret places, not in public. But since the coming of Nazism public shame has ceased, and the more one practices cruelty in public, the better."[39] And so we see a deeper implication of a point made earlier: Incapable of shame, the Nazis' pride in the public display of their cruelty is a major part of what links their assault on the holy within the human to a defilement of their own humanity. Not only do they spill blood—they wallow it in. Refusing to turn their faces away in shame and insisting upon showing their faces in public, they show themselves to be without a face: They show themselves to be inhuman—a status that no animal, however "monstrous," can ever attain. That is what makes the Nazi an instance of monstrosity.

One means by which the Jews who kept diaries sought to maintain their humanity in the face of such monstrosity lay in the recovery of a sense of meaning through the recovery of a sense of time. Like the face, time is the presence of the holy in the human. How is that Divine Presence manifest as time? In the mode of the commandment that has *yet* to be observed. And the first commandment pertaining to the human-to-human relation is the Sixth Commandment: the prohibition against murder. (How much of humanity has *yet* to observe that commanding outcry!) Attesting to the absolute nature of this Sixth Utterance of G-d, the Jew attests to the truth of the First Utterance, which on the Tablets of the Ten Utterances parallels the Sixth: I am *HaShem*. Because the Sixth Utterance is paired with the First, the measure of time is a measure of the Holy One. As Abraham Joshua Heschel has said, "Time is the presence of G-d in the world of space,"[40] so that the harrowing of the Holy One becomes a harrowing of time itself. One place where this assault on time is most visible is in the assault on the holy days.

Life Time, Death Time, and Holy Time

The Nazis cannot mount their ascent as the master race without usurping the Holy One seated on high. And because time is the measure of the holy, the Nazis attack the prayers said in the morning, afternoon, and evening; the Torah, whose portions mark the days of the week; and the deeds of loving-kindness that announce the yet-to-be of our mission in the world. In its metaphysical dimensions, the Shoah is an assailing of the eternal in an attempt to close the portals through which the eternal might make an appearance in time. That is why "the Nazis strictly follow the Jewish calendar," as Mary Berg points out.[41] Scheduling their actions to coincide with the remembrance and observance of holy time, the Nazis would murder the Holy One in the process of murdering the Jews.

Consider, for example, Rosh Hashanah. Rosh Hashanah is observed not on the anniversary of the creation of the world but on the anniversary of G-d's creation of the first human being. It falls on the First of Tishrei, when time begins with the appearance of the human being, because humanity determines its meaning in the embrace of relation that announces our life time. With the appearance of the first human being we have the first appearance of judgment and atonement, both of which are categories that represent the insertion of the eternal into time. That is what makes the days that encompass this time the Days of Awe, the days between and including Rosh Hashanah and Yom Kippur.

The text read on Rosh Hashanah is the *Akeda,* the account of how Abraham raised the knife over his son Isaac. Just as on that day Abraham and Isaac came before a judgment, so does every Jew stand to be judged on Rosh Hashanah. Turning to the Shoah, however, Elie Wiesel reminds us that "we have known Jews who, like Abraham, witnessed the death of their children; who, like Isaac, lived the *Akeda* in their flesh; and some who went mad when they saw their father disappear on the altar, with the altar, in a blazing fire whose flames reached the highest of the heavens."[42] Given these associations with the story of Abraham and Isaac and the tale's connection with Rosh Hashanah, it is not surprising to find so many commentaries on this holiday in the testimonies that emerged from the eye of the deadly storm.

The onslaught against the season, of course, includes an attack on the prayers of the season. For just as the *Shekhinah,* G-d's Indwelling Presence, is associated with the community of Israel (see *Zohar* II, 98a),[43] so is it associated with prayers of Israel. The Baal Shem Tov, founder of Chasidism, for instance, teaches that "when a man begins the Amidah and says the opening verse: 'O Lord, open Thou my lips!' [Psalms 51:17] the Shekhinah immediately enters within his voice, and speaks with his voice."[44] Therefore the annihilation of the Indwelling Presence required the annihilation of prayer. On the eve of Rosh Hashanah 5701, for instance, Chaim Kaplan writes, "Never before was there a government so evil that it would forbid an entire people to pray."[45] A people cannot live a life of value without the holy season that sanctifies all the other seasons of life; and the holy season cannot have any significance without the prayers that define it.

On Yom Kippur the Jews purify their souls with prayer and their bodies with fasting, to become as the angels, who neither eat nor drink. On this day the Jews answer to their name before the Name. In their testimonies from the time of the harrowing of the Name, however, Jews added their diary entries to their prayers of entreaty and recorded the perversion of the season imposed by the enemy's affliction of the body of Israel. In his entry for Yom Kippur 1942, for example, Ringelblum simply jots down, "The practice of torturing Jews in the cities on Yom Kippur."[46] This drenching of the holy day in blood is a means of bleeding the day of its holiness—and the Jew of his name. One means of holding onto his name was to maintain a chronicle of the assault on the Name. This testimony *is not a question of having faith;* rather, it is a matter of sustaining a Jewish name and a Jewish affirmation of Jewish life and of what sanctifies life. Linking their words and their names with the words and the names of Jews everywhere, Jews have sought and continue to seek the ear of the Name in the time of judgment and atonement. That is what makes the testimony of Rosh Hashanah and Yom Kippur so crucial: There is no meaning in life without a mission in life, and there is no mission without this judgment and atonement. It is precisely this judgment and atonement of the Jewish tradition, and not the philosophers' autonomy of the self, that defines the freedom of the human being.

In the Jewish tradition the liberation that brings this freedom happens where the Passover table is laid and the family is gathered. According to the Talmud, "at the time when the Temple stood, the altar used to make atonement for a person; now a person's table makes atonement for him" (*Chagigah* 27a). As the focal point of atonement, the table is the reference point for the soul's liberation. It is the family's gathering about the table for the Passover Seder, therefore, that makes it possible to honor the Talmud's injunction that in every generation we regard ourselves as though we had been liberated from Egypt (*Pesachim* 116b). For this is a liberation not merely from forced labor but from the meaningless power struggle that characterizes idolatry in all its forms, particularly in its most extreme, Nazi form. Passover is about the covenant with divinity and a promise of humanity that draw human beings into a relation with the Name. Where the people of Israel live, the Name lives and life has meaning: That is the Covenant, and the Covenant is the liberation.

Where the people of Israel live in keeping with the Covenant and the commandments of Torah, G-d is One and His Name is One. Which means: The link between what is above and what is below—the *yud-heh* and the *vav-hey*—is manifest. But the Nazis determined that the people of Israel would not live in the Covenant and the commandments of Torah. The wall that imprisons the Jews in the ghetto, therefore, is made of more than brick and mortar: It is made of the evil that is the harrowing of the Name. One tradition maintains that the Name of the Holy One is the Torah itself; since the Torah is made of G-d's commandment, the Nazis assault the Name by assaulting the commandment.[47] Rabbi Shimon Huberband notes, for example, that in the Warsaw Ghetto the use of the *mikveh* or ritual bath "was punishable by death as an act of sabotage."[48] If the liberation from Egypt is manifested through the sanctity of the family gathered about the Passover table, the assault on the family here takes the form of an assault on the laws of family purity, to which the *mikveh* is closely tied. To forbid the use of the *mikveh* is to forbid wives from joining with their husbands and both from joining with the Creator in the process of bringing into the world those souls that issue from the Name. Therefore it is an effort to obstruct the flow of the Name into the world.

In contrast to the first Passover, during the Shoah the Angel of Death from whom the Jews sought deliverance was not the one sent from G-d but was rather the Nazi angel of idolatry. The plague that came upon them, moreover, was not the Plague of the Firstborn; no, it was the Plague of Darkness and Murder, in which "no man could see his brother" (Exodus 10:23). Which is to say: The Nazi could not see the Jew. In many cases this feature of the antiworld only heightened the Jew's need to reconnect himself with the community. In the spring of 1943, for example, Michael Zylberberg relates that, even though he had found safety outside the walls of the Warsaw Ghetto, "the Passover festival was drawing closer and this, also, made me want to return to the ghetto."[49] While he managed to get inside the ghetto for a few days before Passover, he was forced to observe the holy day in isolation: "I went out into the forest and heard the reverberations of the distant gunfire. Sleep was impossible; this was to be a night of wakefulness—a *Lail Shimurim*. I was to hold my own vigil and service, alone, living through their experience on this night of 'blood, fire and pillars of smoke.' These words, from the *Haggadah,* had acquired new meaning."[50] New meaning is imparted to the holy text when it is incorporated into the text of the diary. This new meaning marks the effort to renew the meaning of the Name.

The Jews' endeavor to recover a remnant of life and meaning through a recovery of the Name entails this retrieval of ancient words that take on new meaning by returning a text to its time and a time to its text. Where is this interconnection established? In the community, where the Name below joins with the Name above. If the witness writes in isolation, he does not write merely for himself but in the interest of a community. And searching out renewed meaning in the holy text is essential to the renewal of a community. Just as new meaning is forced into the words, so are new words, words out of place, forced into the season. When the word is torn and twisted from its time, the Jew is cut off from the community, cast into a condition of absolute homelessness, ontologically out of place. Ringelblum provides us with an instance of the word torn from the season that gives it meaning when on 17 April 1941 he writes, "A friend whom I wished a 'calm Passover' (that was last year's motto) replied: 'Rather wish me an easy fast'"—a greeting normally reserved for Yom Kippur.[51] When meaning is removed from words and words from their season, the season of liberation is twisted into a season of destruction. Forced off the calendar and out of its season, "liberation" becomes a synonym for death among the Jews of Nazi Europe—the only "liberation" the Nazis would allow them. The one remaining link between life and liberation is the testimony itself, where the testimony relates not only the greeting but also the *horror* of it.

On each day of the seven weeks from Passover to Shavuot we count the *omer* to indicate that liberation means revelation. For Shavuot is the anniversary of the giving of the Torah at Sinai. On that day the Israelites were gathered at Mount Sinai to hear the Voice of the Holy One. In the ghetto, too, many Jews struggled to hear the Voice of G-d in the chaos and slaughter that surrounded them. Failing to hear that Voice—or fearing the Voice that perhaps they heard—they raised their own voices through their chronicle of the encounter with the One who now seemed to turn toward them quite a different face. Even Adam Czerniakow, head of the Jewish Council of the Warsaw Ghetto and a man known for his secularism, writes, "At 9:30 in the Synagogue on Tlomackie Street I carried the Torah twice around the synagogue. Toward the end of the service (Shavuot) a cantor had a dizzy spell (paralysis)."[52] Like the cantor, the diarist struggles to sanctify the Name of the Holy One in his chronicle of the holy. Like the cantor, he often swoons, and for the same reason: It is the gross incongruity of the imposition of the antiworld upon the world, the collapse and perversion of all distinction, of all *havdalah,* that makes it possible for the holy to manifest itself.

Other examples of the swoon of the witness[53] can be found in the journals of *Oneg Shabbat*[54] members Hersh Wasser and Abraham Levin. Relating the events of Shavuot 5702 (1942), Wasser writes, "All the Jews were driven out of Wojslowice, Sielec, Kumow, and Wolka Leszczanska, to Chelm, and on the way masses were 'rendered cold'—shot down by machine guns. The Jewish blood contribution to world slaughter surpasses understanding and measure."[55] Equally beyond understanding and measure, however, is the determined faith of Rabbi Shlomo Zelichowski of Zdunska Wola, who, according to Levin, sang praises to G-d as he and nine other Jews were hanged in a grisly *minyan* (the quorum of ten required for saying certain prayers) on that same Shavuot.[56] In these incidents we find the extremes of souls rendered cold and souls on fire, extremes that bespeak the extremity of the Nazi assault. Both are instances of the insertion into the world of a Presence from beyond the world, and the pages of these testimonies contain the trace of that Presence.

A holy time during which that Presence is signified by the Light of the Holy One is Chanukah, the Festival of Lights that lasts for eight days. It is a time when we remember not just the victory of the Maccabees over the Greeks who tried to Hellenize the Jews in the second century B.C.E.; more importantly, we remember the reentry of the Name into the world, with the rededication of the Temple and the rekindling of the menorah. During the Shoah, however, the Jews trapped in the Kingdom of Night witnessed the entry of the Nazis into the realm where the remembrance and observance of the holy days would open up a place for G-d to enter. On the first day of Chanukah 5702 (December 1941), for example, one Jew relates, "The entire *minyan* began to say the *Shema Yisroel.* We could hear Jews screaming the same words on the street.... We began to recite the prayers, when suddenly, we once again heard terrible screams and wails form the prison yard. We went over to the window and our blood froze in our veins when we saw a new group of seven Jews being led to the execution area."[57] This conjunction of prayers and screams is yet another example of the incongruity that forces time—the time of the return of G-d's light to the world—out of joint.

When time is out of joint, the holy is out of place, and G-d recedes into the depths of a scream. Indeed, the task of the Nazis who would undo time was to transform the prayer into a scream. And yet, adding his voice to the unholy conjunction of prayers and screams, the Jew joins prayer to outcry and outcry to prayer in an effort to retrieve some remnant of the holy; the chronicle of the harrowing of the Holy One creates a time in which the holy may show itself, even as it is under assault. Therefore Kaplan is careful to observe, "Never before in Jewish Warsaw were there as many Chanukah celebrations as in this year of the wall [1940]."[58] Like the Jews who pray despite the prohibition, the diarist writes despite the darkness and thereby transforms a small piece of the darkness into light. Thus responding to the first utterance of Creation—"Let there be light" (Genesis 1:3)—the Jew affirms meaning of all creation and of all life. The recovery of life and meaning in these daily accounts amounts to the Jew's recovery of the purpose of his Jewishness, both for those who endured the horror and for us, their heirs. For the one who observes and records the events of Chanukah, the holy season itself becomes a means of resisting the assault on time.

Another day that had particular significance for the Jews of Nazi Europe was Purim, when Jews gather in remembrance of their deliverance from the edict of extermination that Haman tried to impose on them in the fifth century B.C.E., during the reign of the Persian king Ahasuerus. The tale is told in the Book of Esther, which is read amidst joyous celebration on the night of 14 Adar (February–March) each year. Here, too, of course, the Jews trapped in the Shoah were faced with a staggering disjuncture between the festive occasion and the days of destruction. While the disjuncture lay in the fact that in this instance they would not be delivered from destruction, very often it was handled by suggesting a similarity between Haman and Hitler. Ringelblum, for example, writes, "People hope for a new Purim—to celebrate the downfall of the modern Haman, Hitler—one that will be commemorated as long as the Jewish people exist."[59]

Not surprisingly, the day of horror that bore particular significance for the Jews of the Shoah was Tisha B'Av, the Ninth of Av, the date of the destruction of both temples as well as numerous other catastrophes. The biblical text traditionally read on Tisha B'Av is the Book of Lamentations. As though adding to that text the latest list of the dead, on 12 August 1940, Czerniakow writes, "Now I must tell their families. One hundred fifty-eight persons are dead out of 260"; and he is careful to add: "Tomorrow is Tisha B'Av."[60] As might be expected, the Nazis marked this date on their calendar as well. Zylberberg, for example, reports that in the Warsaw Ghetto during the summer of 1942 "the first deportation order was issued to us on the 9th of Av, the anniversary of the destruction of the Temple."[61] Here the Jews themselves take the place of the Temple. Like the Temple, they signify the presence of the Holy One in the world; like the Temple, they were consigned to the flames. In the time of the Temple, the light of the Holy emanated from its windows into the world (see, for example, *Tanchuma Tetsaveh* 6); in the time of the Shoah, the light of the Holy One emanated into the world through the testimony of His witnesses.

By now we can see that, like the annihilation of the Jews, the assault on time is a central feature of the assault on G-d that distinguishes the Shoah. And yet, in our consideration of the assault on the Holy One during the holy days, we have not mentioned the holiest of days: the Sabbath. Because it is so fundamental to the Name and the recovery of a name, it requires a special consideration.

The Assault on the Sabbath

Jewish tradition teaches that *Shabbat*, or "Sabbath," is one of the names of G-d (see *Zohar* II, 88b; see also the *Or HaChayim* on Exodus 20:8). Hence it is not for nothing that, when the Nazis invaded Poland, among the first of their decrees was the prohibition against Sabbath observance.[62] Sabbath observance entails entering into a state of "peace" and "rest," of "respite" and "repose," a state of *menuchah*, through an affirmation of the oneness and the sanctity of the Name. Significantly, the root for *menuchah* is *nach*, a verb that means not only "to rest," but also "to dwell." The Sabbath repose is the opposite of the radical homelessness that Primo Levi, for example, describes, when he says that in the concentration camp "the struggle to survive is without respite, because everyone is desperately and ferociously alone."[63] Yes: *ferociously* alone.

Neil
Kochen

What a phrase! It is truly a Holocaust combination of words. How did it find its way into the language? What happens to the language when such a combination of words is possible? What can it mean? Is it that no one hears you scream? That you hear nothing but screams and silence? That you are bereft of everything, from your hair to your name? That, infinitely removed from the Infinite One, you are infinitely homeless? Indeed, living in a camp, in a ghetto, or in hiding, *every Jew in Nazi Europe was homeless.* Here we have a key to the Nazi prohibition against the Sabbath rest: It was a prohibition against Jewish dwelling. For Jewish dwelling is the opening to the dwelling of the Divine in the world. According to the Midrash on Psalms, that is why G-d is called *HaMakom,* or "the Place": He is in the *dwelling place* of the world, for it is He who makes dwelling in the world possible (*Midrash Tehillim* 4:90:10). And in the *Pirke de Rabbi Eliezer,* it is written that G-d is known as *HaMakom* because, in the words of Torah, "In every place *[Makom]* where I record My Name I shall come unto you and bless you" (Exodus 20:24; see *Pirke de Rabbi Eliezer* 35). Tearing the Jews from holiness, the Nazis tear them from the Sabbath; tearing them from the Sabbath, they tear them from the Name.[64]

Further, inasmuch as the Nazis forced the Jews into the desecration of the Sabbath, their assault on the Name is about the obliteration of meaning. As the Maharal of Prague has taught, the six days of Creation correspond to the six directions of physical space: What was created in the first six days was the physical reality of the cosmos. The seventh day, however, transcends the other six to give them meaning: It is the dimension of the holy.[65] Similarly, in his commentary on Parshat Behaalotecha in the *Mei HaShiloach,* Rabbi Mordechai Yosef of Isbitza teaches that the six outer lamps of the menorah point toward the central flame, just as the six days of the week point toward the Sabbath: The central flame, the seventh flame, "stands for intention for the sake of heaven."[66] In Hebraic thinking, of course, "meaning" and "intention" are interconnected, as the word *kavanah* implies. Thus it is the seventh day that makes dwelling viable, because dwelling happens only where there is meaning.

Here we realize that, in a very important sense, the time chronicled in the Holocaust diary is the time of the Sabbath. This day for which all the other days are created is ultimately the basis for the diarists' treatment of the assault on the Name. Without the Sabbath such a chronicle would have no point; with the Sabbath it becomes a matter of absolute urgency. On the Sabbath the Holy One Himself rested from His work and settled into His creation. How? By creating an "additional soul" for the Jews who observe the Sabbath,[67] a soul that transmits the Name through the names of the Jews. Compiling this chronicle of the holy, the Jews struggle to create a place where the Holy One might once more enter His creation. And because this chronicle is generated in the midst of the darkness produced by driving G-d out of the world, it attests to the most fundamental feature of the event's singularity: the assault on the Name.

Refusal and Affirmation of the Name

We have seen the centrality of the harrowing of the Holy One in the testimonies of the Jews who cried out from the core of that assault. Because the assault on the Name is so central to the event, it also dominates Jewish memory of the event: We may refuse G-d or affirm G-d, but we cannot ignore G-d. Indeed, perhaps we can undertake a recovery of the Name after this assault on the Name only by *both* refusing *and* affirming. As Elie Wiesel insists, "G-d is one; He is everywhere. And if He is everywhere, then He is in evil and injustice too, and also in the supreme evil: death. It is man's task to free G-d of this evil."[68] G-d abides not only in the victim but in the executioner as well. This is a condition undreamt of in philosophy.[69]

Fackenheim has noted that, while Nietzsche and Sartre may have found some exhilaration in the idea that G-d is dead or absent, there is only terror in a G-d who is still present but has become an enemy.[70] Here G-d becomes the absolutely Other—Other to Himself—implicating not only His creation in an undoing of the pronouncement that it is "very good," but also the human being created in his image. "It is impossible to believe anything in a world that has ceased to regard man as man," Simon Wiesenthal expresses it. "One really begins to think that G-d is on leave. Otherwise the present state of things wouldn't be possible. G-d must be away. And He has no deputy."[71] The primary representative of G-d in His creation is the one created in His image. The images of creature and Creator are inextricably linked, even—or especially—in their undoing. "At last you must admit, Rabbi," we read in the first of Ka-tzetnik's visions in *Shivitti*, "that G-d of the Diaspora himself is climbing into this truck—a mussulman."[72] And so the ontological assault on the human becomes a metaphysical assault on the divine.

Wiesenthal's remark suggests that the assault on G-d can manifest itself as a loss of belief in G-d. We find a similar sentiment in Wieslaw Kielar's *Anus Mundi,* where he writes, "If He existed—and it is in this belief that I was brought up—how could He allow these murders of helpless human beings, carried out by other human beings whose soldiers wore on the buckle of their belts the words 'G-d with us'?"[73] And, gazing upon the "forlorn and stupefied women" surrounding her, Sara Zyskind confesses that she "began to doubt the existence of G-d.... Perhaps G-d himself had begun to despise His own people."[74] When the human relation that reveals the truth and the holiness of Torah is lost, so is G-d. And yet a trace of G-d remains in the terror over the prospect that He is not simply lost but has become the enemy: Kielar remembers the belt buckles of the murderers that read "G-d with us," signifying Zyskind's fear that perhaps He has come to hate the Jews. Only a believer can lose his belief; only one who is filled with the piety that itself bears the imprint of the Divine can insist on his non-belief. Primo Levi drives home the point in very stark terms: "The experience of the Lager with its frightful iniquity confirmed me in my non-belief.... A prayer under those conditions would have been not only absurd but blasphemous...."[75] Levi refuses belief because he refuses the blasphemy and impiety of the nonbeliever. G-d cannot be ignored.

Levi's refusal is filled with a longing for G-d that affirms the holiness of the Holy One. He does not pray because it would be unholy. Thus his refusal is in keeping with the Talmudic tradition that says G-d likes to be overcome by His children (see *Bava Metzia* 59b), particularly in the light of what befalls His children. After listening to the screams of children being slaughtered, Kitty Hart writes, "You find it hard to believe that any faith in a benevolent G-d could be of value.... Yet I longed to produce Jewish children to make up, in however small a way, for so many who had been exterminated."[76] This desire to have children is an expression of faith despite faith. For the person of faith, G-d "vanishes to the rear," as André Neher has said, but "there is no purpose in seeking Him in that rear, for G-d is already out there in front, on the horizon-edge of a Promise which only restores what it has taken, without ever being fulfilled."[77] The child that Hart would have is the embodiment of this Promise "out there in front," revealed not in its fulfillment but in the human being's longing for what was lost, for the benevolence of the G-d who was lost. In that longing abides G-d's memory of and longing for Himself, for His own deliverance from the valley of the shadow of death. If G-d reveals Himself through the disturbance of the witness, He reveals Himself perhaps most profoundly in the rebellion of the witness.

Indeed, it is this anger of a believer that underlies Wiesel's refusal to accept G-d's silence, his refusal in *Night* to fast on Yom Kippur.[78] In *One Generation After* he explains: "He who says no to G-d is not necessarily a renegade. Everything depends on the way he says it, and why. One can say anything as long as it is for man, not against him."[79] This specifically Jewish tradition goes back to Abraham's argument with G-d over the fate of Sodom and Gomorrah; in fact, after his show of hospitality toward the three strangers who approached his tent, this is Abraham's first interaction with G-d after he had sealed the Covenant. It is precisely as the People of the Covenant that the Jews take up their remembrance of G-d and their argument with G-d. "There comes a time," says Wiesel, "when only those who do believe in G-d will cry out in wrath and anguish."[80] And so he raises his outcry:

> Whether G-d is silent
>
> Or weeps,
>
> *Ani maamin.*
>
> *Ani maamin* for him,
>
> In spite of him.
>
> I believe in you,
>
> Even against your will.
>
> Even if you punish me
>
> For believing in you.[81]

This is the song that turns memory against G-d in a turning of G-d against Himself. It is a song that reveals the sanctity of the *question* underlying the harrowing of the Holy One.

The Hebrew word for "question" is *shelah;* in the middle of that word is the word *el,* the word for "G-d." Which means: G-d is in the question.[82] That is where we wrestle with the angel. And so "man raises himself to-ward G-d by the questions he asks Him," Moshe teaches Eliezer in Wiesel's *Night.*[83] What sort of questions? The survivors provide us with a few ex-amples. "Did G-d take leave of his senses?" asks Isabella Leitner.[84] Pushing the question further, Eugene Heimler asks more boldly of G-d Himself, "Almighty G-d, why have you done this to us?…You are wicked, O Lord, as wicked as man."[85] Jewish tradition holds that G-d is the shadow of man; when men do nothing, G-d folds His arms. Therefore, as Heimler suggests, there is a parallel between the movements of G-d and the actions of human beings. The slumber of the one is the sleeping sickness, the sickness unto death, of the other.

Hence Ana Vinocur cries out to awaken both humanity and the Guard-ian who, according to tradition, neither sleeps nor slumbers (see Psalms 121:4). Both must be stirred if the Name is to be recovered. "It may be too late by the time you wake up," she cries out to the world. "And G-d…? I sometimes thought that the crying of the children was too weak to reach Him. But He had to hear them, because there was more and more crying. O G-d! Wake up and see what they have done to the people who have always kept faith with you!"[86] The Guardian of Israel is the essence of Is-rael, so that if the Sleepless One should sleep, then Israel would no longer be Israel (a point certainly not lost to the Nazi killers). How is G-d to be awakened? How shall we get the Nameless One to answer to His Name? By addressing Him in these words of memory that address humanity, by the very memory of Him who lives in the memory of humanity.

"G-d's final victory," Gergor's father tells him in Wiesel's *The Gates of the Forest,* "lies in man's inability to reject Him. You think…you're cry-ing out your hatred and rebellion, but all you're doing is telling Him how much you need His support."[87] And, in the light of what has been said, it may be that through the outcry of the Jews G-d is telling us how much *He* needs *our* support. Revealing Himself through our conduct as well as through our outcry, G-d assumes a human aspect, and the human being takes on a divine image. The recovery of the Name, both His and ours, is a recovery of this image and aspect of the human and the divine. Therefore we pray in the Name of *HaShem.*

Prayer To the Name, for the Name, in the Name

In contrast to the Greek *deomai* and the Latin *precari*—which imply supplication, entreaty, and pleading—the Jewish *tefillah* is associated with decision, thought, analysis, and judgment; its cognate *naftulim* means "struggles" or "wrestlings," so that here prayer is not a request submitted for oneself but an encounter—at times adversarial—between G-d and the soul, as when Jacob wrestled with the angel at Peniel. (This distinction should be kept in mind when we refer to "Jewish prayer" below.) If prayer is for the sake of redemption, moreover, it is for the redemption of the Name, and not merely for oneself. We do not pray *in* the Name of anyone; we pray *for the sake of* the Name in order to take on a name. To be sure, at the end of the Eighteen Benedictions that Jews pray three times a day it is a custom to recite a verse from the Scriptures that contains the same first and last letters as the first and last letters in one's name, so that, through prayer, we may remember our name, for the sake of the Name.

Which is to say: Prayer is for the sake of the community *Knesset Yisrael*, which is the *Shekhinah* in exile. Jews do not retreat to the cloister to pray; rather, they pray in a *minyan*, standing as a community before the Holy One. The Baal Shem Tov maintained that prayer and the *Shekhinah*, G-d's Indwelling Presence, are of a piece; in the words of a *tsaddik*, "Men believe they pray before G-d, but this is not so, for the prayer itself is divinity."[88] The prayer takes holds of the one who prays and sets a task before him: To pray is to be commanded to act. Through prayer, therefore, we do not speak to G-d—G-d speaks to us, declaring, "Hear, O Israel" through our own lips.

Since the destruction of the Holy Temple, prayer not only takes the place of sacrifice but is more dear than sacrifice. Even prior to the Temple's destruction, says the Midrash, G-d said to King David, "The one prayer which you stand and pray before me is more precious in my sight than the thousand burnt-offerings which Solomon your son is destined to offer up before me" (*Ruth Rabbah* 3:2). Viewed as the elevation of the soul, or as the soul's drawing nigh unto the Holy One, prayer has much the same purpose as sacrifice. For "sacrifice" in Hebrew is *karbon*, a cognate of the word *karov*, meaning "near": Like sacrifice, prayer is a drawing near to the Infinite One who at times seems to be infinitely distant. "Our devotion in prayer," writes the eleventh-century sage Bachya ibn Paquda, "is nothing but the soul's longing for G-d" (*Chovot Halevavot* 8:3). If in the Shoah there is a harrowing of the Holy One—if G-d and the prayer are one and if the soul emanates from G-d—then in the Shoah there is likewise a harrowing of the soul. As the breath or *neshimah* that G-d breathes into the human being, the soul or *neshamah* is like a part of G-d Himself, and the longing of the soul is G-d's longing for Himself.

Prayer, then, is a form of G-d's self-presence, a manifestation of the *Shekhinah,* in His Creation. "As the Shofar cannot emit any sound except when blown by man," the Chasidic Koretzer Rebbe teaches, "no man can raise his voice in prayer except when the *Shekhinah* prays through it."[89] Hence "prayer," notes Harry Rabinowicz, "is part of the *Shekhinah,* which may be why the *Shekhinah* itself is called prayer."[90] Because in Jewish tradition the *Shekhinah* is identified both with prayer and with the word,[91] prayer is above all a dialogue, and dialogue—when it is truly dialogue—bears the aspects of prayer. Both are a hearing in the midst of response and a response that is a hearing. Thus prayer can transform the silence of divine muteness into the response that can come only in the form of silence. G-d is, as it were, forced into a dialogue in which even His silence is a response. "Thanks to prayer," Wiesel explains, "the Supreme Judge, the Father of humanity, leaves His celestial throne to live and move among His human creatures. And, in turn, the soul transported by its prayer leaves its abode and rises to heaven. The substance of language, and the language of silence—that is what prayer is."[92] And that is what the Jew struggles to become in his or her struggle to once again wrestle a name from the Angel after the harrowing of the Name.

With regard to the Shoah, which entailed a radical assault on prayer, memory is itself a form of praying that is a wrestling for the sake of one's humanity. Particularly when it is the memory of prayer. "It's prayer which makes you a human being," Filip Müller recalls the words of a Jew named Fischl, an inmate of Auschwitz.[93] Humanity derives from sanctity, and sanctity derives from prayer. It is not a question of belief; prayer precedes belief and overtakes nonbelief. Since Fischl had no tefillin, Müller relates, he would mime the ritual of wrapping the phylacteries around his arm and head. "It seemed sheer madness to pray in Auschwitz," says Müller. "But here on the border-line between life and death, we obediently followed his example, possibly because…we felt strengthened by his faith."[94] The men pray despite themselves. They pray because the prayer, steeped with the One to whom it is offered, has a life of its own. They pray because, just as they behold Fischl's invisible tefillin, so do they hear a silent summons arising from the prayer itself. The prayer is itself the Name.

It is neither by chance nor by sentiment that in many quarters the memory of the Shoah has become part of the Jewish liturgy of prayer. The liturgy's *Siddur,* or prayer book, itself draws forth this memory, as it happened with Vladka Meed when, at the end of the war, she surveyed the rubble of the Warsaw Ghetto. "My eyes fell upon the remains of a torn, soiled *Siddur,*" she recalls, "and I see again my home—my father and mother."[95] The image of the *Siddur* in ruins is precisely an image of the Jewish people, the Jewish G-d, and the Jewish tradition—the Holy Name and the Holy One—in ruins. For the torn *Siddur* is the torn Word, the torn Name, that brings about the ascent of the human and the descent of the Divine. It is the book that draws the People of the Book nigh unto the Giver of the Book. And when this book of blessings emerges from the pages of the book of memory, it struggles, like Jacob wrestling with the Angel, to recover the blessing of life.

The recovery of the Name is the recovery of life, and the witness's memory of prayer is often a memory of that recovery. Moshe Sandberg, for instance, summons the memory of a Jew in Dachau who was constantly immersed in his prayer book, "until he collapsed and was taken to the hospital"; the man, in fact, survived when by every rational measure he should have died, "according to himself thanks to his prayers."[96] Paul Trepman relates that while he and his comrades hid in the tight confines of a dark cellar, they recited the Shema; "it was an upsurge of religious feeling, and it kept us sane after a fashion"[97] —"sane" in a place where prayer itself might appear to be insanity. Here, of course, "sane" does not mean "rational" so much as maintaining the hale and whole relation to G-d that sanctifies the relation to other human beings; here, remaining "sane" means remaining human.

If those who were in hiding might thus maintain their sanity and their humanity, how much more might be said of those in the murder camp who kept their sanity and their humanity even in the midst of the Nazi dehumanization and humiliation? According to Samuel Pisar, for instance, there were Jews in Majdanek who said their prayers during the High Holy Days under the direct threat of death. "In the darkness," he writes, "with prison caps for yarmulkes, every man stood in front of his bunk, facing Jerusalem. Without the chants of a cantor to guide him, every man mumbled softly, lest we be heard by the roaming guards and their vicious dogs, whatever prayers he could remember."[98] Why these prayers despite the death that breathes down their necks? Because without these prayers these Jews are dead as Jews, dead, therefore, as human beings. Without these prayers the Jews have no name.

Pisar's image of prison caps turned into yarmulkes—a mark of death made into a sign of life—exemplifies the dialectical nature of prayer in the midst of memory. You have turned us over to death? No matter: Our memory will return us to life. You would reduce our tradition to ashes? Then we shall fetch from those ashes the fire that ignites our prayers.[99] We shall dance, like souls on fire, in remembrance of the flames that consumed our souls, in remembrance of Rebbe Leib, son of the great Maggid of Mezeritch, who cried out to his fellow Jews, "Your dancing counts for more than my prayers."[100] After all, was it not Moshe Leib of Sassov who said, "When somebody asks something impossible of me, I know what I must do: I must dance"?[101] And the impossible was precisely what G-d was asking of the Jews in the Shoah.

Thus, in prayers transformed into dance, praying as they danced, a group of one hundred rabbis danced at Birkenau in the shadow and by the terrible light of the crematoria. The Angel of Death, Mengele himself, had ordered them to dance. But then, Sara Nomberg-Przytyk remembers, they began chanting the *Kol Nidre:* "Now they were no longer singing in obedience to Mengele's orders."[102] They were singing their affirmation of the One G-d, who alone determines the absolute prohibition against the murder that the Nazis perpetrated. Should they have rejected G-d? No: If they had, the Nazis would have had a victory both over the rabbis and over G-d. Perhaps, on the other hand, their piety was itself a show of defiance. No one can say for certain. What is certain is this: Prayer turns mockery into devotion, just as it turned prison caps into yarmulkes. It turns death into life and thus recovers the Name that was consigned to death by transforming the Name into a dance. It is not enough to learn Torah: One must dance Torah. For if we do not have Torah, we do not have prayer.

If, as Heschel argues, the true content of prayer is the response to it,[103] then there is no prayer without the deed—without the *mitzvah*. For according to Jewish teaching, the response to prayer is not G-d's reply to a request but our engagement in action. What is a *mitzvah?* In the words of Heschel, it is "a prayer in the form of a deed."[104] It is part of our dialogue with the Holy One: what we *do,* we *say* to G-d. Therefore any post-Holocaust Jewish identity that might emerge must emerge through the Jewish prayer in the form of a deed, that is, through the *mitzvah.* For a *mitzvah* is not just a good deed; it is a *commanded* deed. Indeed, the Talmudic sage Rabbi Chanina teaches that one who acts because he is commanded is greater than one who acts without being commanded (*Avodah Zarah* 3a). There is no other way to answer, "Here I am!" to the One who asks each of us, as He asked Adam, "Where are you?" (Genesis 3:9). As Lévinas has said, G-d is not love, as the Christian teaching maintains (1 John 4:16); rather, G-d is the *commandment* to love.[105] Therefore, in the harrowing of the Holy One, the Nazis undertake an assault not only on the Jews but also on the *mitzvah.*

The Nazis' Assault on the *Mitzvah*

Rabbi Kalonymos Kalmish Shapira has pointed out that, since the word *mitzvah* contains the four-letter Holy Name *(yud-heh-vav-heh),* G-d, *HaShem,* is *in* the *mitzvah.*[106] While the last two letters of the Name, *vav-hey,* are apparent, the first two are hidden in the *mem-tsadi* of *mitzvah.* For when transformed according to the *At-bash* method of interpretation,[107] the *mem* and *tsadi* become *yud* and *heh,* the first two letters of the Name. The *mitzvah,* therefore, is a vessel or a portal through which the Holy Name enters the world.

We have seen that in the Holocaust the assault on G-d's Chosen is quintessentially an assault on G-d Himself. The assault on G-d, in turn, invariably takes the form of an assault on the Torah through which He commands and sanctifies His Chosen with *mitzvot.* Indeed, just as he declared G-d and prayer to be one, the Koretzer Rebbe taught, "G-d and Torah are one. G-d, Israel, and Torah are one."[108] One means the Nazis employed for destroying the Jews and their teachings concerning the *mitzvah* was the destruction of Torah scrolls wherever they could find them. Rabbi Huberband points out, for example, that whenever Jews were found with Torah scrolls, they were tortured and the scrolls were burned or desecrated.[109] And in his diary from the Vilna Ghetto, Zelig Kalmanovitch writes, "A war is being waged against the Jew. But this war is not merely directed against one link in the triad [of Israel, G-d, and Torah] but against the entire triad: against the Torah and G-d, against the moral law and Creator of the universe."[110] Waged against Israel, G-d, and Torah, the war against the Jews is a war against the *mitzvah,* against the prayer in the form of the deed, and against places of prayers that might be made into deeds.

Just as the *mitzvah* is itself a prayer, the prayer is itself a *mitzvah.* Therefore the Nazis transformed places of prayer into latrines, stables, scrap depots, and other such facilities. In many cases, however, the Nazis were not content merely to desecrate the places of prayer; they put them to the torch, often with praying Jews inside, thus consigning G-d Himself to the flames.[111] The assault on the synagogue is an assault not on a building or a space but on the commandment and the encounter between G-d and the soul that characterizes prayer: In order to assail G-d, the Nazis launched an attack on the prayer that is itself divinity. The diarists bear witness to this assault. On the eve of Tisha B'Av 5700 (1940), for example, Chaim Kaplan writes, "Public prayer in these dangerous times is a forbidden act. Anyone caught in this crime is doomed to severe punishment. If you will, it is even sabotage, and anyone engaging in sabotage is subject to execution."[112] Note well: The Nazis deem prayer *an act of sabotage.* Why? Because prayer, and prayer alone, affirms the Divine, transcendent *authority* behind the *mitzvot,* particularly the one that prohibits murder. Does that mean one must be "religious" or "in the Covenant" to be ethical? No. But it does mean that being ethical has no meaning without the testimony that being ethical is Divinely commanded. And where being ethical, in truth, has meaning, the Holy One has a dwelling place. Which means: There is a place for prayer.

Indeed, humanity's task is to create a dwelling place for the Creator in the midst of His creation.[113] And this *mitzvah*—the most fundamental of all the *mitzvot*—has its roots in marriage, home, and family. The marriage that declares life to be sacred is the foundation for the home as a center of sanctity, which is what makes the home a dwelling place through which the *Shekhinah* may enter into the world. And wherever the *Shekhinah* enters, we have a commandment, a *mitzvah.* Thus, just as the place of prayer came under assault, so did the place of *dwelling,* a place constituted and consecrated by deeds of kindness and hospitality. One of the most significant symbols of the home's sanctity is the *mezuzah*, which is attached to the doorposts of the home and contains portions of the Torah that commands us to act in a certain manner. The *mezuzah* is embossed with the letter *shin*, which stands for *Shadai* or "Almighty" and is one of the names of G-d. And so we realize the importance of the *mezuzah:* It is the sign of G-d's presence at the threshold of the home, a sign of the sanctity of home and family. The destruction of the *mezuzah*, then, signifies an attempt to destroy the Name of G-d.

Here Ringelblum notes, "At the beginning of the Ghetto period, *men of valor* [Nazis] tore down the *mezuzot* from the doorposts of Jewish apartments."[114] This destruction of the *mezuzah* is an assault not only on the particular homes violated but on the very notion of home as the site from which life derives its value: Home is the place where our name is first uttered, where we are first called upon to act for the sake of another, where we first engage the *mitzvah*. There is a connection, then, between the assault on the home and the assault on the names of those Jews who engaged in the observance of the *mitzvot*; where one comes under attack so does the other. That is why "the Germans collected *taleysim, talis kotons,* and *kitls.* These holy garments were given to Jews to wash floors, automobiles, and windows."[115] When a Jew puts on these holy garments or lays tefillin with the appropriate prayers on his lips, his very body is transformed into a cry of "Here I am!" in an answering to his name before the One who summons him by name to observe these *mitzvot.* It is a saying of *Hinehni!*—"Here I am, ready to act!" The destruction and desecration of such ritual objects, then, are tied to the assault on the *mitzvah*, which is precisely an assault on Torah, Israel, and G-d.

The performance of a *mitzvah* requires not only the hands and the lips but the entire body; indeed, for a Jew the body itself embodies the *mitzvot*.[116] Therefore the features of the body exemplifying the Jew's observance of the *mitzvot* came under severe attack; among Jewish men, for example, the feature that distinguishes the face as a face turned toward G-d is the beard. Thus Rabbi Huberband notes, "If a bearded Jew was caught, his life was put in danger. They tore out his beard along with pieces of flesh, or cut it off with a knife and a bayonet."[117] Similarly, describing an *Aktion* staged in the Lvov Ghetto, David Kahane writes, "First they seized old men with beards and sidelocks. Not even a work card could save a bearded Jew."[118]

The Talmud tells us that the beard is the glory of the face (*Shabbat* 152a). If it is the *glory* of the face, then it makes the face into a sign of the Holy One, who sanctifies the life of the human being through His commandments, beginning with the Divine prohibition against murder.

Because the *mitzvah* defines who the Jew is, the Nazis' assault on the *mitzvah* is an assault on the Jew's being *in the world;* to be sure, that the Jews' crime was the ontological crime of *Dasein,* of being there. But it was also a metaphysical crime, for it lay neither in simply being there nor in having committed a transgression but in signifying that we are commanded from on high—commanded by One who transcends the justifications of race—to *do* something *in the world.* Where prayer takes the form of a deed, human life is a participation in life and in the creation of life. As we have seen, many of the *mitzvot* revolve around getting married, having children, and establishing homes—that is how we live *in the world* and join our voice to the voice of the Creator to declare that life is good.

The assault on the *mitzvah* that came with the murder of the Jews entailed the murder not only of mothers, fathers, and children, but of the very notion of mother, father, and child. For in the Jewish tradition it is the *mitzvah,* and not "culture," that shapes the essence of a mother, a father, or a child. And of these the notion of a child is perhaps the most crucial. In the time of the Shoah, "children were old, and old men were as helpless as children," Elie Wiesel once stated it.[119] The old men were taken. And the children grew as old as G-d. Remember these lines from Wiesel's *Ani Maamin:*

These children

Have taken your countenance,

O G-d.[120]

Hence the memory of the living G-d lies in the memory of the dead child. That is where the harrowing of the Holy One is most harrowing. And the Nazis knew it.

The Murder of the Child

The most overwhelming of the memorials at Yad Vashem, the Holocaust memorial center in Jerusalem, is the Children's Memorial. Entering the memorial is like entering a tomb. But there are no bodies laid to rest in the tomb. On the contrary, there is an abysmal sense of unrest. That is the reason for the handrails: It is not the darkness—it is the swoon of the aftermath, of feeling the ground crumble from beneath your feet. No, there are no bodies: Instead of bodies there is a darkness seared by a million and a half points of light generated by using mirrors to reflect the light of five candles. Instead of bodies there are names, hundreds of thousands of names. Every few seconds you hear the name, the age, and the birthplace of a murdered child. Every few seconds your soul is racked not by the million and a half little ones but by *this one*. And in that utterance of each name you hear the utterance the Name. You hear your own name. You hear the Angel of Death asking you: "What is your name?"

The researchers at Yad Vashem have identified less than a third of the names of the murdered children. It takes three years to get through the list of names.

Emil Fackenheim observes that "once Moses offered his life in behalf of the children and succeeded. Adam Czerniakow did not merely offer but gave his life for the children. However, unlike Moses he failed. The enemy was more sleepless and slumberless than the G-d of Israel."[121] The children were among those who were first targeted for extermination, not only to annihilate the Jewish future that they represented but also to destroy the Jewish tradition that they sustained. Says Wiesel, "It was as though the Nazi killers knew precisely what children represent to us. According to our tradition, the entire world subsists thanks to them."[122] To be sure, many texts from the tradition attest to the importance of the child both to the life of the tradition and to the Holy One whose presence is revealed through the tradition. In the Midrash, for example, it is written, "R. Judah said: Come and see how beloved are the children by the Holy One, blessed be He. The Sanhedrin were exiled but the *Shekhinah* did not go into exile with them. When, however, the children were exiled, the *Shekhinah* went into exile with them" (*Eichah Rabbah* 1:6:33). Similarly, the Talmud teaches that all of Creation endures thanks to the breath of little school (*Shabbat* 119b), and not by the pillars of power, as invoked by the Greek image of Atlas holding up the world on his shoulders. And in the Zohar we read, "Who is it that upholds the world and causes the patriarchs to appear? It is the voice of tender children studying the Torah; and for their sake the world is saved" (*Zohar* I, 1b). One can see that the murder of the child is central to the harrowing of the Holy One. And in the death of the child we see Him in the throes of death.

Elie Wiesel drives home this point with devastating pathos in *Night*, where we encounter one of the most dreadful of all the memories that now haunt Jewish memory: the hanging of a child. In the assembly of prisoners forced to witness the hanging, the young Eliezer hears a Jew next to him asking, "Where is G-d? Where is He now?" And from within his soul comes the terrifying reply: "Where is He? Here He is—He is hanging here on these gallows."[123] Then there is Issachar's wife, the woman in Wiesel's *A Jew Today*, who sees dead children everywhere. "They are G-d's memory," she repeated over and over.[124] That is to say, they are G-d's memory of us, as well as our memory of G-d. If, as it is written in the *Tikunei Zohar*, children are "the face of the *Shekhinah*,"[125] it is because in this remembrance of the child we come face-to-face with the harrowing of the Holy One.

Because children are the face of the Divine Presence, the Nazis rooted out that presence by creating realms that were void of Jewish children. "In the ghetto streets no children played," Ka-tzetnik recalls. "In the ghetto there were no children. There were small Jews and there were big Jews—all looking alike."[126] In his memoir George Lucius Salton recalls the moment when, upon his liberation from Wöbbelin, he saw children for the first time "in years." They were German children: "The Jewish children had all been gassed. Probably by the fathers or uncles of these children here."[127] Even where children remained, they were transformed into nonchildren. "When I saw them with toys in their hands," Wiesenthal remembers, "they looked unfamiliar, uncanny, like old men playing with childish things."[128] In the play of the child lies the movement of life, the celebration of life and meaning signified by the child. When that play ceases, life loses its significance. With this in mind, we recall a passage from Alexander Donat's memoir, where he says of his three-year-old son, "The lively child whose nature had been movement and playfulness now sat for hours at a time without moving. Whenever I seemed to be leaving him, his only reaction was to tighten his grip on me, uttering only the single word: *'Daddy.'*"[129] This single word not only undoes the father; it announces the ontological undoing of being, for it is a word that both demands a response and makes all response impossible.

The evil of the pain that Lévinas describes as "the explosion and most profound articulation of absurdity"[130] lies not so much in the pain experienced by a father in a moment like the one Donat relates but in the suffering of the child himself. If the profound absurdity is proclaimed in the word to which it is impossible to respond, it explodes in the child whom it is impossible to save.[131] That is the insoluble problem: The child *as such* is precisely the one whom we must save if we are to return to the Name that is under assault. This claim of the child upon us is what links the name of the child to our own name. So we try desperately to save the little one. But in the antiworld the child is condemned even in the midst of rescue. Who can forget in this regard the haunting figure of a man trying to save a child in Wiesel's *Ani Maamin*:

> I run,
>
> And while I run,
>
> I am thinking:
>
> This is insane
>
> This Jewish child
>
> Will not be spared.
>
> I run and run
>
> And cry.[132]

As in Wiesel's vision, so in Wiesenthal's nightmare about a ghetto child named Eli: "His father brought him to me in his arms. As he approached he covered his eyes with his hands. Behind the two figures raged a sea of flames from which they were fleeing. I wanted to take Eli, but all that existed was a bloody mess."[133] And Sim Kessel's nightmare followed him from the antiworld into the world: "I still dream of the children at Drancy, clutching at their mothers' skirts and crying incessantly."[134] The dreams that invade the nights of Wiesel, Wiesenthal, and Kessel are the stuff of which the antireality of the Kingdom of Night is made. And the invasion takes place night after night.

In the Jewish tradition we are taught that we must take especially good care of the widow, the stranger, and above all the orphan because they are the ones closest to G-d (see, for example, Exodus 22:20–21). In the antiworld engineered by the Nazis, however—a realm whose essence is not just murder but the murder of *children*—those who are nearest to G-d are precisely the ones most distant from G-d's help. That is why the child is the one nearest to our memory, the one who invades our memory, inexorably, like the scream that reverberates throughout Sara Nomberg-Przytyk's memory of the slaughter of children burned alive: "Suddenly, the stillness was broken by the screaming of children,...a scream repeated a thousand times in a single word, 'Mama,' a scream that increased in intensity every second, enveloping the whole camp. Our lips parted without our being conscious of what we were doing, and a scream of despair tore out of our throats.... At the end everything was enveloped in death and silence."[135] If the Shoah is characterized by an assault on the Name, it is an assault on this name by which each of us first knows the *other* human being, the name that is the first meaningful word to emerge from our mouth, the name of the one who first calls us by name: Mama.

That is the name that signifies our being as a human being, because that is the name that signifies our being as a *child*. In the Nazis' perversion of the very significance of the child, the silence of which Nomberg-Przytyk speaks is what the child aflame comes to signify. When the child's coming into being is designated a crime against being, it is a *novum* in history, as Fackenheim rightly points out.[136] Yet the memory of the *novum* instills it with a history, so that the process of remembrance opens up a prospect for tearing asunder what should never have been joined together; it opens up a path toward the recovery of our name.

One cannot collide with the accounts of what became of the children without erupting in a scream. But a scream is not a response. If the child and the Holy One to whom he is bound to are to be recovered, then this recovery can happen only in an act of response and responsibility. Couched in the memory of the assault on G-d as well as in the memory of the murder of the child is the summons to a responsibility for the child, which is a responsibility to bear a name and to transmit a name. It arises not from the head or the heart of the individual but from beyond the human being, from the tradition that insists on the association between the Holy One and the holiness of the little one, between the Name and the name. In Paul

Trepman's memoir we find an illustration of this point. There he remembers a remark made by Mira Jakubowicz in the Warsaw Ghetto: "For many years I was far away from Jewish tradition, from the Jewish way of life that is so full of trials and sorrows. But the suffering which has come to our people now has only strengthened me in my resolve never to abandon our Jewish children."[137] In that resolve we have the resolve never to abandon the Name.

Primo Levi offers us an important variation on this theme in his memory of a three-year-old boy called "Hurbinek" (they did not know his real name), whom he met in Auschwitz after the Russians liberated the camp on 27 January 1945. "Hurbinek, the nameless," Levi describes him, "died in the first days of March 1945, free but not redeemed. Nothing remains of him: he bears witness through these words of mine."[138] While the child remains nameless, the Holy Name speaks through the words of the witness, often despite the witness. The testimony of the witness places the lost child on another shore, over *there*. Thus the disturbance of the witness situates the child in all the "theres," which is the literal meaning of the Hebrew word for "heaven," *shamayim,* the abode of the Holy One whom tradition associates with the child. The means of reaching across the distance that separates us from Him is prayer. There, too, there most of all, we wrestle with the Angel.

According to Jewish tradition, only when our prayers come from the lips of our children, untainted as they are by sin, do those prayers reach the ears of G-d. Since the day when the Sanctuary was destroyed, explains the Maggid of Dubno, the gates of prayer have been locked; only through the child can we be redeemed. "For the outcry of children," says the Maggid, "is formed by the breath of mouths unblemished by sin, and is therefore capable of piercing the windows of Heaven."[139] In the memory of the Holocaust, however, the child's prayer is buried in a shriek of silence. Wrestling with the Angel, we wrestle with that silence and with that shriek, so that the wrestling itself becomes our prayer. For from the wrestling we take the shriek—that is why we limp.

No child, of course, is born by itself; the babe has a mother who, along with the infant, brings into the world a renewal of the world, a participation in the work of the Creator. Born to die, however, the child is no longer a child, the mother no longer a mother, Creation no longer Creation.

Thus in the Nazis' harrowing of the Holy One we arrive at an assault on the Name that manifests itself as an assault on the origin of our name, on the one who first utters our name with loving-kindness. For at the origin lies the sanctity of life and of the Name and of all we do to answer to our name. At the origin—in the womb of the mother—the very sanctity of humanity and Creation is decided. Thus the Nazis made motherhood a capital crime.

Notes

1. See also Maimonides, *The Commandments*, vol. 1, trans. Charles B. Chavel (New York: Soncino, 1967), 218.

2. Cf. Emmanuel Lévinas, *Ethics and Infinity*, trans. Richard A. Cohen (Pittsburgh: Duquesne University Press, 1985), 105.

3. See Herman Kruk, *The Last Days of the Jerusalem of Lithuania: Chronicles from the Vilna Ghetto and the Camps, 1939–1944*, ed. Benjamin Harshav, trans. Barbara Harshav (New Haven: Yale University Press, 2002), 311.

4. Ignaz Maybaum, *The Face of G-d after Auschwitz* (Amsterdam: Polak and Van Genep, 1965), 25–26. Cited in Steven T. Katz, *Post-Holocaust Dialogues: Critical Studies in Modern Jewish Thought* (New York: NYU Press, 1983), 156–57.

5. See Oskar Rosenfeld, *In the Beginning Was the Ghetto: 890 Days in Łódź*, ed. Hanno Loewy, trans. Brigitte Goldstein (Evanston: Northwestern University Press, 2002), 134.

6. Cited in Emil L. Fackenheim, *Jewish Philosophers and Jewish Philosophy*, ed. Michael L. Morgan (Bloomington: Indiana University Press, 1996), 122.

7. Elie Wiesel, *Legends of Our Time* (New York: Avon, 1968), 230.

8. Recall here the teaching from the Tosefta: "Why was Adam created alone? So that in this world the righteous could not say, 'Our children are righteous, and yours are evil'" (*Sanhedrin* 8:4). And: "So that the great among the nations could not claim that the King of kings created the world for them alone" (*Sanhedrin* 8:5).

9. Leo Baeck, *The Essence of Judaism*, trans. Victor Grubenweiser and Leonard Pearl (New York: Schocken Books, 1948), 153.

10. Louis Newman, ed., *The Hasidic Anthology* (New York: Schocken Books, 1963), 83.

11. Emil L. Fackenheim, *What Is Judaism?* (New York: Macmillan, 1987), 109.

12. See Hillel Seidman, *Tog-bukh fon Warshever geto* (New York: Avraham Mitlberg, 1947), 67.

13. Yitzhak Katznelson, *Vittel Diary*, trans. Myer Cohn, 2nd Ed. (Tel Aviv: Hakibbutz Hameuchad, 1972), 83–84.

14. Emmanuel Ringelblum, *Notes from the Warsaw Ghetto*, trans. and ed. Jacob Sloan (New York: Schocken Books, 1974), 24.

15. Josef Katz, *One Who Came Back: The Diary of a Jewish Survivor*, trans. Herzl Reach (New York: Herzl Press and Bergen-Belsen Memorial Press, 1973), 153.

16. See Louis Finkelstein, *Akiba: Scholar, Saint, and Martyr* (New York: Atheneum, 1981), 103.

17. In the words of Lévinas, in the face we have "the conception of G-d in which He is welcomed in the face-to-face with the other, in the obligation towards the other." See Emmanuel Lévinas, "Revelation in the Jewish Tradition," trans. Sarah Richmond, in *The Levinas Reader,* ed. Sean Hand (Oxford: Basil Blackwell, 1989), 204.

18. See Lévinas, *Ethics and Infinity,* 86. Because the face signifies holiness, Lévinas goes on to say, "The face is signification, and signification without context. I mean that the Other, in the rectitude of his face, is not a character within a context. Ordinarily,...the meaning of something is in its relation to another thing. Here, to the contrary, the face is meaning all by itself" (86–87).

19. A fearsome and graphic illustration of this point can be found in Harry James Cargas, *Shadows of Auschwitz: A Christian Response To the Holocaust* (New York: Crossroad, 1990), 116–17.

20. Salmen Lewental, *Manuscript of a Sonderkommando Member,* trans. Krystyna Michalik, in Jadwiga Bezwinska, ed., *Amidst a Nightmare of Crime: Manuscripts of Members of Sonderkommando* (Oswiecim: State Museum, 1973), 136.

21. Cf. Didier Pollefeyt's essay "Horror Vacui: A Catholic Perspective on God and Evil in/after Auschwitz," in John K. Roth and David Patterson, eds., *Fire in the Ashes: God, Evil, and the Holocaust* (Seattle: University of Washington Press, 2005), 219-30.

22. Chaim A. Kaplan, *The Warsaw Diary of Chaim A. Kaplan,* trans. and ed. Abraham I. Katsh (New York: Collier, 1973), 129.

23. David Kahane, *Lvov Ghetto Diary,* trans. Jerzy Michalowicz (Amherst: University of Massachusetts Press, 1990), 67.

24. Emil L. Fackenheim, *To Mend the World: Foundations of Post-Holocaust Jewish Thought* (New York: Schocken Books, 1989), 209.

25. Katznelson, *Vittel Diary,* 94.

26. Ibid., 152.

27. Ringelblum, *Notes,* 39.

28. Ibid., 225–26.

29. Ibid., 218.

30. Ibid., 35.

31. Ibid., 135.

32. Katz, *One Who Came Back*, 244.

33. See chapter 3 for a detailed examination of the assault on the mother.

34. Katz, *One Who Came Back*, 206.

35. Moshe Flinker, *Young Moshe's Diary*, trans. Shaul Esh and Geoffrey Wigoder (Jerusalem: Yad Vashem, 1971), 75.

36. Emmanuel Lévinas, *Collected Philosophical Papers*, trans. Alphonso Lingis (Dordrecht: Martinus Nijhoff, 1987), 180.

37. This point is, of course, the theme of Silvano Arieti's Holocaust novel *The Parnas* (Philadelphia: Paul Dry Books, 2000).

38. Recall here an incident that Emmanuel Ringelblum relates: "A police chief came to the apartment of a Jewish family, wanted to take some things away. The woman cried out that she was a widow with a child. The chief said he'd take nothing if she could guess which of his eyes was the artificial one. She guessed the left eye. She was asked how she knew. 'Because that one,' she answered, 'has a human look.'" See Ringelblum, *Notes*, 84.

39. Kaplan, *Warsaw Diary*, 331.

40. Abraham Joshua Heschel, *The Sabbath: Its Meaning for Modern Man* (New York: Farrar, Straus & Giroux, 1981), 100.

41. Mary Berg, *The Warsaw Ghetto: A Diary*, trans. Norbert and Sylvia Glass, ed. S. L. Schneiderman (New York: L. B. Fischer, 1945), 103.

42. Elie Wiesel, *Messengers of G-d*, trans. Marion Wiesel (New York: Random House, 1976), 95.

43. See also Gershom Scholem, *Kabbalah* (New York: New American Library, 1974), 31, 111.

44. See Newman, *Hasidic Anthology*, 337.

45. Kaplan, *Warsaw Diary*, 202.

46. Ringelblum, *Notes*, 314.

47. Nachmanides, for instance, notes that, according to the mystical tradition, "the entire Torah is composed of Names of the Holy One blessed be He, and each and every section [of the Torah] contains a [Divine] Name upon [the basis of] which a particular matter was formed or accomplished or is dependent for existence." See Nachmanides, *Writings and Discourses*, vol. 1, trans. Charles B. Chavel (New York: Shilo, 1978), 112. A variation of this teaching holds that the Torah itself, with all its words written together as a single word, is regarded as the name of G-d: says the Zohar, "The whole Torah is an enfolding of the Divine Name, the most exalted Name, the Name that comprehends all other names" (*Zohar* II, 124a).

48. Shimon Huberband, *Kiddush Hashem,* trans. David E. Fishman, ed. Jeffrey S. Gurock and Robert S. Hirt (Hoboken, NJ: Ktav and Yeshiva University Press, 1987), 61.

49. Michael Zylberberg, *A Warsaw Diary* (London: Valentine, Mitchell & Co., 1969), 94.

50. Ibid., 95.

51. Ringelblum, *Notes,* 154.

52. Adam Czerniakow, *The Warsaw Ghetto Diary of Adam Czerniakow,* ed. Raul Hilberg, Stanislaw Staron, Joseph Kermisz, trans. Stanislaw Staron, et al. (New York: Stein and Day, 1979), 245.

53. Recall here Lévinas's statement that the Infinite One is revealed in the disturbance of His witness; see *Ethics and Infinity,* 109.

54. The *Oneg Shabbat* circle was a group of people from all walks of life assembled by Emmanuel Ringelblum to keep diaries and gather other accounts of the Nazis' activities in the Warsaw Ghetto as well as throughout Poland. The term *Oneg Shabbat* means "delight in the Sabbath," which is a delight in the entry of the Eternal One into time.

55. Hersh Wasser, "Daily Entries of Hersh Wasser," trans. Joseph Kermish, *Yad Vashem Studies,* 15 (1983): 275.

56. Abraham Levin, "Extract from the Diary of Abraham Levin," *Yad Vashem Studies* 6 (1967): 317. If this example is not enough to make the point about the monstrous nature of the Nazi evil, here is another: A survivor once related to me a scene he witnessed in his small Polish hometown. The Nazis arrested a Jew for studying Torah. Not only did they sentence him to a public hanging in the town square, but, as the crowd gathered and the Jew's family cried out to G-d, the Nazis took the Jew's eldest son to the gallows and ordered him: "Put the noose around your father's neck and pull the lever. Or we shall hang your entire family, one by one, here and now." His horror now running deeper than his grief, the Jew's son did not know what to do. So his father begged him: "Hang me, my son! Hang me!" That is the perversion of world and reality that the Nazis engineered in the anti-world: They devised a system that would lead a father to *beg his son to hang him* for studying Torah. This evil was even beyond the evil that the Romans could conceive, when they tortured Jews to death for studying Torah.

57. Huberband, *Kiddush Hashem,* 166.

58. Kaplan, *Warsaw Diary,* 234.

59. Ringelblum, *Notes,* 139.

60. Czerniakow, *Warsaw Ghetto,* 184.

61.   Zylberberg, *A Warsaw Diary*, 75.

62.   See Huberband, *Kiddush Hashem*, 40.

63.   Primo Levi, *Survival in Auschwitz*, trans. Stuart Woolf (New York: Simon & Schuster, 1996), 88.

64.   For those who are interested in gematria, according to the method of squaring the letters, the square of each letter of the Divine Name *(yud-hey-vav-hey)*—that is, 100 + 25 + 36 + 25 = 186, which is the numerical value of *Makom*.

65.   From *Gevurot Hashem* 46, cited in Pinhas H. Peli, *The Jewish Sabbath: A Renewed Encounter* (New York: Schocken Books, 1988), 11–12. See also Avraham Yaakov Finkel, *Kabbalah: Selections from Classic Kabbalistic Works from Raziel HaMalach To the Present Day* (Southfield, MI: Targum Press, 2002), 152.

66.   Mordechai Yosef of Isbitza, *Mei HaShiloach*, trans. and ed. Betsalel Philip Edwards (Northvale, NJ: Jason Aronson, 2001), 281.

67.   It is written in the Torah that on the seventh day G-d *shavat veyinafash*, "rested and was refreshed" (Exodus 31:17), where the root of the word "was refreshed," *veyinafash* is the same as the root for "soul," *nefesh*. In his commentary on this verse, therefore, Sforno explains that the word *veyinafash* is a reference to an additional soul that a person receives on the Sabbath in order to attain the purpose of G-d's Creation: To live a life in keeping with Torah.

68.   Elie Wiesel, *From the Kingdom of Memory: Reminiscences* (New York: Summit Books, 1990), 25.

69.   But it is more than dreamt of in Lurianic Kabbalah, the primary mystical influence on the Chasidic teachings in which Wiesel was raised. The Lurianic view of evil is based on a teaching from the Zohar. There it is written that the divine contraction that is necessary for Creation produces a kind of fallout called *kelipot* or "shells" (*Zohar* I, 19b), which nevertheless contain divine "sparks," since nothing can exist outside of the Divine Presence. Luria's teacher Rabbi Moses Cordovero (1522–70) compares the process to the digestion of food (*Pardes Rimonim* 25:1). As the body absorbs just so much nourishment and then produces waste, so does the physical world absorb just so much holiness and then produces "shells" or "fragments." Because the *kelipot* veil G-d's holiness, they are the source of evil, sustained not so much by physical matter as by the ego that would equate being with the thinking "I," as is the case with modern speculative philosophy. Here our task is to elevate Creation by releasing the sparks of holiness within the *kelipot*. Only through human actions can holiness be released into the world; only through human agency can evil flourish.

70.   Fackenheim, *To Mend the World*, 250.

71. Simon Wiesenthal, *The Sunflower,* trans. H. A. Piehler (New York: Schocken Books, 1976), 14–15.

72. Ka-tzetnik 135633, *Shivitti: A Vision,* trans. Eliyah De-Nur and Lisa Herman (New York: Harper & Row, 1989), 7.

73. Wieslaw Kielar, *Anus Mundi: 1,500 Days in Auschwitz/Birkenau,* trans. Susanne Flatauer (New York: Times Books, 1980), 177.

74. Sara Zyskind, *Stolen Years,* trans. Margarit Inbar (Minneapolis: Lerner, 1981), 195–96.

75. Primo Levi, *The Drowned and the Saved,* trans. Raymond Rosenthal (New York: Vintage Books, 1988), 145.

76. Kitty Hart, *Return To Auschwitz* (New York: Atheneum, 1982), 156.

77. André Neher, *The Exile of the Word: From the Silence of the Bible To the Silence of Auschwitz,* trans. David Maisel (Philadelphia: Jewish Publication Society, 1981), 123.

78. Elie Wiesel, *Night,* trans. Stella Rodway (New York: Hill and Wang, 1960), 75.

79. Elie Wiesel, *One Generation After,* trans. Lily Edelman and Elie Wiesel (New York: Pocket Books, 1970), 216.

80. Elie Wiesel, *Evil and Exile,* trans. Jon Rothschild (Notre Dame: University of Notre Dame Press, 1990), 20.

81. Elie Wiesel, *Ani Maamin: A Song Lost and Found Again,* trans. Marion Wiesel (New York: Random House, 1973), 107.

82. Cf. Elie Wiesel, *Against Silence: The Voice and Vision of Elie Wiesel,* vol. 3, ed. Irving Abrahamson (New York: Holocaust Library, 1985), 297.

83. Wiesel, *Night,* 16.

84. Isabella Leitner, *Fragments of Isabella,* ed. Irving Leitner (New York: Thomas Crowell, 1978), 4.

85. Eugene Heimler, *Night of the Mist,* trans. Andre Ungar (New York: Vanguard, 1959), 30.

86. Ana Vinocur, *A Book without a Title,* trans. Valentine Isaac and Ricardo Iglesia (New York: Vantage, 1976), 66.

87. Elie Wiesel, *The Gates of the Forest,* trans. Frances Frenaye (New York: Holt, 1966), 33.

88. See Martin Buber, *The Legend of the Baal Shem,* trans. Maurice Friedman (New York: Schocken Books, 1969), 27.

89. See Newman, *Hasidic Anthology,* 335-36.

90. Harry M. Rabinowicz, *Hasidism: The Movement and Its Masters* (Northvale, NJ: Jason Aronson, 1988), 35.

91. See, for example, Joseph Gikatilla, *Sha'are orah: Gates of Light,* trans. Avi Weinstein (San Francisco: Harper, 1994), 337.

92. Elie Wiesel, *Paroles d'étranger* (Paris: Éditions du Seuil, 1982), 171–72.

93. Filip Müller, *Auschwitz Inferno: The Testimony of a Sonderkommando,* trans. Susanne Flatauer (London: Routledge and Kegan Paul, 1979), 28.

94. Ibid., 29.

95. Vladka Meed, *On Both Sides of the Wall,* trans. Benjamin Meed (Tel Aviv: Hakibbutz Hameuchad, 1973), 334.

96. Moshe Sandberg, *My Longest Year,* trans. S. C. Hyman (Jerusalem: Yad Vashem, 1968), 89.

97. Paul Trepman, *Among Men and Beasts,* trans. Shoshana Perla and Gertrude Hirschler (New York: Bergen-Belsen Memorial Press, 1978), 65.

98. Samuel Pisar, *Of Blood and Hope* (Boston: Little, Brown, 1979), 61.

99. Here one may recall a story from the Shevet Yehuda, the sixteenth-century martyrology compiled by Solomon ibn Verga. The story is about a father who lost his family members one by one, until finally he cried out to G-d: "You want me to cease believing in You, to cease praying to You, to cease invoking Your Name to glorify and sanctify it. Well, I tell You: No, no—a thousand times no! You shall not succeed! In spite of me and in spite of You, I shall shout the Kaddish, which is a song of faith, for You and against you." See Steven T. Katz, ed., *Interpretations of Judaism in the Late Twentieth Century* (Washington, DC: B'nai B'rith Books, 1991), 376–77.

100. See Elie Wiesel, *Souls on Fire: Portraits and Legends of Hasidic Masters,* trans. Marion Wiesel (New York: Vintage, 1973), 46.

101. See Elie Wiesel, *Somewhere a Master,* trans. Marion Wiesel (New York: Summit Books, 1982), 110.

102. Sara Nomberg-Przytyk, *Auschwitz: True Tales from a Grotesque Land,* trans. Roslyn Hirsch (Chapel Hill: University of North Carolina Press, 1985), 106.

103. Abraham Joshua Heschel, *Man's Quest for G-d: Studies in Prayer and Symbolism* (New York: Charles Scribner's Sons, 1954), 16.

104. Ibid., 69.

105. See Emmanuel Lévinas, "Useless Suffering," trans. Richard Cohen in *The Provocation of Levinas: Rethinking the Other,* ed. Robert Bernasconi and David Wood (London: Routledge, 1988), 176–77.

106. See Kalonymos Kalmish Shapira, *Sacred Fire: Torah from the Years of Fury, 1939–1942,* trans. J. Hershy Worch, ed. Deborah Miller (Northvale, NJ:

Jason Aronson, 2000), 61. It is likely that Rabbi Shapira received this teaching from the commentary of the *Or HaChayim* on Leviticus 18:4, where, based on the same method of *At-bash* (see note 107 below), he writes, "Performance of each *mitzvah* also results in G-d's name, or rather part of it, coming to rest on the sinew which that *mitzvah* represents."

107. The *At-bash* transformation is a means of interpretation, whereby the first letter of the alphabet is interchanged with the last letter, the second letter of the alphabet with the penultimate letter, and so on.

108. Newman, *Hasidic Anthology*, 147.

109. Huberband, *Kiddush Hashem*, 44.

110. Zelig Kalmanovitch, "A Diary of the Nazi Ghetto in Vilna," trans. and ed. Koppel S. Pinson, *YIVO Annual of Jewish Social Studies* 8 (1953): 52.

111. I cannot help but recall what my late friend and teacher, Emil Fackenheim, used to relate to me. Over the years that I knew him, Fackenheim would on occasion tell to me a story about the one or two Jews who would rush into synagogues that the Nazis had set aflame in order to save the scrolls of the Holy Torah. "They maintained that the Jews were rats," he said. "But rats do not run into burning buildings to save Torah scrolls."

112. Kaplan, *Warsaw Diary*, 179.

113. This is why the Torah begins with the letter *beit,* a word that also means "house," which is to say: The foundational meaning of the first letter of Torah is the "house" or "family" signified by the *beit,* a point discussed at greater length in the next chapter. See also Michael J. Alter, *Why the Torah Begins with the Letter Beit* (Northvale, NJ: Jason Aronson, 1998), 145–48.

114. Ringelblum, *Notes,* 152.

115. Huberband, *Kiddush Hashem,* 35.

116. While Rabbi Simlai teaches that the 365 commandments correspond to the 365 days of the year (see *Makkot* 23b), we also have the tradition of the 613 commandments, 248 correspond to the 248 bones of the body, and 365 to the 365 sinews of the body (see, for example, *Makkot* 24a; *Zohar* II, 165b; Chayyim Vital's *Shaarei Kedushah* Part 1, Gate 1; the commentary on Deuteronomy 20:11 in the *Or HaChayim; Keter Shem Tov* 53; or Yaakov Yosef of Polnoe in *Toledot Yaakov Yosef, Shemini* 2). The 248 positive commandments, says the Zohar, correspond to the 248 "upper organs," whereas the 365 negative commandments correspond to the 365 "lower organs" (see *Zohar* II, 165b).

117. Huberband, *Kiddush Hashem,* 135.

118. Kahane, *Lvov Ghetto Diary,* 45.

119. See David Patterson, *In Dialogue and Dilemma with Elie Wiesel* (Wakefield, NH: Longwood Academic, 1991), 21.

120. Wiesel, *Ani Maamin,* 57.

121. Emil L. Fackenheim, *The Jewish Bible after the Holocaust* (Bloomington: Indiana University Press, 1990), 47.

122. Elie Wiesel, *A Jew Today,* trans. Marion Wiesel (New York: Random House, 1978), 178–79.

123. Wiesel, *Night,* 71.

124. Wiesel, *A Jew Today,* 81.

125. Cited in Nehemia Polen, *The Holy Fire: The Teachings of Rabbi Kalonymus Kalman Shapira* (Northvale, NJ: Jason Aronson, 1999), 102.

126. Ka-tzetnik 135633, *Kaddish,* trans. Nina De-Nur (New York: Algemeiner Associates, 1998), 30.

127. George Lucius Salton, *The 23rd Psalm: A Holocaust Memoir* (Madison: University of Wisconsin Press, 2002), 218.

128. Wiesenthal, *The Sunflower,* 47.

129. Alexander Donat, *The Holocaust Kingdom* (New York: Holocaust Library, 1978), 94.

130. Lévinas, "Useless Suffering," 157.

131. I remember sitting with Emil Fackenheim in his apartment in Jerusalem and listening to him speaking about his efforts to respond to the Holocaust. Suddenly, as if struck by a bolt of realization, he stopped in mid-sentence. His bottom lip trembling and tears now running down his cheeks, he said, "I just realized what I have been trying to do for the last thirty years: I've been trying to undo it! But I can't!… I can't!"

132. Wiesel, *Ani Maamin,* 89.

133. Wiesenthal, *The Sunflower,* 71.

134. Sim Kessel, *Hanged at Auschwitz,* trans. Melville Wallace and Delight Wallace (New York: Stein and Day, 1972), 46.

135. Nomberg-Przytyk, *Auschwitz,* 81.

136. Fackenheim, *The Jewish Bible after the Holocaust,* 87.

137. Trepman, *Among Men and Beasts,* 194.

138. Primo Levi, *The Reawakening,* trans. Stuart Wolf (Boston: Little, Brown, 1965), 22–23.

139. Quoted in Eliyahu Kitov, *The Book of Our Heritage,* vol. 1, trans. Nathan Bluman (New York: Feldheim Publishers, 1973), 75–76.

CHAPTER THREE

THE DESECRATION OF THE ORIGIN

The silent face of my mother—
With her last glance turned to the sky;
And her last thoughts, most likely of her children;
Mother was set ablaze. A mother burns!
—Ka-tzetnik 135633, *Kaddish*

☙

IN ORDER TO UNDERSTAND HOW THE DESECRATION OF
the origin is tied to the Nazi assault on the Name, we must understand
how the Name, as it is manifest in Torah and Talmud, is tied to the
origin—that is, how it is tied to the one who gives birth to the Jew. For
if the crime of the Jew is his or her being in the world, then the one most
"culpable" in that crime is the one who might give birth to the Jew. And
from a Jewish standpoint she is the most holy.

Written in Hebrew, "woman" is *ishah,* which breaks down into *esh-hey,*
or *Esh HaShem,* the "Fire of G-d." Indeed, the word *isheh* means "burnt
offering" or "sacrifice": It is the fire that belongs to G-d and that elevates
Creation.[1] Does that mean that woman is to be a *karban,* a "sacrifice" to
G-d? Assuredly not: It means that she is *karov,* "near" to G-d. It means that
she burns with the black fire on white fire of Torah (see, for example, the
Mekilta de Rabbi Ishmael, Bachodesh 4). As the "Fire of G-d," woman draws
us upward and nearer to G-d. And what is the Fire of G-d? It is not a con-
flagration that may burn a house down; rather, it is the fire of the hearth

that lights up and warms a dwelling. Unlike a coat, which warms only the illusory self, the hearth warms all who draw nigh unto it. And the hearth is the center of the home, as suggested by a Hebrew word for "hearth," *moked,* from the verb *miked,* meaning to "focus." The word *moked* also refers to the "altar" in the Temple: The center of dwelling in the world is the center of dwelling in the home. At the core of that center is woman.

Already we see that a relation to the origin is essential to a sense of dwelling in the world. This point will prove to be a key to the Nazis' desecration of the origin in their assault on the Name. In order to take our understanding of the relation between woman and dwelling to a deeper level, however, we must examine the significance of the feminine in Jewish thought and in the sacred tradition.

Woman in the Sacred Tradition

In modern times the Jewish thinker who most profoundly articulates that significance is Emmanuel Lévinas. In *Ethics and Infinity,* for example, he comments on the relation between woman in the sacred and the implications of that tradition for Jewish thought, saying, "The feminine is described as the *of itself other,* as the origin of the very concept of alterity."[2] Thus understood, the feminine comes to bear not only in the relation between man and woman but in any relation between one human being and another, a relation that is itself antithetical to Nazi teaching. Where there is human relation, there is a difference that has been transformed into nonindifference. In Jewish thought, the "feminine," or *nekevah,* makes possible the establishment of a difference that is nonindifference, from which all issues of meaning and sanctity derive. For, in accordance with the meanings of the cognate verb *nakav,* the feminine "marks" or "distinguishes" a person for *this* relation to *this other* human being. Therefore it is a Jewish mother, and not a Jewish father, that makes a Jew a Jew. To have an origin—to have a mother—is to be already marked for a mission: Origin implies destiny, when that origin is seen as a *mother* and not as some primeval ooze. Situated at the origin of human sanctity, woman represents not the primeval but the immemorial, the remembrance of something that transforms everything afterward into *a something.*

Signifying an immemorial past, woman also signifies an open-ended future and therefore the mystery of the *yet to be,* of what is yet to be revealed, and yet to be consummated.[3] The alterity represented by the feminine, then, is not an otherness already contained in being; it is the otherness of what is more than being, beyond being, and *better* than being. The feminine is both what already is and what is yet to be. Thus, like meaning, dwelling unfolds where a future designated by the feminine unfolds. To have meaning is to have a direction, and to have direction is to approach a realm where we have yet to arrive: Meaning is what is yet to be realized. Hence the prophet's pronouncement: "Behold, a young woman will conceive and give birth" (Isaiah 7:14). What designates this future as the future of a life is the origin of life situated in the home: To have meaning—to have the very possibility of redemption, in other words—is to have a *mother.* Thus when we say of some unsavory character that he too has a mother, we are saying that even his life has meaning and value.

We are also saying that he too is loved: To have a mother is to be the recipient of a caress, which in Hebrew is *letifah.* Looking more closely at this word, we realize that to have an origin is to have a source of kindness, of what is *latif,* or "kind." The Nazi assault on the Name as it manifests itself in the desecration of the origin is an assault on *kindness.* To be sure, they prohibited all non-Jews in the vicinity of the ghettos and camps from showing any kindness toward the Jews. Thus, in the words of Primo Levi, the Nazis devised a realm in which "everything is hostile."[4] *Everything* is hostile. Which means: Here there are no mothers. Embodied in the feminine, the kindness of the caress draws us into a relation with what is forever sought but never touched. Like the act of loving-kindness performed "for nothing," the caress, says Lévinas, "consists in seizing upon nothing, in soliciting what ceaselessly escapes its form toward a future never future enough, in soliciting what slips away as though *it were not yet.* It *searches.*"[5] Here one may recall that the two words at the very center of the Torah are *darosh darash,* which translates as to "search diligently" but which literally means to "search and search again." Thus the Torah ends its first half with searching and begins again with searching: The Torah, like woman, is about searching. It is about what is revealed only in the caress.

What woman signifies in the Jewish tradition can be seen in the tale of the creation of the first woman. Here Lévinas comments by saying, "Woman does not simply come to someone deprived of companionship to keep him company. She answers to a solitude inside this privation and—which is stranger—to a solitude that subsists in spite of the presence of G-d; to a solitude in the universal, to the inhuman which continues to well up even when the human has mastered nature and raised it to thought."[6] Of course, woman mitigates the solitude of being not as a mate but as a *wife* and as a *mother;* it is not for nothing that the creation of woman includes the commandment to get married and have children (Genesis 2:24). Therefore the Midrash teaches that when He created Eve, G-d plaited her hair, brought her to the wedding canopy, and performed a marriage (see *Bereshit Rabbah* 18:2 and 18:4; see also Talmud tractate *Eruvin* 18a–18b). Thus exceeding the ontological landscape "nature," woman—the origin—is the one who cannot be possessed, who is beyond the projects of our labor in the world. Created from the side of man, which is hidden even when he stands naked, she consists of the hidden: As the origin, she is the one beyond our grasp (see *Bereshit Rabbah* 80:5).[7]

Hence "the souls of women" says Jiří Langer (murdered by the Nazis), "come to this earth from higher worlds than the souls of men. The Law therefore sets women free from those commandments whose fulfillment is limited to a particular period, to a particular time of day or season [*Rosh Hashanah* 30a; *Chagigah* 4a; *Kiddushin* 29a]. For the world in which the souls of women have their origin is raised above the conception of time."[8] Woman, then, is not just the other; beyond such categories, she opens up the very otherness of the interrelation that defines humanity as well as the mystery of divinity, as a giving, over against a conquering. Forever sought and eternally future, woman is the one through whom holiness enters the world. Therefore, says the Talmudic sage Rabbi Chelbo, only through a man's wife does blessing come to a home (*Bava Metzia* 59a). "A man who has no wife," it is written in the Midrash, "lives without good, help, joy, blessing, and atonement"; in fact, says the Midrash, without woman a man is not an *adam,* not a human being (*Kohelet Rabbah* 9:9:1).[9]

In the Jewish tradition the feminine manifestation of the Holy One is represented by the *Shekhinah;* she enters the world through the marriage between G-d and Israel,[10] a relation that can be articulated in the relation between any husband and wife. Says the great mystic of sixteenth-century Safed, Rabbi Moshe Cordovero, "As long as a man has not married, the *Shekhinah* is not with him, since she relates to man mainly through the female aspect. For man stands between two female aspects—his wife below in the physical world, who receives 'sustenance, clothing, and conjugal rights' from him [see Exodus 21:10]; and the *Shekhinah* above him, who blesses him with all these so that he will give again and again to the wife he has chosen in the covenant of marriage."[11] Similarly, the thirteenth-century mystic Rabbi Joseph Gikatilla asserts that the *Shekhinah* "in the time of Abraham our father is called Sarah and in the time of Isaac our father is called Rebecca and in the time of Jacob our father is called Rachel."[12] Therefore, says the Zohar, "When a man is at home, the foundation of his house is the wife, for it is on account of her that the *Shekhinah* departs not from the house" (*Zohar* I, 50a)—or from the world. And what comes into the world, through this origin that is woman? It is Torah, as the Maharal of Prague has taught: "If the home possesses Torah it possesses that which sustains it. Understand this."[13] Which is to say: If it possesses Torah, it possesses the origin.

In the Talmud it is said that the *Shekhinah* is not only a feminine presence but is also a maternal presence (see *Kiddushin* 31b). When she accompanies Israel into exile, then, it is as a mother looking after her children. Because the *Shekhinah* accompanies Israel into exile, the Jews are able to endure life without succumbing to the alienation of exile. What is the sign of this accompaniment? It is the Torah itself, which the Jews bear with them in their wanderings.[14] According to an ancient teaching, the Torah had to be accepted first by the women at Mount Sinai before it could be received by the men. For the House of Jacob mentioned in Exodus 19:3 precedes the reference to the Children of Israel, and the House of Jacob refers the women among the Hebrews (see, for example, Rashi's commentary on Exodus 19:3; see also *Mekilta de-Rabbi Ishmael, Bachodesh* 2; also *Zohar* II, 79b). It is through the feminine, who is the mystery of value and meaning, that we have the Torah and a dwelling place in the world.[15] For if the Torah is the foundation of Creation, the mother, through her tie to the *beit* in which the Torah originates, is the foundation of the Torah itself; she is the origin of the origin. To be sure, the first letter in the Torah is *beit,* a letter that is associated with the womb from which Creation is born. Significantly, the *beit* also designates a "house," the place that a mother transforms into a *dwelling* place.

"At the level of Divinity," Rabbi Yitzchak Ginsburgh points out, "the house symbolizes the ultimate purpose of all reality: to become a dwelling place below for the manifestation of G-d's presence. Not as Abraham who called it [the Temple site] 'a mountain,' nor as Isaac who called it 'a field,' but as Jacob who called it 'a house.'"[16] Hence the wives and mothers of Israel are known as the *House* of Jacob. Thus we see more clearly than ever that, through her tie to the *beit* at the origin of Torah, the mother is both the foundation of Torah and the center of the dwelling place. For there is no dwelling in the world without the Word, without the Torah, that comes from G-d. Thus linked to the Creator and the dwelling He makes possible, the mother lies at the origin of Creation and the center of the dwelling place. And what is a dwelling place? It is a space into which we invite another—the space opened up by the mother.

In the Zohar it is written that only with the advent of Jacob "did the worlds take their final form, and were not again demolished as heretofore" (*Zohar* I, 154b). Why? Because only with the House of Jacob—with woman—is there room for a world and a space for dwelling. The mystery of value and meaning unfolds wherever we make room for another—that is the meaning of dwelling: We do not usurp the place of another. Woman opens up space, has space, where there is no physical space. Hence she is precisely the one who does not usurp the place of another. Rather, miraculously, she creates room for another life within herself, in the very depths of her physical being. What she embodies, metaphysically, then, is the radical opposite of the ontological interest, which is the Nazis' interest in *Lebensraum,* a term that designated the usurping of the place and the space of another.

Lévinas has pointed out in this connection that the being of the ego is always suspect because, as ego, I must always "ask myself if my being is justified, if the *Da* of my *Dasein* is not already the usurpation of somebody else's place."[17] As the one who harbors a womb, which is the hidden *inner space* of the origin, woman is the one who precisely does *not* usurp the place of another but rather makes room for another to dwell in the world, quite literally and quite graphically, by conceiving and giving birth. There is no giving more profound than giving birth, no giving more profoundly holy. Dwelling happens where woman is present because woman represents a dwelling *place* or *Makom* that does not usurp the place of another but rather opens up a place *for* the other. That is why *Makom* is one of the names of G-d. Like G-d, woman as such is *other*-oriented; she is the opposite of the ego and is the essence of presence.

We have spoken of the Hebrew word for "woman." Here we consider the Hebrew word for "mother": It is *em,* a word that, as *im,* also means "with," as when a mother says to her little one, "It's all right, I'm right here with you." Therefore, in that familiar photo of a mother holding her child in her arms, with the Nazi's rifle aimed at the back of her head, we see the embodiment of the Third Reich in its desecration of the origin. We see, in short, what the Nazi makes of the mother's being *with* her babe. And we the infinite extent to which a mother is prepared to *be with* her little one.

Defining the mother is the "womb" that is *rechem;* it is a cognate of *racham,* which means to "love" or to "have compassion" as only a mother can love and have compassion.[18] Joined with *rachamim*—that is, "compassion" or "love"—the father becomes the Holy One, as in the expression *Av HaRachamim,* "the Father of love and compassion" or "the loving and compassionate Father"—the Father who is also Mother. Without G-d the Mother we have no access, no relation, to G-d the Father. That is why it is not good for a man to be alone, as it is written (Genesis 2:18): The teaching of the Father must join with the love of the Mother to instill the human being with the image of the holy. Thus the *adam* who had begun as both male and female is split into two distinct beings, so that each could enter into a *relation* with the other, and neither would be alone.[19] The Oneness of G-d is a singularity that entails the Oneness of the Supernal Mother and the Heavenly Father; when these two origins are *uniquely* One, the purpose of reality becomes clear: to create a home. The one created in the image of the Holy One is created male and female—and then that one is separated into two—because both are required to make creation into a dwelling place for the Creator. Both are required for bringing life into the world.

We see more clearly now what it means to say that through the mother we have the Torah: Bearing life into the world, she bears Torah into the world. For the Torah *is* life; it is the *Ets Chayim,* the "Tree of Life" that sustains all life (see, for example, Proverbs 3:18; see also *Berakhot* 32b and *Taanit* 7a; also *Vayikra Rabbah* 35:6). Thus the Talmud compares the Torah to a woman (*Kiddushin* 30b). Thus in the Zohar it is written: "First came *Ehyeh* (I shall be), the dark womb of all. Then *Asher Ehyeh* (That I Am), indicating the readiness of the Mother to beget all" (*Zohar* III, 65b). The "I shall be" posits the yet-to-be that is the horizon of meaning; the

"That I am" or "What I am" is the manifestation of meaning along that horizon: Begetting all, the mother begets meaning. Begetting all, the Zohar says further, the Supernal Mother begets all of humanity: "The [Supernal] Mother said: 'Let us make man in our image'" (*Zohar* I, 22b). Bearing in mind the association between the mother and the House of Jacob, we note that this principle is also stated in the Midrash: "The Holy One, blessed be He, said to His world: 'O My world, My world! Shall I tell thee who created thee, who formed thee? Jacob has created thee, Jacob has formed thee'" (*Vayikra Rabbah* 36:4). For the House of Jacob signifies the mother of creation. From the depths of the mother's compassion—from the *rechem* within the *rachamim*—human life itself begins to stir. Thus the mother links us to the Creator, to the absolute origin of all things.

Only a mother, moreover, can beget a mother: What lies at the core of an immemorial origin of the Jew lies also at the heart of an ongoing creation of the Jew, so that the *anticipation* of an ongoing Jewish presence in the world becomes a definitive element of creation. Says André Neher, "G-d starts creating, and He distributes creation over seven days. *Time* itself is of the uppermost importance. Creation manifests itself by the appearance of time."[20] Thus, for Jewish presence in the world—the presence that the Nazis deemed ontologically criminal—the tenses and the intensity of time comprise a fundamental aspect of an origin that is not only behind us but is forever before us: The origin is the future. They realized, therefore, that the destruction of the Jewish future required the desecration of the Jewish origin. And so they set out to murder the Jewish mother.

A Memory of the Murder of the Mother: Ka-tzetnik 135633

One man whose life and writings reveal the *how* and *why* of the Nazi assault on the mothers of Israel is Yehiel De-Nur, the author known as Ka-tzetnik 135633. Ka-tzetnik 135633 is not precisely a pen name for De-Nur. It is the name with which he was baptized in Auschwitz. Yehiel De-Nur was born in 1909; Ka-tzetnik 135633 was born in 1943. In the late spring of 1945, still wearing the tattered striped outfit of an Auschwitz inmate, Ka-tzetnik lay dying in an Italian hospital. But before death could overtake him, he resolved to fulfill a promise he had made to the dead. So he asked for writing materials and put to paper what he had seen in the Kingdom of Night. Some two weeks later he produced a manuscript. He also made a miraculous recovery, as though his testimony had brought him back from the grave. The escaped Auschwitz inmate entrusted his book to a Jewish soldier. Noticing that the manuscript had no author's name, the soldier asked, "Who shall I say wrote this?"

"Who wrote it, you ask?" the man replied from the other shore. "*They* wrote it! Go on, put *their* name on it: Ka-tzetnik!"

It was the name given to all the inhabitants of the concentrationary universe, the name of all those whose voices went into this voice. Thus appeared *Sunrise over Hell,* the first novel to bear witness to the Shoah. Thus appeared the author Ka-tzetnik.

Throughout his life Ka-tzetnik gave no public lectures and never appeared on a talk show. When his children were in high school in Israel they read his works, but they did not know that he was their father, Yehiel De-Nur. He never participated in the ceremonies for the Ka-tzetnik Award, a literary prize named after him. Nor did he ever hold special seminars for the future teachers of Israel, as he was often requested to do.

"My wife tells me I should," he once explained to me. "And I know she is right. But for some reason I cannot. It isn't me. It's the others. I have always tried to keep Yehiel De-Nur separate from Ka-tzetnik."

I first met Yehiel De-Nur when I visited him at his Tel Aviv apartment in July 1989. His wife Eliyah warmly greeted me at the door. From the moment I entered their home she treated me as if she had known me for years, while Yehiel at first cautiously waited to see who I was. Eliyah was known throughout Israel as a poet, humanitarian, and translator of her husband's works into English. His "savior," Yehiel called her. After *Sunrise over Hell* was published in Israel in late 1945, she spent more than a year tracking down its author. The book was in every Israeli home, but no one, not even the publisher, knew the identity of its author. Eliyah found him at last, however, and they were married. Ka-tzetnik tells much of their story in his novel *Phoenix over the Galilee.*

Once Eliyah's trust had convinced him that he could trust me, Yehiel asked me about my work on the Holocaust. He listened with his characteristic intensity, his eyes riveted to mine, as I offered my faltering response to his question. Suddenly he went to his desk, pulled out a manuscript, and cried, "Here: This is the key! You will take it. You will read it. This is the key! My books are about Auschwitz. This one *is* Auschwitz!"

It was the manuscript of the English translation of *Shivitti*. He told me I could read it in only an hour, but that night back in Jerusalem I spent more than six hours poring over Ka-tzetnik's harrowing tale of how he had overcome thirty years of sleeplessness. Every night the nightmares would come, so that he had to catch what sleep he could in afternoon naps. Finally, Eliyah took him to Holland, where he underwent five LSD therapy sessions to free himself of the dreams. *Shivitti* is his account of those sessions. And yet he could not write it until ten years after the experience, when the first line of the book came to him: "LSD treatment of Mr. De-Nur, Session One..."

"For two weeks," he told me, "from the first word to the last, I wrote continuously. I have no memory of anything else, until I noticed other things on the desk, the picture of Eliyah. And somehow I knew I was finished. Oh, yes, there was one other thing: the cry of a child outside my window. It was a cry of life."

The voice of a child came to him through one window as he peered through another. The voice of a child called to him from one world as he passed through another.

What he recorded in the book called *Shivitti* consists of visions rivaling those of Ezekiel. And yet Ka-tzetnik is not Ezekiel, for whom the dry bones came to life. Ka-tzetnik is Ka-tzetnik, before whose eyes the very bones of the dead were reduced to dust.

"They called it a factory," he told me one day, his eyes fixed on something only he could see. "But I could not understand what it produced. Later I found out that at the same time men were making something at a place called Los Alamos. The product was much the same. G-d created us in His image and gave us the imagination to create Him in turn. G-d did not make Auschwitz. Neither did a devil. It was man. And in making Auschwitz, man made a new image of G-d. That new god is Nucleus! The hard water it took to create that god was made of the blood of more than a million and a half children."

The next time I saw Yehiel De-Nur was the last time I saw Eliyah. It was in June 1991. I had traveled to Israel by way of the murder camp sites at Treblinka, Majdanek, and Auschwitz-Birkenau. When he greeted me at the door, Yehiel hesitated for a moment, a bit puzzled: He did not recognize me at first.

"David, you are so different," he said.

He could not put his finger on it, but he insisted that I had changed dramatically. I could not imagine what he was talking about. But then I realized: It was the ashes that had left their mark on me, and my eyes had been transformed by what they had seen.

But Eliyah insisted that I had not changed a bit. Eliyah had a way of seeing through the ashes.

But she had changed. It was only two years since I had last seen her, but she looked ten years older. Her face was marked with the pain and the sickness of cancer. When she excused herself to go rest, her eyes had the look of a last look. She knew. And so did I.

Yehiel immediately asked me about my visits to the sites of the murder camps in Poland. There was a strange desperation in his voice. He wanted to know whether any of the wooden blocks are still standing in Birkenau, whether they were as he has described them in his books. It was as if he were not quite sure that they had ever existed, as if he were trying to confirm for himself that he had not gone insane and invented it all.

Yes, Yehiel, I assured him, the plank beds are there in the blocks, just as you describe them. Yes, the stone oven runs down the middle of each block. Yes, opposite the tracks where the Jews were unloaded and selected for the gas chambers stand the barracks made from the bricks of the village of Birkenau. You did not make it up, Yehiel. You have not gone mad. (Or have you? How have you kept from going mad?)

Yehiel De-Nur died in July 2001. But I wonder whether Ka-tzetnik 135633 does not live in all of us, curled up in the nagging ashes of the dead that invade our bread and whose voices reverberated in his voice. Yes: I wonder.... He offered us a key, however, in *Shivitti*. But what does it unlock?

For one thing, it unlocks a trace of what was consumed at Auschwitz and reveals what underlies the plight of the world in the post-Holocaust era. I do not know if Ka-tzetnik was a prophet. But what Martin Buber once said of the prophets surely applies to Ka-tzetnik: "They always aimed to shatter all security and to proclaim in the opened abyss of the final insecurity the unwished for G-d who demands that His human creatures become real…and confounds all who imagine that they can take refuge in the certainty that the temple of G-d is in their midst."[21] A major theme that concerned the prophets was the destruction of the Temple. Just so, among the terms used to refer to the Holocaust is the word *Churban,* the word used to refer to the destruction of the Temple. It is no accident. For each Churban entailed the obliteration of the flow of G-d's light into the world. By the light and in the darkness of the flames that consumed the Temple of Israel—the Jewish people—the visions in *Shivitti* unfold.

This is what he sees: "Darkness in my mouth. I can taste it."[22] The darkness in the mouth is the darkness of silence: The Kingdom of Night is the Kingdom of Silence, the realm where Silence is King. The monarch emerges in *Sunrise over Hell,* where the cry of those marked for death "split the heavens, but Heaven remained lofty and silent as though G-d had deserted its temples."[23] Through the rift in the heavens pours darkness, emptiness, night—all the new synonyms of silence, a silence that is precisely the opposite of a maternal word of loving-kindness. Describing the inauguration of this silence in the Kingdom of Exile, Ka-tzetnik writes, "No screams here, no speech. The Site of Silence… Night here had an essence all its own. Night here was at the beck and call of an omnipotent sovereign, a sovereign supreme over the Planet. Night muffled, stealing inaudibly on tiptoes to envelop you, inaudibly, so as to keep from trespassing upon the terrifying silence reigning supreme."[24] No screams. No speech.

Recalling the mystical teaching that the *Shekhinah* manifest in woman is the origin of speech,[25] we realize that this imposition of an irreducible silence is a defining feature of the desecration of the origin. And we see a definitive connection between the desecration of the origin and the muting of creation. Such is the silence of the exile that inserts itself into the mouth of the witness. And it is a sovereign over the *planet,* extending beyond the electrified barbed wire, as Ka-tzetnik suggests in *Star of Ashes:* "Silent are the heavens, silent the yellowed fields; silent the readied rifles, silent the ghetto hovels."[26] In his novel *Atrocity,* Ka-tzetnik underscores this mute condition. When the boy Moni, the novel's hero, first entered the Auschwitz barracks, the prisoners "received him the way the pile behind the block receives a skeleton just dumped by the block orderlies. Here no one utters a word. Here speech is extinct."[27] Death wordlessly receives death; death is precisely this wordlessness. Then there is Professor Raphael, the scholar who knew ten languages, yet "only three words ever break from Professor Raphael's mouth: the names of his wife and two children,"[28] the single source of blessing in his world. But his wife and children, the source and symbols of life, are no more. Hence the *Shekhinah* is no more; speech is no more. This is the wordlessness that the witness struggles to convey with words.

Where, then, does the word go when it leaves the mouth filled with darkness? It curls up in the darkness of the eyes of those who are fed into the gullet of nothingness. And yet, in *Shivitti*, Ka-tzetnik manages somehow to pray,

> G-d
>
> Give me this day the silent word, like
>
> the one
>
> Their eyes gave on Their way to
>
> The crematorium[29]

This is the word that the man seeks from G-d, snatched from the mouth and laid into the eyes. This is the word of the prolonged prayer that is *Shivitti*. Reading this text, we peer into their eyes. Responding to this text, their eyes penetrate into us, until we behold a single word, as it was branded into the forehead of Shlamek's father in Ka-tzetnik's *House of Dolls:* It is the word *Jude*. "Blood gave from the seared word," we read. "And the word was as clear as the blood oozing from it. As though it were quite natural that the word *Jude* should give blood."[30] Here the distinction between word and meaning is especially pronounced, and the draining of meaning from the word is especially graphic. Drained of its lifeblood, the exiled word is drained of meaning. G-d, give us this day the silent word that bleeds from the eyes in tears of blood!

In the Age of Auschwitz that being which is human being is stamped with the bleeding word *Jude*. For this is the word that reveals who we are, the word that contains our blood and our name. "Give me this day the silent word" amounts to "return to me my harrowed name, and in my name my soul." The prophetic witness who reveals the exile of the word thus unveils the fragmentation of the Name that plagues a nameless post-Holocaust humanity.

Buber has held that with the prophet a voice from beyond the man invades him, a Presence that descends from "the divine sphere."[31] In *Shivitti,* however, the divine sphere cracks, and what descends upon the man is an imposed nothingness, a *shav,* to use the Hebrew word, which is a cognate of *Shoah.* Yet it is a nothingness that is not merely nothing; it haunts the discourse that would constitute the name and soul of the witness. "The *I* of Then and the *I* of Now," Ka-tzetnik states it, "are a single identity divided by two."[32] And between the two looms a presence made of absence, a soul other than and at odds with its name. In the fragmentation of the name of the one now called Ka-tzetnik, it is not the author as I who undertakes his task but the author as other, who has lost his I and who articulates that loss through his character. In *Phoenix over the Galilee,* for instance, the author's persona Harry Preleshnik declares, "My name was burned with all the rest in the crematorium at Auschwitz."[33] Like his author and in an expression of the authorial splitting of the self, Harry eventually becomes an author in *Phoenix over the Galilee.* The bond between character and author is emphasized by the number they share, the number that eclipses their name and splinters their soul.

"All I've ever written is in essence a personal journal," says the man whose soul was split in half, "a testimonial on paper of I, I, I: I who witnessed…I who experienced…I who lived through…I, I, I, till half through a piece, I suddenly had to transform *I* to *he.* I felt the split, the ordeal, the alienation of it."[34] Reading these lines, one cannot help but notice the splitting of the I into something other than itself that occurs in the process of bearing witness. Becoming a witness is "a tearing away from oneself despite oneself," as Lévinas puts it.[35] The I of the witness "means *here I am,* answering for everything and for everyone. Responsibility for others has not been a return to oneself, but an exasperated contracting, which the limits of identity cannot contain."[36] The witness's stance of being-for-the-other, moreover, is assumed by a creature of flesh and blood. In its most basic form the fragmentation of the soul is the fragmentation of the body. For the body is a fundamental element in the relation between one human being and another, the relation in which the life of the soul comes to bear. And it is most fundamental in the relation between mother and child, where the body of the one emerges from the body of the other.

Thus Ka-tzetnik comes to the most dreadful of his visions in *Shivitti,* a vision in which he beholds what his novels could not contain:

> My mother. I see her naked and marching in line, one among Them, her face turned towards the gas chambers. "Mama! Mama! Mama!" A voice comes rolling down to me out of the Auschwitz sky. The echo of each separate word is a hammer crashing on my eardrums. It's my mother, naked. She's going to be gassed. I run after her. I cry out, "Mama! Mama!" I, outside that line, run after her: "Mama Listen to me! Mama!" My mother naked. Going to be gassed. I behold my mother's skull and in my mother's skull I see me. And I chase after me inside my mother's skull. And my mother is naked. Going to be gassed. I'm choking![37]

In case one may have wondered where the mother has been in all of this, here we have the answer.

The Hebrew edition of *Shivitti* is titled *Tsofen: E.D.M.A.*, which means *Code: E.D.M.A.* "E.D.M.A." is an acronym for *Elohei De Meir Anani*, or "G-d of Meir, answer me" (see *Avodah Zarah* 18a). It is a phrase used by the followers of the great Talmudic sage Rabbi Meir whenever they fell into danger under the Roman oppression. This code appears on the title page of every novel that Ka-tzetnik published, yet he himself claimed to not know what it meant. All he knew was that he would utter this code whenever the abyss of the Shoah was about to swallow him, and somehow he would survive. It seems, however, that the E.D.M.A. could not save him from this horrific vision of his mother. For this vision is far more than a memory from an individual's past. It is a revelation of the primal mother of all the children of the earth, a vision of the Supernal Mother, who is buried with the ashes of her children, herself reduced to ash. It is a vision of the *Shekhinah* herself going to be gassed, here and now.

The world has known orphans before, many times over. But the world itself has never been so orphaned. Why an "orphaned world"? It is not merely the fact that almost all of the survivors whose memories we inherit were orphans. Rather, it is because these are not orphans whose mothers have passed away—they are orphans whose mothers were murdered in a realm where it was *illegal* to be a Jewish mother. In the Holocaust Kingdom not a single Jewish mother died. No, they were all murdered. Let us consider now the orphans' memory of the murder of the mother.

The Cry of the Orphan and the Orphaned Outcry

If, as it is often said, the Nazis destroyed souls before they destroyed bodies, a key component of such an assault lies in the assault on the mother. For our initial sense of who we are—our first inkling of substance and meaning—comes from the relation to the mother. It is she who initially intones our name with love and conveys to us the sense that we *matter*. When the mother is lost, the word that bespeaks the dearness of the human being is lost; hence the human image is lost. For the mother is our original and most immediate tie to the Creator, to that absolutely Other who is revealed in the absolute nonindifference of love. Inasmuch as the Holocaust entails a radical assault upon the soul, it entails a radical assault upon the mother and, through the mother, upon the One in whose image the soul is created.

By now we can see that the Nazis' calculated murder of Jewish mothers was tied to the murder of the Supernal Mother, the One whose four-letter Name ends in the feminine vowel sign *kamats*. Similarly, we see that a people and a world are ontologically orphaned, with their essence redefined as the essence of the orphan. Sara Zyskind begins her memoir, for example, with the memory of her mother's last Mother's Day.[38] And the memory of an outcry rises to the surface of her page: "I don't want to be an orphan, Mother!"[39] Similarly, while standing at the window of a Nazi prison cell, Paul Trepman looks out into a courtyard, where Jews stand naked, waiting to be murdered, and from the silent suffering of that crowd a terrible vision comes to him. "My mother," the horror overwhelms him, "had probably perished in the same way in the Warsaw ghetto, along with my sister, and the rest of my family. Now, for the first time, I felt truly orphaned."[40] Now, for the first time, he belongs to no one's memory.

The cry of "I don't want to be an orphan" is a cry of "I don't want to be forgotten." The orphan's memory is the memory of the loss of the one who will never forget our name, even if we should forget. The emptiness the orphan experiences is the void of being forgotten—by force, by murder, not by an act of G-d. Losing those hands and that face, the child loses her own hands and face, her own deeds and words. She is not left alone in the world.

No, she is left alone in the antiworld, "the shadow of another shadow," as Ana Vinocur expresses it.[41] When the mother is turned to ash, creation is returned to the *tohu vevohu,* to the chaos and the void, antecedent to every origin. Significantly, the first word in Vinocur's *Book without a Title* is *mother.* From this word arise all other words, beginning with her name.

"The greatness of Israel," it is written in the Midrash, "is compared… to a woman bearing child" (*Shir HaShirim Rabbah* 8:19). If the Covenant that distinguishes the Jews is definitively linked to the Creation, then the murder of the mother is inextricably bound to the extermination of the Covenant. The bearer of Creation and Covenant, the mother bears life into the world. As the bearer of Creation and Covenant, she is the bearer of Torah, and Torah, in turn, signifies the presence of the Name, of *HaShem,* in the world. From that Presence life derives its meaning and its sanctity, its substance and its sense. When, upon their arrival at Birkenau, mothers are sent to the left and their children to the right, it is not simply the division of a transport into two groups, one condemned and the other yet to be condemned; what transpires is a rending of the Covenant itself and the tearing of a wound into the heart of Creation.

Isabella Leitner's memory of the moment when her mother was torn from her upon their arrival in Birkenau, will drive the point home: "Mama! If you don't turn around I'll run after you. But they won't let me. I must stay on the 'life' side. Mama!"[42] No good-bye. No last look. Such exchanges belong only to the world that comes from the hand of the Creator, only to the world where there are mothers, not to the antiworld where Mengele orchestrates the annihilation of the mother with a wave of his baton. Etched into the memory of Auschwitz is the memory of this essence of Auschwitz, of this obliteration of the mother who signifies the obliteration of the world and its origin, of the name and the Name. The mother is the strength of Israel, Jewish tradition maintains. In that mass of Jews consigned to the flames it is she who is on her way to the gas chambers, every Jewish mother in every Jew and every Jew in every Jewish mother.

Initially a person comes into the world as a Jew because his mother is a Jew; then he is reborn as a Jew through the memory of his Jewish origin, a memory manifested through a sense of Jewish responsibility. For one who must now wrestle a name from the Angel, this remembrance entails a movement toward the womb of the origin that arises not afterward but from the depths of the Horror itself, from the time of the origin's obliteration. One example of that moment is found in Ka-tzetnik's *Star of Ashes*, where he remembers the children who "push against their mother's belly as if seeking to get inside once more. Their scream, embryonic, unuttered, howls out of the mother's eyes."[43] That mother's eyes bore into our own eyes, as we push against the belly of the Supernal Mother. As we seek to merge with the womb of the origin, the mute scream rises up from the origin, not in a howl of pain or despair but in a cry for help—a cry for *our* help. At stake in our response to that summons is our very humanity, as Nathan Shapell suggests when, upon the death of his mother, he laments, "It was the end. My life had no further meaning. I had no function as a human being anymore."[44] A cry rose up from the ghetto. It was the Jewish children weeping for their mother Rachel. And they would not be comforted. For she was no more.

In the Jewish tradition, as in most traditions, the mother is associated with the earth. Planet Auschwitz, however, rests not upon the earth but upon several feet of Jewish remains, on the mothers' ashes that now veil the Mother Earth. The loss of the human image that Shapell experienced upon the loss of his mother is expressed in other memoirs as an eclipse of the earth. It is the earth—and, symbolically, the mother—of which Agnes Sassoon speaks when she says, "My memories are of darkness and doom; heaviness, depression, desolation…. I cannot remember spring or summertime, or seeing flowers and greenery."[45] In short, she cannot remember the life that rises up from the womb of the earth, since her every link to that origin has been severed by a darkness that the light cannot comprehend. And, through memory, she struggles to emerge from that desecrated womb.

In those days of destruction, in that destruction of days, the earth moved not with the stirring of life but with the throes of death. Donna Rubinstein, for instance, recollects the mass graves at Krasnostav: "They covered up the graves but the soil heaved."[46] And, as though in a state of delirium, Judith Dribben writes, "They bury them half-alive…or half-dead…and the soil was moving…the soil was moving…they bury them half-alive…and the soil was moving…."[47] The soul reels at such an image! The earth that heaves is not an earth that we can walk. With the annihilation of the *adam,* the *adamah* churns; the origin itself shifts under the weight of the children forced back into her womb. The ground itself crumbles in a mute, embryonic howl that reverberates throughout the memory of the survivor who struggles to regain a name.

And yet within the memory of the loss of the earth there springs a trace of the recovery of that earth. At times this recovery lies in the remembrance of a garden in a ghetto where there should be no garden, a sowing of the soil with life rather than death. Ana Vinocur was among those who planted such a garden and who remembers, "That dialogue in which the earth's answer was expressed so eloquently and in such a comforting way, brought to my mind that expression which is now so meaningful: Mother Earth."[48] The act of sowing and thus affirming life at its origin enables the human being to hear the eloquence of the origin and to thus move toward the origin. That movement is a movement toward the Name. Vinocur's characterization of her relation to the earth as a dialogue is also significant: The divine aspect of the mother imparts to the dialogue an aspect of prayer. Eugene Heimler, for instance, writes, "If I was in trouble, all I had to do was to close my eyes, imagine my mother's face hovering before me—and pray to her."[49] G-d may have turned away, but the prayer still finds its way to the Supernal Mother.[50]

For Sara Zyskind, this tie to the Supernal Mother is revealed in the form of intervention on the occasion of her father's illness in the Łódź Ghetto. When he was finally allowed to enter the hospital, she writes, "I ran to the cemetery to tell Mother about what happened. There was no doubt in my mind that the miracle had taken place thanks to Mother's intervention with the Divine Powers."[51] Here the dialogue with a mound of earth becomes a pathway to the Heaven of heavens; the one who signifies the human tie to the divine origin—precisely *because* she signifies that bond—has the power to intervene with the Divine Powers. Donna Rubinstein also expresses this conviction when, upon her liberation and return to her hometown of Krasnostav, she cries, "O, my dear Mama, did you intervene for me? Is it you who helped me survive the war? Please, Mother dear, guide me in my future the way you have until now."[52] Even when she has passed, the mother is still present; even from the past, she is still the origin of the future. The annihilation of the origin, then, entails not only the destruction of the past but, in that very destruction, it includes the obliteration of the future, without which there can be no life. Just as there can be no life without the mother.

The mother's intervention with the Creator is a manifestation of the compassion, or the *Chesed,* that lies at the root of Creation. But this intervention did not always occur; or, if it did occur, it did not always succeed. In many cases all that was experienced was the terrible absence of the mother and an infinite isolation from her compassion. While imprisoned with a group of orphaned women in Stutthof, for example, Sara Nomberg-Przytyk recalls, "We felt that we…could not even succeed in raising a trace of compassion. That was how it remained until Liza started singing a song about a Jewish mother, and we, who had lost our mothers so cruelly, could not keep ourselves from crying."[53] Upon the annihilation of the origin that the mother represents, the void overtakes the origin and swallows up every word. The emptiness into which the words of these women fade is the emptiness that emerges with the loss of the mother and of the love that makes the mother who she is. The song about a Jewish mother is, after all, a song about love in its most sacred form.

The Loss of the Love That Lies at the Origin

In the sixteenth century Rabbi Yitzchak Luria raised a question: "If *Binah* or Understanding, which is associated with the Mother, is a mental process, why is it said to be in the heart, and not in the head?" Aryeh Kaplan explains: "The heart is actually the Personification of Imma-Mother, which is Binah-Understanding, where She reveals herself."[54] In the injunction to love G-d, the first thing with which we are called upon to love is the heart, *b'kol levavkha* (Deuteronomy 6:5). One also recalls that the *lamed* and the *beit* of *lev,* the Hebrew word for "heart," are the last and the first letters of the Torah. The heart, therefore, contains all of the Torah: It is on the heart, indeed, that the Teaching is to be inscribed (Deuteronomy 6:6). Personified as the heart, then, the mother signifies not only the origin of life but also the center of life. The heart bears this significance because it is the seat of Torah, which is the love and the teaching of G-d. And the loving-kindness shown by one human being toward another is the highest expression of that love and teaching centered in the heart and personified by the mother.

Hence, Rabbi Ginsburgh reminds us, "loving-kindness is the means through which G-d's presence is ultimately revealed,"[55] and it is originally revealed through the mother. In the Tanya, moreover, the Alter Rebbe, Rabbi Schneur Zalman, maintains that loving-kindness in the form of charity is feminine and, by implication, maternal, for "it receives a radiation from the light of the *Ein Sof* [the Infinite One] that [like a womb] encompasses all worlds."[56] From a Jewish perspective, therefore, maternal love is not just a feeling or a state of mind but is the manifestation and revelation of the Most High in our very midst. In the annihilation of that love we find once again that the ontological assault on the mother moves to a metaphysical level. Like the light created upon the first utterance of G-d, the mother's love is the mainstay of life, even and especially during the reign of death.

We see this in Leon Wells's memoir when he says, "I began to observe to my disgust that I, too, was coming very near to developing the indifference and apathy of so many others. I was saved from succumbing to these feelings only by the thought of those at home, and the determination that my mother should see me alive."[57] And: "Nothing could disturb me. I had seen my mother again. It had been the happiest day in my life for a long, long time."[58] Representing love in its holiest aspect, the mother embodies the opposite not only of human indifference but of ontological indifference, the opposite of what Lévinas calls the "there is" or "the phenomenon of impersonal being."[59] This "impersonal being" is a being that is empty of any maternal aspect, completely neutral and utterly indifferent. Maternal love, on the other hand, represents a loving nonindifference that comes from beyond the human being to awaken a nonindifference within the human being. If, as Olga Lengyel declares, "inhumanity was the natural order of things at Birkenau,"[60] it is because Birkenau is the phenomenological manifestation of an ontologically indifferent, antimaternal realm. For in Birkenau motherly love was carefully eliminated from the order of being; in Birkenau motherly love was a capital crime.

Maternal love is not part of the fabric of being—it is a breach of being. Through that love the mother opens up a small portal through which the Divine reveals itself from beyond the mute neutrality of all there is. "Mothers never thought of themselves," writes Vinocur. "They were sublime, special beings, divine!"[61] Only where we have a connection to these "special beings" do we have a connection to life. Why? Because as they love, so do they command us to love, as it is written in the Torah: "And you shall love your neighbor as yourself" (Leviticus 19:18). As we saw in chapter 1, this "as yourself," *kamokha,* means "that is what you are." In other words: "You shall love your neighbor, for that loving *is* your self," the soul and substance of who you are. That love for the other is the meaning of our life. And that commandment is what the mother conveys. The memory of the mother's love is a memory of this commandment to love, regardless of reward, regardless even of the presence of the loved one who might return the look of love. Indeed, the act of remembrance is itself an act of love.

If one of the aims of memory is to recover some link with life, it should come as no surprise to find that the orphan's tie to the mother is an essential aspect of his or her memory. In a statement reminiscent of Leon Wells's remarks cited above, Kitty Hart writes, "One thing I needed very much: regular visits to my mother."[62] Why? Because every other image and entity she encountered in the concentrationary universe declared to her that she was a nonentity, not a child or a person at all but a mere shadow about to be swallowed up by the Night. Through her mother's eyes, however, she could retrieve some trace of herself as someone who is loved and who is therefore alive: Through her mother she could wrestle her name from the Angel of Death. When she fell ill with typhus, in fact, Kitty once again received life from her mother. "Mother talked to me," she remembers, "though all she got in return was rambling nonsense. I did not even recognize her. But she persevered, slowly and steadily drawing me back to life."[63] In these lines we see that maternal love is as unconditional as it is deep, absolutely unconditional, and is therefore a reflection of the Absolute.

"Mother talked to me": The mother speaks, which is to say, the mother loves, without the reinforcement of response or recognition. She loves, then, without ground or limitation, infinitely and eternally, as G-d loves. And so she summons from the child a love that also transcends the boundaries of time and death, as one may see from a memory recorded by Sara Nomberg-Przytyk: "A young girl whose mother was assigned to the gas did not want to be separated from her. She wanted to die with her mother. They tore her from her mother by force."[64] Here the assault on maternal love takes the form of an assault on the love for the mother, even unto death. Not only are the mother and child consigned to death, but the love between them is also condemned through the elimination of the embrace that arises *between* them. The space *between* the two, where this love abides, is obliterated by forcing each to die separately, in isolation from one another: no more visits, no more being together. Not even in the gas chamber.

And yet the memory of the mother reestablishes a certain between space, where the visitation of maternal love comes from beyond the grave, from the other side of the sky that became her grave. For Isabella Leitner, this visitation assumes the form of an epiphany of the face. "My mother's face," she writes in the present tense, "her eyes, cannot be described.... She knows that for her there is nothing beyond this. And she keeps smiling at me, and I can't stand it. I am silently pleading with her: 'Stop smiling.' I gaze at her tenderly and smile back."[65] One swoons at this silent exchange! "The face speaks," as Lévinas says.[66] But the mother's face does more than speak. The mother's face *loves,* silently and absolutely, transcending all the limits of discourse. "Her face has an otherworldly look," Leitner continues her memory of her mother. "She wants us to live, desperately. All these years I've carried with me her face of resignation and hope and love."[67] The commandment to love that signifies the Divine Presence is a commandment to live. Like the Good that chooses us before we make any other choices, maternal love calls us by name and commands us to live, even as that life is about to be consumed. If memory is able to traverse time, it is because maternal love is able to transcend time. More than the remnant of a life, the survivor is the bearer of a life. For she bears the loving gaze of the mother who bore her. She bears the memory and the name of the mother.

Because maternal love is of such a transcendent nature, the image—no, the *presence*—of the mother manifests itself despite death. Eugene Heimler, for example, lost his mother just prior to his deportation. Yet, while riding the train to Auschwitz with his wife Eva, he notes, "Everybody to whom I belonged was either unconscious or dead. Eva, too, was lying in a coma by my feet. And then I saw my mother's face approaching from the distance."[68] Once more the epiphany of the face announces the maternal love that overcomes the ferocious isolation that the Nazi would impose upon the Jew. Once more the memory of maternal love invokes a moment in life over which death has no power. Saul Friedländer also recalls an instant of horror and panic during the time when, as a child, he was hiding from the Nazis. It too happened on a train; although the train was not bound for the death camps, the incident took place after his mother and father had been deported. "I screamed in terror," he writes. "But suddenly, by a miracle, my mother, who had set out in search of me, appeared. I ran to her, threw myself in her arms sobbing,… I opened my eyes: it was Madame Chancel stroking my forehead to calm me."[69] Once again we find the language of apparition and the image of a loving caress reaching across the chasm of death, as though his mother moved the hands of his protector, Madame Chancel.

But if the mother is dead, what does memory recover? Among other things, it recovers a name and, with the name, a world in which the human being may belong. To retrieve a name from the void is to draw the word out of exile and, if only for a moment, rejoin the word with its meaning, the name with its soul. Which word? Thomas Geve tells us in his memoir, where he recalls receiving a certain message from the women's camp in Birkenau: "News of my luck spread quickly and soon I was surrounded by dozens of roommates who, claiming to be my best friends, wanted to hear details—but above all to see the word 'mother.' There was a double reason for rejoicing: someone had found a mother, the being dearest to all of us."[70] Here the word *mother* is itself a message, a conveyor of meaning and of love, that appears in the midst of an antiworld dominated by everything that is opposed to love and the meaning it fosters.

Just as young Geve's fellow inmates gather around this word, so do we gather around this memory rendered through the word. Just as they see in this message not only *his* mother but *the* mother, so do we see in this memory a trace of maternal love as such. For if this love succumbs to the annihilation aimed at it, then this word loses its meaning, and the soul loses its name. But if the word is there, if a life is risked to transmit this word, if memory can smuggle it into the present through the veils of the past—then the name that is the vessel of life might be recovered. Suddenly these orphans lost in an orphaned world have a mother. Suddenly the block assumes the air of a home. But only for an instant.

A Name and an Address

Here we come to a deeper elaboration of the connection between the feminine and the origin discussed earlier. "The feminine aspect of the soul," Rabbi Ginsburgh points out, "and, in general, the woman in Judaism is symbolized by the house."[71] The reverse is also the case: The home, which is a sanctuary for life, is symbolized by the woman, who also houses life within her womb. Other associations and explanations also come to mind; one recalls, for example, Rashi's commentary on Numbers 26:64, where he writes, "The decree consequent upon the incident of the spies had not been enacted upon the women, because they held the Promised Land dear. The men had said, 'Let us appoint a chief and return to Egypt' (Numbers 14:4), while the women said, 'Give us a possession in the Land' (Numbers 27:4)." If the sum of the Torah lies in the commandment to love, it is because the commandment to love opens up a dwelling place, a place where children and families may come into being. As we have seen, the mother is the incarnation of that love; hence the mother is the personification of the home. And the Nazi Reich is precisely the opposite of the home.

The Nazi Kingdom of Night, then, is also the Kingdom of Exile. If, as Buber has said, "'Good' is the movement in the direction of home,"[72] the Nazi evil manifest in the murder of the Jewish mother is a movement away from home and into exile. It was not for nothing that the language of extermination included terms such as "resettlement." We also see why, for the Nazis, simply killing the Jews was not enough. Waging an ontological war against the Jews, the Nazis had to annihilate their home and their concept of home; they had to drive them from their homes and thus render them homeless prior to killing them. The fact that all six of the murder camps were located in Poland, therefore, had a particularly devastating irony for the three and a half million Polish Jews, as Harry Rabinowicz points out: "So closely did the Jews associate themselves with this homeland that its name was etymologically interpreted in Hebrew either as *Polin* ('Here ye shall dwell') or *Polaniah* ('Here dwells the Lord')."[73] In the Nazi assault on the mother we see the fundamental human problem of dwelling in its most extreme form: The murder of the maternal love that distinguishes the origin of life is engineered by the devastation of the home. Once the mother is eliminated, the reign of exile and homelessness is inaugurated. And the mother herself, the very one who had symbolized the home, becomes the symbol of exile, an embodiment of the *Shekhinah* in exile, which is the exile of the Name.

The Nazi project aimed at the devastation of the home assumed a variety of forms. There were times, for example, when the house lost the sanctity and sanctuary of a home by the mere appearance of the Nazis, who would come and go as they pleased. Such was the case in the Polish town of Bielitz, where prior to being forced out of her house, Gerda Klein recalls, "The sanctity of our home was gone, the chain of tradition broken, the shrine built by love and affection desecrated."[74] In just a few words Klein articulates the scope of the loss: An entire history, the time of tradition, was destroyed by the violation of this small space. Epitomized by the mother, the love that distinguishes the family is the love that constitutes the Jewish tradition. And the center of the life nurtured by Jewish tradition is the home.

What Gerda Klein invokes with words Lily Lerner conveys by means of an image. After being forced out of their home in the Hungarian town of Tolcsva, she and her family were forced to find shelter in Miskolc. "We no longer sat around the kitchen table," she writes. "The kitchen in Miskolc was too small to have one. In a strange sense, the family had lost a little of its magnetic core when it lost that table."[75] The sense of this loss is not so strange when we recall that in the Talmud, Rabbi Yochanan and Rabbi Elazar both teach that "as long as the Temple was in existence, the altar was [the means of] atonement for Israel, but now [since there is no Temple], each man's table is [the means of] atonement" (see *Menachot* 97a; *Chagigah* 27a). Thus the Code of Jewish Law compiled by Rabbi Joseph Caro in the sixteenth century is known as the *Shulchan Aruch,* or *The Set Table.* The table is where family members and guests join with one another in the act of sharing a piece of bread. Thus the life of the family has its origin in the mother, both literally and symbolically; from her womb come the children and from her hands the bread on which the blessing is said at the table. It is she who sets and orders the table, she, then, who creates the place of *dwelling*.

And so one understands why Jean Améry insists that "there is no 'new home.' Home is the land of one's childhood and youth. Whoever has lost it remains lost to himself."[76] A man can have no new home any more than he can have a new mother or a new identity. The "new" one is always a counterfeit and invariably leads to the alienation experienced by Saul Friedländer when, as a child, he and his parents tried to find a new home in Paris after they had fled from Prague. There, he remembers, he could find a place neither among the Christian nor among the Jewish children: "I was tied to a tree and beaten...by Jewish children because they thought I was different from them. So I belonged nowhere."[77] The violence done to the home translates into violence done to the child. Here the Jew becomes the one who, by definition, belongs nowhere, and this violence shows up not only in bruises on the body, but also in an absence imposed upon the soul. Thus, when Friedländer recalls his mother's words, "we can no longer exist legally,"[78] it is the memory of being cast outside the parameters of life itself. And that memory is articulated in the words of the *mother:* It is she who expresses the child's loss of being and belonging, since it is she who embodies the home that makes possible all belonging—something that the Nazis made impossible for the Jews *by law,* or by a kind of antilaw. Here lies a most insidious aspect of the ontological evil that National Socialism represents: Once it becomes a crime for a Jew to have a home, it is a crime for a Jew to have a name, a crime for a Jew to be.

If the concentrationary universe has been deemed an antiworld, it is because, among other reasons, it is antithetical to the home. Like the child whose "being" consists of not belonging, the home appears in this antiworld as the absence of the one thing needful, the absence of an entire world. All the fixtures and furnishings that constitute a life in the world are absent from the antiworld; indeed, the whole of the antiworld seemed to be gathered into those ruins that had once been a home. In the case of Filip Müller the devastation of the home is signified not by the ruins of a house but by the ruins of memory itself. "The memory of my parents," he writes, "my family and my early youth in my home town had faded."[79] If the Shoah was essentially a war against memory, it was a war against the memory of home and all that the home symbolizes. Without the home the human being has neither a name nor an address; without the home the human being has no being. Because without the home the human being has no mother.

This linkage between home and mother is quite explicit in Kitty Hart's *Return To Auschwitz.* After she and her mother were completely shaved upon their arrival at the camp, she relates, "When I turned to look for my mother I couldn't make her out at first.... Had we come here straight from home? Home: the word had ceased to mean anything."[80] In Thomas Geve's memoir we find a similar collapse; upon seeing his mother for the first time in Auschwitz-Birkenau, he asserts, "I hardly recognized Mother. Still in her early thirties, she looked as harsh as her companions."[81] In both instances the loss of recognition of the mother is directly tied to the loss of the meaning of the word *home;* it is in her face, overflowing with maternal love, that the meaning of *home* is inscribed. When the Nazis deface the mother's face they erase the very notion of home. And yet the memory of the loss as a loss entails an affirmation of the dearness of what was lost. Sustaining that memory is essential to sustaining a name. For it is essential to sustaining a family, and there can be no home without a family, no family without a name.

Assuming the form of the memory of a name, the longing for the home expresses itself as a longing for the family. When Moshe Sandberg and his comrades, for example, were transported from a Hungarian labor crew to Dachau, the first thing they asked the inmates of Dachau was whether they might join members of their families who had been sent there. They met only with cynical laughter, however, since those in Dachau knew, says Sandberg, "that we would also go the way of our families with whom sooner or later we would be reunited, yes, reunited in another world, in the world of the dead."[82] In the antiworld the family is relegated to a realm that is eternally *after, later, not yet*. Thus the memory of the family—and, by implication, the memory of the mother—becomes a memory of the future; in the act of remembrance what *was not then* becomes what is *yet to be*. Why? Because once memory affirms the dearness of what was lost, the thing lost becomes the thing *sought*.[83] A memory that came to Zivia Lubetkin during the darkest hours of the Warsaw Ghetto Uprising comes to mind: "My imagination drew my thoughts away to our ancestral Homeland, to my many friends there."[84] The ancestral homeland is the home where she has yet to arrive, *ancestral* not because she has already come from there but because it is the origin that summons her toward a future, even when there appears to be no future.

Once memory is future-oriented—once it is for the sake of a future—it becomes a voice that addresses me. Which is to say: Memory assumes a *face*. And when the memory is the memory of the murdered mother, it is the face of the mother that speaks, the face of the origin, of love, and of home. The mother, who abides at the origin of life, is herself the origin of memory: In a very important sense, the mother writes the memory of the orphan's loss. In that writing, then, a trace of the mother, who is antecedent to the utterance, is present in the utterance. From the depths of the orphan's page the voice of the mother summons all who come before this page to a recovery of the origin, the love, and the home that were lost. For the desecrated origin belongs to each of us.

Therefore the little girl who cries out in Livia Bitton-Jackson's memoir cries out to me. I am the one called to listen, the one whom she addresses when she screams, "Mommyyy! Where are you? Mommy! They are killing my mother! Everybody, listen! Can't you hear? Oh, Mommy! Oh, G-d, they are killing my mother!"[85] Can the soul endure *this* memory? Can it endure the words and the memory of Isabella Leitner, when she says, "The air was filled with the stench of death. Unnatural death. The smoke was thick. The sun couldn't crack through. The scent was the smell of burning flesh. The burning flesh was your mother"?[86] Note the shift from the third person to the second person: "your mother." Leitner addresses *me*. *My* mother!? Suddenly I am the one who must do the work of recognition and remembrance. Suddenly I am the one who is orphaned. Because the mother is definitively linked to the origin that gives birth to a teaching and a tradition, the memory of her loss is a memory that becomes part of a tradition and therefore part of a common memory. Thus I too am the one who, in an act of response and remembrance, must affirm the dearness of what was lost. I too am the one who must attest to the teaching and the tradition. I too must wrestle a name from the Angel.

The Murder of the Moral in the Assault on Motherhood

Most fundamental to the Torah that comes to us from the origin of all things is the Divine prohibition against murder. It is the first principle of all moral relation. In the previous two chapters we saw that the Nazis set out to eliminate both the prohibition and its Divine source. Here we collide with perhaps the most heinous form of that assault: The calculated murder not only of mothers but also of motherhood through the undoing of the moral.

In November 1941, for example, Emmanuel Ringelblum notes in his diary that "Jews have been prohibited from marrying and having children. Women pregnant up to three months have to have an abortion."[87] In the concentration camp at Ravensbrück, Germaine Tillion recalls, "the medical services of the Revier were required to perform abortions on all pregnant women. If a child happened to be born alive, it would be smothered or drowned in a bucket in the presence of the mother."[88] (Yes, *in the presence of the mother!*) And in the murder camps pregnancy was neither a medical condition nor a blessing from G-d—it was a capital crime. The testimony of these two witnesses alone reveals a unique aspect of the Holocaust as the murder not only of human beings but of the very origin of human life and of human sanctity, which is the basis of the prohibition against murder.

But there is more. On 5 February 1942, Vilna Ghetto diarist Herman Kruk wrote, "Today the Gestapo summoned two members of the Judenrat and notified them: No more Jewish children are to be born. The order came from Berlin."[89] Six months later, in his diary from the Kovno Ghetto, Avraham Tory noted, "From September on, giving birth is strictly forbidden. Pregnant women will be put to death."[90] Recalling the significance of the mother within the tradition, we realize that when a pregnant woman is put to death, more than a mother and her babe is murdered, both physically and metaphysically. This point becomes even clearer when on 4 February 1943, Tory laments, "It was terrible to watch the women getting on the truck; they held in their arms babies of different ages and wrapped in more and more sweaters so that they would not catch cold on the way [to their death]!"[91] Exceeding the horror of slaughtering pregnant women, it seems that the Nazis waited until many of these mothers held their babies in their arms before murdering them and their infants with them.

What are these mothers to say that would declare their love to their little ones, as they wrap them in another sweater to keep them from catching cold on their way to the cold and the darkness of a mass grave? There is no reply to such a question; every attempt to reply is transformed into a crescendo of horror. And the horror that overwhelms Tory oozes from the words of Yitzhak Katznelson when he cries out, "These mothers with babes in their wombs! This murderous German nation! That was their chief joy! To destroy women with child!"[92] It was their chief joy because it was an expression of their primary aim; it was the joy of those who bask in the satisfaction of a job well done.

Since a mother is a mother by virtue of a certain relation to her child, the assault on the mothers of Israel included an assault on that very relationship, an assault not just on the body but on the being of the mother, an ontological assault. We have seen a variation of this onslaught in Tory's account of the women who wrapped their little ones in sweaters as they were being taken to a mass grave. In his diary Josef Katz records a similar incident, one related to him by a woman from the ghetto in Liepaja. "When the SS surrounded the ghetto," she told him, "I thought our last hour had struck. I took my little children and dressed them in their woolen socks and their best little dresses. I thought my children should be nice and warm when they go to their deaths."[93] Nice and warm: One might take this to be an example of the invincibility of a mother's care for her children, but it cannot be understood in such a manner, since a mother's care is a care for life. In the world of humanity a mother dresses her children "nice and warm" for a cold winter's day, not for their last day. Here, then, not just the mother but the loving relation that makes her a mother is twisted out of the world and turned over to the antiworld.

Perhaps better than anyone else, Emil Fackenheim understood the implications of this murder of mothers and motherhood. "The very concept of holiness," he argues, "must be altered in response to the conjunction, unprecedented in the annals of history, of 'birth' and 'crime.'"[94] And with the unprecedented conjunction of these categories there arises within the murder camps a singular, unprecedented moral dilemma, a dilemma that is itself part of the assault on motherhood. Isabella Leitner offers us a devastating description of that impossible dilemma, of the choice that is no choice. It is a description of what transpired upon the birth of a child in Auschwitz:

> Most of us are born to live—to die, but to live first. You, dear darling, you are being born only to die. How good of you to come before roll call though, so your mother does not have to stand at attention while you are being born. Dropping out of the womb onto the ground with your mother's thighs shielding you like wings of angels is an infinitely nicer way to die than being fed into the gas chamber. But we are not having *Zeil Appell,* so we can stand around and listen to your mother's muffled cries. And now that you are born, your mother begs to see you, to hold you. But we know that if we give you to her, there will be a struggle to take you away again, so we cannot let her see you because you don't belong to her. You belong to the gas chamber. Your mother has no rights. She only brought forth fodder for the gas chamber. She is not a mother. She is just a dirty Jew who has soiled the Aryan landscape with another dirty Jew. How dare she think of you in human terms? And so, dear baby, you are on

your way to heaven to meet a recent arrival who is blowing
a loving kiss to you through the smoke, a dear friend, your
maker—your father.[95]

Of course, the little one born here is born not just to die but to be murdered: The angel whose wings surround the infant is the Angel of Death.
And yet the Angel of Death might here be mistaken for a maternal angel
of mercy: For the task of making the babe into fodder for the gas chamber
falls to compassionate women who with loving hands take the infant from
the mother and see to its death—women who might themselves be mothers.

It is they who recall, "For a moment, for just a moment, we had a
real smell of a real life, and we touched the dear little one before she was
wrapped in a piece of paper and quickly handed to the *Blockelteste* so the SS
wouldn't discover who the mother was, because then she, too, would have
had to accompany the baby to the ovens. That touch was so delicious. Are
we ever to know what life-giving feels like? Not here. Perhaps out there,
where they have diapers, and formulas, and baby carriages—and life."[96]
The babe was hidden from the SS, but who could hide the mother from
herself? And where were the others to hide, those women who gave the
child over to death?

There are no diapers in the antiworld—that is what makes it an antiworld. A world in which there are diapers and formulas and baby carriages—even a world in which a mother may die in order to save her child—is
a world that retains its ontological order, one upon which G-d may still
pronounce, "It is very good." The reversal of this order is the mark of the
antiworld ruled by the SS antigod, ruled by Mengele, who once explained,
"When a Jewish child is born…I can't set the child free because there are no
longer any Jews who live in freedom. I can't let the child stay in the camp
because there are no facilities in the camp that would enable the child to
develop normally. It would not be humanitarian to send a child to the ovens without permitting the mother to be there to witness the child's death.
That's why I send the mother and the child to the gas ovens together."[97]
If the humanitarian belongs to the moral, then Mengele may understand
himself to be acting morally in killing mothers with their infants. What,
then, is the moral response to that morality? And what becomes of the

moral demand to save the life of a mother?

When a woman named Esther announced to Sara Nomberg-Przytyk that she was going to have a baby, Sara's reaction was: "I turned to stone."[98] Not "Oh, how wonderful!" or even "How could you be so foolish?" but the silence of turning to stone. That is the response elicited by these glad tidings in the midst of the antiworld. For Sara was well aware of Mengele's humanitarianism. And she was well aware of the humanitarian measures that must be taken into order to counter the humanitarianism of Mengele. "Our procedure," an inmate explained, "is to kill the baby after birth in such a way that the mother doesn't know about it.... We give the baby an injection. After that, the baby dies. The mother is told that the baby was born dead. After dark, the baby is thrown on a pile of corpses, and in that manner we save the mother. I want so much for the babies to be born dead, but out of spite they are born healthy."[99] When Esther gave birth to her baby, "the attendants tried to convince her not to feed the baby so that it would die of hunger. Esther would not hear of it. She gave the baby her breast and talked with wonder about how beautifully it suckled. The supervisor of the infirmary had a duty to report all births, but somehow she delayed. She had pity on Esther."[100] The result of this pity was that three days later both Esther and her baby were gassed. What sort of pity, then, is one to have?

Here the singular horror, the ethical and metaphysical horror, that belongs to the realm of the Holocaust, is that one is led to kill not to destroy but to save, to kill out of love, both for the mother and for the child. "No one will ever know," writes Gisella Perl, a woman who served as a doctor in Auschwitz, "what it meant to me to destroy these babies. After years and years of medical practice, childbirth was still to me the most beautiful, the greatest miracle of nature. I loved those newborn babies not as a doctor but as a mother and it was again and again my own child whom I killed to save the life of a woman."[101] My own child: To destroy one's own child is to destroy a defining dimension of one's own being. For the child signifies meaning in the life of the mother as well as in the life of the one who loves the child like a mother. She who strangles the child wrings her own heart and soul. Here too we glimpse an aspect of the singularity of the Event as a desecration of the origin.

We also see why at times it may have been very difficult for Dr. Perl to destroy a child even to save the mother. She relates an incident, for example, that occurred when she was unable to bring herself to kill a baby born to a woman named Yolanda. After two days, however, she says, "I could hide him no longer. I knew that if he were discovered, it would mean death to Yolanda, to myself and to all these pregnant women whom my skill could still save. I took the warm little body in my hands, kissed the smooth face, caressed the long hair—then strangled him and buried his body under a mountain of corpses waiting to be cremated."[102] The incongruity of the caress of love coupled with the touch of death is staggering. The loving embrace of the child consecrates the moral relation that imparts humanity to the human being. But in a realm where the moral relation is expressed by killing the child, both the relation and the meaning it consecrates are turned on end. A time came when, according to Dr. Perl, Mengele would exploit this overturning even further, declaring that, while babies still had to be destroyed, the women who delivered them would be spared. But no sooner were 192 expectant mothers identified than Mengele "changed his mind" and had all of them "loaded on a single truck and tossed—alive— into the flames of the crematory."[103] Thus Dr. Perl received a demonstration of why she must do what she must do.

We are taught in the Mishnah that the world is sustained by three things: Torah, worship, and acts of loving-kindness (*Avot* 1:2). And an act of loving-kindness is a *mitzvah* commanded from on high. What is the greatest *mitzvah*, the most profound utterance to G-d in the form of a deed, the *mitzvah* that overrides all other *mitzvot?* It is the saving of a life, which is the saving of a world. Thus the Mishnah teaches that saving a single life is like saving the entire world (*Sanhedrin* 4:5). In the same verse, however, it says that to destroy a single life is like destroying the entire world. Where, then, is the *mitzvah* in killing an infant to save the mother? What does *this* prayer in the form of a deed say to G-d? And what becomes of Dr. Perl's maternal love in *this* act of loving-kindness?

Her comrade Olga Lengyel has a response, if not an answer, to these questions, for she sees a terrible implication of the situation into which these women are thrown in their effort to save a mother. "The Germans succeeded," she laments, "in making murderers of even us. To this day the picture of those murdered babies haunts me. Our own children had perished in the gas chambers and were cremated in the Birkenau ovens, and we dispatched the lives of others before their first voices had left their tiny lungs."[104] But have the Nazis, who would displace the Creator by removing the mother from creation, indeed succeeded in recreating these women in their own image? Are these women who kill the children they love like a mother indeed made into murderers? Do they have the moral status of a murderer?

To these questions we must answer No. For even in the antiworld— even in the midst of the Nazi desecration of the origin—the Jewish mothers retain their sanctity. The Jewish mothers remain mothers *despite* the assault on motherhood, despite killing babies. Let us see why.

Mothers *Despite* Killing Babies

Mothers *despite* killing babies? Anyone with even a shred of moral sensibility reels at this combination of words. To entertain for even a moment the idea that there might be a moral justification for killing babies is a moral outrage. And yet...

As it often happens when dealing with the Holocaust, there looms an insistent *and yet*. In order to demonstrate the justification for killing these infants, we must first distinguish the context for this killing of babies in the camps from other contexts. It happened, for example, that babies were killed by people who were in hiding, so that the cries of the little ones would not give them away. Aryeh Klonicki-Klonymus faced such a dilemma. "I had some heated encounters," he relates, "with fellow Jews who were in hiding. They demanded that I allow the strangulation of my child. Among them were mothers whose children had already met this fate. Of course I replied to them that as long as I was alive such a thing would not come to pass."[105] It did not come to pass. Although Klonicki-Klonymus and his family were indeed murdered by the Nazis, it was not the result of their having been given away by the cries of the babe—cries that in the world announce the dearness of life and not the threat of death.

The act of killing babies in hiding was not committed in response to a prohibition against birth—the Nazi prohibition that is diametrically opposite the Divine prohibition against murder. The women who killed babies born in the camps, however, did so in order to protect the mother against the Nazi prohibition, both despite and because of the Divine prohibition. Not only were they interested in saving the life of another, but they acted at the risk of their own lives; what these women feared was not their own death but the death of the other, of the one bearing the child, in the face of a capital prohibition against birth. As the basis of one person's responsibility for another, this fear of the death of another is the basis of the moral relation to another.[106] And, as we have seen, without the mother there is no moral relation, since without the mother there is no Torah. In the antiworld, killing babies became the only remaining moral response to the moral outrage of the Nazi prohibition against birth.

The dilemma of course arises when we note that the mother is not the only other person in this situation: In addition to the mother who is saved there is the child who is killed. Here it might be argued that these women in fact became accomplices to the Nazis, who themselves were bent on the slaughter of Jewish infants. Indeed, it may be argued, these women could have said, "Take these babies with their mothers, if that is your wish. But it is not our wish, and our hands will not be soiled by having any share in your design. We refuse to play any part in your efforts to murder our people in the murder of our mothers and their infants. They will go to G-d as mother and child. And, if there is a G-d, you will go to hell!" They cannot be viewed as accomplices, however, because they did not intend the annihilation that their captors intended: They chose to kill infant children to save mothers, whereas the Nazis were bent on the elimination of mother and child *as such*. One might also object that these mothers, like all Jews, were already marked for the gas chambers, so that the attempt to save them was futile. But the fact that some survived demonstrates another fact: The death for which they were marked as Jews was not the necessary death that awaited them if they had been found to have borne a Jewish child into the world. As we have seen, in the case of the Jewish mothers, the crime of giving birth was added to the crime of being Jews.

Other objections to this killing can be raised. It may be said, for example, that killing a woman's newborn robs her of her status as mother and thus plays into the Nazis' assault on the mother. To this objection we answer that those who were saved have the potential to becomes mothers once again, if they should survive the camp. Although it is true that a woman derives her *meaning* as mother from the child, the child derives his or her *being* from the mother: She is the origin, and her preservation is a preservation of the origin. Saving the mother, therefore, does not amount to destroying motherhood as the Nazis would have destroyed it; on the contrary, it affirms the dearness of the one who gives birth and thereby affirms motherhood. As horrible as it may sound—and it is horrible—the women who made the decision to offer up the lives of these little ones were justified in their decision. Those lives were given up for the sake of many lives, for the lives not only of their mothers but also for their future brothers and sisters. Therefore the women who were determined to save the mother were determined to save the future, which is the realm not only of hope but of meaning. By preserving the mother—even at the terrible price of killing the little one—women like Gisella Perl and Olga Lengyel preserved a basis for pursuing a path into the future, for engaging a mission, without which there is no meaning, no humanity. Thus preserving a future, they resisted the Nazi murder machine even as they resorted to killing the most innocent of the innocent.

If we should turn to Jewish law to seek further justification for this position, it might seem that we have found it in the Mishnah, where it is written, "If a woman is in hard travail, one cuts up the child in her womb and brings it forth member by member, because her life comes before that of [the child]" (*Oholot* 7:6). Yet this flight to *halakhah* not only fails to provide justification; it makes justification even more problematic. For if we read further in the same Mishnah, we discover that Jewish law serves more to complicate than to clarify the dilemma: "But if the greater part [of the infant] has proceeded forth, one may not touch it, for one may not set aside one person's life for that of another." *Halakhah,* however, is Jewish law for life lived in a Jewish community, and not for life turned over to the machinery of death aimed at the obliteration of that community. Therefore we must ask: Does the mother's life come before the child's life, or does she lose that precedence once the child is born? But we must also ask: What if the thing threatening the life of each is not a medical condition but a Nazi murderer? That is, what if it is a question not of which we allow to die but of which we allow to be *murdered?* To this question even the *halakhah* has no answer.

Yes, the women in the camps took the lives of infants, but they did not do so in an act of murder. Rather, they did so in order to prevent two acts of murder. Murder is not only the intended taking of the life of another; it is the appropriation of another's life as one's own, a taking possession of another's life to serve one's own "interests," in such a way that we lay the life of the other upon an altar erected to ourselves. That is what made Cain's slaying of Abel an act of murder. But the women in the camps are not Cain. If G-d should put to anyone the questions He put to Cain—Where is your brother? and What have you done?—He puts them not to the women who killed those babies but to the Nazis who prohibited their birth. Unlike Cain, who took a life in an effort to undermine the origin of life, the women who killed babies in the camps sought to save the mother and thereby preserve the sanctity of the origin.

The origin of what? The origin of life, certainly. More than that, as we have shown, the mother is the origin of the *sanctity* of life and therefore of the very prohibition against murder. Hence, as Lévinas has rightly argued, without woman—without the mother—man knows "nothing which transforms his natural life into ethics, nothing which permits living a life, not even the death that one dies for another."[107] And, we might add, without the mother man knows nothing of the prohibition against taking the life of another. Even as they killed these infants, the women in the camps preserved the prohibition against murder in their preservation of the mother. Why? Because, situated at the origin, the mother represents a transcendent ground beyond being, from which all that appears in being derives its meaning and its value. Thus the moral dilemma that confronted the women in the death camps entailed the salvation of the ground of morality itself. Without the preservation of the mother, this discussion would itself be rendered pointless.

Which brings us to one last insight: As a desecration of the origin, the Nazi assault on G-d and humanity was neither immoral nor amoral—it was antimoral. Had these women been caught killing an infant, it would have meant their death—not for killing the infant but for failing to see to it that the mother was murdered along with the infant. The women who killed babies in order to save other women did so not in order to sustain the Kingdom of Night but to sustain the prospect for a return to another kingdom, to a world where moral dilemmas are intelligible. Refusing to allow a mother to join her child in death was their only means of choosing life. If, as we are taught in the Torah, choosing life means choosing good (see Deuteronomy 30:15), then the choice they made was the only moral choice they could have made—if it still makes sense to speak of a moral choice in such a realm. Hence the singularity of the moral dilemma facing the women who decided to take the lives of the little ones is inextricably connected to the uniqueness of the Holocaust itself.

Finally, perhaps the only legitimate response to the desecration of the origin is to refrain from indulging in moral arguments such as this one and silently attend to these words from Isabella Leitner. "Mother, I will keep you alive," she says, after seeing her mother led away to death.[108] How does she keep her mother alive—and with her mother, motherhood—so that she may find her way back into a world of moral dilemmas? She tells us: "Mama, Mama, I'm pregnant! Isn't that a miracle, Mama? Isn't it incredible, Mama? I stood in front of the crematorium, and now there is another heart beating within that very body that was condemned to ashes. Two lives in one, Mama—I'm pregnant!...[My baby] has started the birth of the new six million."[109] There can be no doubt that when she felt that life stir within her, she remembered those mothers who were robbed of their motherhood. Yes, perhaps that is the way to answer the desecration of the origin: to become mothers and fathers in a sanctification of the motherhood that was a capital crime in the Nazi murder camps. More convincingly than any argument, that is what Isabella Leitner and women like her may teach us each time they give birth to a Jewish child: bear Jewish life into the world and transmit to those souls a memory and a name.

But, as we shall see in the chapters that follow, the matter is not as simple as that.

Notes

1. Those who are familiar with the esoteric teachings in Judaism will recall that fire is associated with the letter *shin,* which is one of the three letters known as the "mothers." Fire is also associated with the *sefirah* of Binah, or "Understanding," which is known as the Supernal Mother (see, for example, chapter 1 of the *Sefer Yetzirah*).

2. Emmanuel Lévinas, *Ethics and Infinity,* trans. Richard A. Cohen (Pittsburgh: Duquesne University Press, 1985), 66.

3. The relationship with the feminine, Lévinas explains, is a relationship "with the future, with what (in a world where there is everything) is never there, with what cannot be there when everything else is there—not with a being that is not there, but with the very dimension of alterity." See Emmanuel Lévinas, *Time and the Other,* trans. Richard A. Cohen (Pittsburgh: Duquesne University Press, 1987), 88.

4. Primo Levi, *Survival in Auschwitz,* trans. Stuart Woolf (New York: Simon & Schuster, 1996), 42.

5. Emmanuel Lévinas, *Totality and Infinity,* trans. Alphonso Lingis (Pittsburgh: Duquesne University Press, 1969), 257–58.

6. Emmanuel Lévinas, *Difficult Freedom: Essays on Judaism,* trans. Sean Hand (Baltimore: Johns Hopkins University Press, 1990), 33.

7. Here we have the secret of the *Megilat Esther,* the Book of Esther, which is literally the "Revelation of the Hidden," revealed as that which is hidden. Just as Esther saved the Jewish people, it is thanks to woman, who is the embodiment of the holiness hidden from the eye, that the Jewish people endure.

8. Jiří Langer, *Nine Gates to the Chassidic Mysteries,* trans. Stephen Jolly (New York: Behrman House, 1976), 136.

9. While this may be, admittedly, a "man's point of view," it is not reducible to a "man's point of view." Jewishly speaking, it is a point of view that comes from *HaShem.* And what married man reading these lines would not admit that he is in fact a better man thanks to his wife and the mother of his children?

10. As it is written: "At Mount Sinai G-d went forth to meet them; like a bridegroom who goes forth to meet the bride, so the Holy One, blessed be He, went forth to meet them to give them the Torah" (*Pirke de Rabbi Eliezer* 41).

11. Moshe Cordovero, *The Palm Tree of Devorah,* trans. Moshe Miller (Southfield, MI: Targum, 1993), 128.

12. Joseph Gikatilla, *Sha'are Orah: Gates of Light*, trans. Avi Weinstein (San Francisco: HarperCollins, 1994), 204.

13. Yehuda Loeve, *Nesivos Olam: Nesiv Hatorah*, trans. Eliakim Willner (Brooklyn: Mesorah, 1994), 322. For this reason it is written in the Talmud that whenever he heard the sound of his mother's footsteps, Rabbi Joseph would say, "I shall rise before the *Shekhinah* that is approaching" (*Kiddushin* 31b).

14. Emil Fackenheim recalls an image from his childhood. It is a painting of "Jews fleeing from a pogrom....The fleeing Jews in the picture are bearded old men, terrified, but not so much as to leave behind what is most precious to them. In the view of antisemites these Jews would doubtless be clutching bags of gold. In fact each of them carries a Torah scroll." See Emil L. Fackenheim, *What Is Judaism?* (New York: Macmillan, 1987), 60.

15. That is why in the sixteenth century Rabbi Yehuda Loeve, the Maharal of Prague, declared, "Woman is the consummation of man's existence, for through her, man becomes complete. When a man has his own woman [a bride], his existence is essential, not casual. When he has an illicit relationship with a woman, however—when the lust strikes him—his very existence is casual. Thus 'He who has illicit relations with a woman lacks a heart' [Proverbs 6:32]. The Torah, too, completes man; it is often compared to a woman [see, for example, *Kiddushin* 30b] because, like woman, it makes man complete." See Loeve, *Nesivos Olam*, 106.

16. Yitzchak Ginsburgh, *The Alef-Beit* (Northvale, NJ: Jason Aronson, 1991), 46.

17. Emmanuel Lévinas, "Ethics as First Philosophy," trans. Sean Hand and Michael Temple, in *The Levinas Reader*, ed. Sean Hand (Oxford: Basil Blackwell, 1989), 85.

18. Lévinas sheds light on these connections when he says, "*Rachamim* (Mercy)...goes back to the word *Rechem*, which means uterus. *Rachamim* is the revelation of the uterus to the other, whose gestation takes place within it. *Rachamim* is maternity itself. G-d as merciful is G-d defined by maternity." See Emmanuel Lévinas, *Nine Talmudic Readings*, trans. Annette Aronowicz (Bloomington: Indiana University Press, 1990), 183.

19. See Rashi's commentary on Genesis 1:27.

20. André Neher, *The Prophetic Existence*, trans. William Wolf (New York: A. S. Barnes, 1969), 131.

21. Martin Buber, *The Eclipse of G-d: Studies in the Relation of Religion To Philosophy*, trans. Maurice Friedman et al. (New York: Harper, 1957), 73.

22. Ka-tzetnik 135633, *Shivitti: A Vision*, trans. Eliyah De-Nur and Lisa Herman (New York: Harper & Row, 1989), 4.

23. Ka-tzetnik 135633, *Sunrise over Hell,* trans. Nina De-Nur (London: W. H. Allen, 1977), 78.

24. Ibid., 158.

25. See, for example, Joseph Gikatilla, *Sha'are Orah: Gates of Light,* trans. Avi Weinstein (San Francisco: Harper, 1994), 337.

26. Ka-tzetnik 135633, *Star of Ashes,* trans. Nina De-Nur (Tel Aviv: Hamenora, 1971), 53.

27. Ka-tzetnik 135633, *Atrocity,* trans. Nina De-Nur (New York: Kensington, 1977), 92.

28. Ibid., 136.

29. Ka-tzetnik 135633, *Shivitti,* 108.

30. Ka-tzetnik 135633, *House of Dolls,* trans. Moshe M. Kohn (New York: Pyramid, 1958), 125.

31. Martin Buber, *The Prophetic Faith,* trans. Carlyle Witton-Davies (New York: Harper and Brothers, 1960), 64.

32. Ka-tzetnik 135633, *Shivitti,* 100.

33. Ka-tzetnik 135633, *Phoenix over the Galilee,* trans. Nina De-Nur (New York: Harper & Row, 1969), 28.

34. Ka-tzetnik 135633, *Shivitti,* 71.

35. Emmanuel Lévinas, *Otherwise than Being or Beyond Essence,* trans. Alphonso Lingis (The Hague: Nijhoff, 1981), 74.

36. Ibid., 114.

37. Ka-tzetnik 135633, *Shivitti,* 100–101. In a later work Ka-tzetnik wrote, "On her way to the crematorium my mother saw my face. I know it because I, too, on my way to the crematorium, saw my mother's face." See Ka-tzetnik 135633, *Kaddish,* trans. Nina De-Nur (New York: Algemeiner Associates, 1998), 122.

38. Sara Zyskind, *Stolen Years,* trans. Margarit Inbar (Minneapolis: Lerner, 1981), 11.

39. Ibid., 44.

40. Paul Trepman, *Among Men and Beasts,* trans. Shoshana Perla and Gertrude Hirschler (New York: Bergen Belsen Memorial Press, 1978), 130.

41. Ana Vinocur, *A Book without a Title,* trans. Valentine Isaac and Ricardo Iglesia (New York: Vantage, 1976), 107–07.

42. Isabella Leitner, *Fragments of Isabella,* ed. Irving Leitner (New York: Thomas Crowell, 1978), 19–20.

43. Ka-tzetnik 135633, *Star of Ashes,* 52.

44. Nathan Shapell, *Witness To the Truth* (New York: David McKay, 1974), 93.

45. Agnes Sassoon, *Agnes: How My Spirit Survived* (Edgeware, England: Lawrence Cohen, 1983), 34.

46. Donna Rubinstein, *I Am the Only Survivor of Krasnostav* (New York: Shengold, 1982), 39.

47. Judith Dribben, *And Some Shall Live* (Jerusalem: Keter Books, 1969), 85.

48. Vinocur, *Book without a Title,* 45.

49. Eugene Heimler, *Night of the Mist,* trans. André Ungar (New York: Vanguard, 1959), 102.

50. One recalls in this connection the Chasidic tradition that maintains that when we pray, the *Shekhinah* speaks through our lips. See, for example, the teachings of the Baal Shem Tov and the Koretzer Rebbe in Louis I. Newman, *Hasidic Anthology* (New York: Schocken Books, 1963), 335–36.

51. Zyskind, *Stolen Years,* 61.

52. Rubinstein, *I am the Only Survivor,* 90.

53. Sara Nomberg-Przytyk, *Auschwitz: True Tales from a Grotesque Land,* trans. Roslyn Hirsch (Chapel Hill: University of North Carolina Press, 1985), 6–7.

54. See Aryeh Kaplan's commentary in *The Bahir,* trans. with commentary by Aryeh Kaplan (York Beach, ME: Samuel Weiser, 1979), 127–28.

55. Ginsburgh, *Alef-Beit,* 88.

56. Schneur Zalman, *Likutei Amarim Tanya,* trans. Nissan Mindel (New York: Kehot, 1981), 593.

57. Leon Wells, *The Death Brigade* (New York: Holocaust Library, 1978), 74–75.

58. Ibid., 86.

59. Lévinas, *Ethics and Infinity,* 48.

60. Olga Lengyel, *Five Chimneys* (London: Granada, 1972), 94.

61. Vinocur, *Book without a Title,* 88.

62. Kitty Hart, *Return To Auschwitz* (New York: Atheneum, 1984), 104.

63. Ibid., 106.

64. Nomberg-Przytyk, *Auschwitz,* 35.

65. Leitner, *Fragments of Isabella,* 6.

66. Lévinas, *Ethics and Infinity,* 87–88.

67. Leitner, *Fragments of Isabella,* 16.

68. Heimler, *Night of the Mist,* 31.

69. Saul Friedländer, *When Memory Comes,* trans. Helen R. Lane (New York: Avon, 1980), 101–2.

70. Thomas Geve, *Youth in Chains* (Jerusalem: Rubin Mass, 1981), 82–83.

71. Ginsburgh, 45.

72. Martin Buber, *Between Man and Man,* trans. Ronald Gregor Smith (New York: Macmillan, 1965), 78.

73. Harry Rabinowicz, *Hasidism: The Movement and Its Masters* (Northvale, NJ: Jason Aronson, 1988), 1.

74. Gerda Weissmann Klein, *All But My Life* (New York: Hill and Wang, 1957), 31.

75. Lily Gluck Lerner, *The Silence* (Secaucus, NJ: Lyle Stuart, 1980), 55.

76. Jean Améry, *At the Mind's Limits,* trans. Sidney Rosenfeld and Stella P. Rosenfeld (Bloomington: Indiana University Press, 1980), 48.

77. Friedländer, *When Memory Comes,* 45.

78. Ibid., 78.

79. Filip Müller, *Auschwitz Inferno: The Testimony of a Sonderkommando,* trans. Susanne Flatauer (London: Routledge & Kegan Paul, 1979), 17.

80. Hart, *Return To Auschwitz,* 62.

81. Geve, *Youth in Chains,* 83.

82. Moshe Sandberg, *My Longest Year,* trans. S. C. Hyman (Jerusalem: Yad Vashem, 1968), 59.

83. Recall here Lévinas's remark cited in note 3 above.

84. Zivia Lubetkin, *In the Days of Destruction and Revolt,* trans. I. Tubbin (Tel Aviv: Hakibbutz Hameuchad, 1981), 151.

85. Livia E. Bitton-Jackson, *Elli: Coming of Age in the Holocaust* (New York: Times Books, 1980), 70.

86. Leitner, *Fragments of Isabella,* 94.

87. Emmanuel Ringelblum, *Notes from the Warsaw Ghetto,* trans. and ed. Jacob Sloan (New York: Schocken Books, 1974), 230.

88. Germaine Tillion, *Ravensbrück,* trans. Gerald Satterwhite (New York: Doubleday, 1975), 77.

89. Herman Kruk, "Diary of the Vilna Ghetto," trans. Shlomo Noble, *YIVO*

Annual of Jewish Social Science 13 (1965): 20.

90. Avraham Tory, *Surviving the Holocaust: The Kovno Ghetto Diary*, trans. Jerzy Michalowicz (Cambridge, MA: Harvard University Press, 1990), 114.

91. Ibid., 195.

92. Yitzhak Katznelson, *Vittel Diary*, trans. Myer Cohen (Tel Aviv: Hakibbutz Hameuchad, 1972), 109.

93. Josef Katz, *One Who Came Back: The Diary of a Jewish Survivor*, trans. Hilda Reach (New York: Bergen Belsen Memorial Press, 1973), 103.

94. Emil L. Fackenheim, *The Jewish Bible after the Holocaust* (Bloomington: Indiana University Press, 1990), 87.

95. Leitner, *Fragments of Isabella*, 31–32.

96. Ibid., 49.

97. Quoted in Nomberg-Przytyk, *Auschwitz*, 69.

98. Ibid., 68.

99. Ibid., 69.

100. Ibid., 71.

101. Gisella Perl, *I Was a Doctor in Auschwitz* (New York: International Universities Press, 1948), 82.

102. Ibid., 84.

103. Ibid.

104. Lengyel, *Five Chimneys*, 111.

105. Aryeh Klonicki-Klonymus, *The Diary of Adam's Father*, trans. Avner Tomaschiff (Tel Aviv: Hakibbutz Hameuchad, 1973), 31.

106. Cf. Lévinas, *Ethics and Infinity*, 119.

107. Lévinas, *Difficult Freedom*, 34.

108. Leitner, *Fragments of Isabella*, 95.

109. Ibid., 96.

CHAPTER FOUR

THE DEATH OF THE ANGEL OF DEATH

I have returned to tell you the story of my own death.
—Moshe the Beadle in Elie Wiesel, *Night*

ᚥ

FOR ONE CREATED IN THE IMAGE AND LIKENESS OF THE Holy One, death is not a natural phenomenon that transpires after three score and ten years; rather, it is a moment in the life of the soul, a testimony and a task to which each of us is summoned, from our very origin. But what can be said of death in the antiworld, where the origin has been erased? There too it is not a natural phenomenon; there are no natural phenomena in the antiworld. But what is it? And if death is in some sense a return to the origin, where does the soul return to if the origin has been obliterated? Can there be a return of the soul? Can there, in fact, be any death? And if in the concentrationary universe there is neither origin nor death for the Jew, then how does the Jew affirm his name in response to the Angel of Death? What, indeed, becomes of the Angel of Death? And with whom shall the Jew wrestle into order to attain a blessing and a name in the wake of the assault on the Name?

Ka-tzetnik describes Auschwitz as "a death undreamed by Death itself."[1] For Death could never dream the death of the Angel of Death. In this chapter we shall consider how it is that, with the assault on the very meaning of G-d and humanity, with the desecration of the origin of the soul, there comes a singular assault on the Angel of Death. As we saw in the introduction, the Nazis did not want the Jew alive. They did not want

137

the Jew dead. No, they wanted to eliminate every predicate from the Jew, to reduce him or her to the namelessness of the *Muselmann*. Setting out to murder the name of the Jew, the Nazis created the *Muselmann* over against the Jew precisely by making the Jew into a *Muselmann*. That is what defines the Nazis, just as the Torah defines the Jews. That is why Primo Levi sees embodied in the *Muselmann* "all the evil of our time in one image."[2] Embodied in the *Muselmann* is the antihuman image, the image emptied of the divine image and the name annihilated in the assault on the Name. It is why Emil L. Fackenheim sees in the *Muselmann* the Nazis' "most characteristic, most original product."[3] If Auschwitz signifies the Holocaust, the *Muselmann* signifies Auschwitz.

Far more than the victim of starvation and brutality, the *Muselmann* is the Jew whose prayers were regarded as an act of sedition, whose holy days were defiled, whose very origin was desecrated. He is the Jew for whom marriage and childbirth were forbidden, for whom schooling was a crime, for whom there was no protection under the law. He is the Jew both widowed and orphaned, forced to witness the murder of his family, and rendered "ferociously alone"[4] before being rendered ferociously faceless. Hence Fackenheim describes the *Muselmann* as "a *novum*"[5] or "a new way of human being in history."[6] And yet Levi wonders whether it is a way of *human* being at all: "Non-men" he calls them.[7] They have no name, no origin—no death. Hesitating to call their death death, we realize that one of the defining features of this singular horror lies in the death of the Angel of Death.

The assault on the one who asks us our name, however, begins well outside the gates embossed with the promise *Arbeit Macht Frei*. It begins in the ghetto, where we discover that the concentrationary universe extends far beyond the camps. The ghetto was not a place to live or even a place to die; it was a nonplace of nonbeing. Windows facing outside the ghetto had to be covered, and Jews were forbidden to even look outside its borders. We shall begin, therefore, with the inside that was outside the annihilation camps; we shall begin with the diaries written in the ghettos, with the diaries that attest to the difference between death and ghetto death. Then we shall move to the inside from the outside, as we examine the memory of the death of the Angel of Death that transpired in the core of the concentrationary universe, where there was no burying the dead, no getting it over with.

When Life and Death Were Brethren

When scholars examine life in the ghettos that the Nazis created for the Jews, they often overlook what is most ubiquitous: death. True, they point out, with horror, the pervasiveness of death, but they seldom examine its essence or its significance for a deeper understanding of the Shoah. Perhaps it is left unexamined because it is so pervasive, like the air that we do not notice we are breathing. Many explore starvation, disease, and other forms of murder that were used against the Jews in the ghettos, but the phenomenon of death in the ghetto is seldom distinguished from the phenomenon of death outside the ghetto, in the world where human beings are human beings. Ghetto life has been thoroughly studied, but ghetto death and what it means to an understanding of the Nazis' assault on Jewish life have been all but ignored.

Assuming that the ghetto is indeed an abnormal realm in which death may have an abnormal status, we must first ask about the role of death in a "normal" realm of Jewish life. The eleventh-century sage Rabbi Bachya ibn Paquda explains how death is regarded within the Jewish tradition: "Life and Death are brethren, dwelling together closely to one another, inseparable, holding fast to the two ends of a tottering bridge over which all the world's creatures pass. Life is at its entrance; Death is at its exit. Life builds, Death breaks up. Life sows, Death reaps. Life unites, Death divides. Life strings together, Death scatters what has been strung together."[8] While the Torah enjoins us to choose life (Deuteronomy 30:19), making this choice does not mean that we no longer pass away from this earth; it does not entail the removal of death from the world. Rather, it means that in choosing life we understand death to be part of the process of sanctifying life through Torah study, religious observance, and deeds of loving-kindness.[9]

That is why, according to Jewish teaching, kindness can be shown even toward the dead. Like life, death is situated within the contexts of the sacred. It is the culmination, not the negation, of life. Murder is evil; in itself death is not. Standing by while people die is evil; in itself dying is not. Taking death to be part of life, Jews begin the Kaddish, the Prayer for the Dead, with a magnification and sanctification of the Name, in whom all life originates, and they end by declaring, "Amen." Placed on its proper ground, death in the Jewish tradition becomes an occasion for humanity's affirmation of the dearness of life.

In the Jewish tradition, moreover, "dearness of life" is dearness of the life of the *other* human being. Only in that relation, says the Sforno in his commentary on Genesis 2:18, can the purpose of our being created in the image and likeness of the Holy One be realized: To live in that image is to live in relation to another, for the sake of another. Ultimately, it is to make our dying part of our living, by dying for the sake of another. How, then, can we tell whether we are living and dying according to the task inscribed in our name? The Chasidic master Moshe Leib of Sassov answers, "Ask yourself whether it brings you closer to your fellow human being."[10] In the relation to our fellow human being we have life; therefore it is good. What is *lo-tov,* "not good," is being alone in the isolation of our illusory ego (Genesis 2:18): Alone, the human being has no identity, no name, and—what is the same thing—no love. Jewishly understood, even in death we are not alone. And so, upon the creation of the human being, G-d pronounces creation to be not merely "good" but "very good" (Genesis 1:31): Only for a human being is relation an issue in the life of the soul.

When we join our voice to the Voice of the Creator to declare creation to be "very good," we affirm the dearness of life. To choose life is to choose this "very good" that distinguishes the living from the nonliving. It inheres in the *neshamah* or the soul that the Name breathes into the human being by giving him a name; it is life itself, both in its physical and in it spiritual manifestations. Having thus received a life and a name, we are summoned to answer to and for the life of another. Therefore, choosing this "very good" means realizing the dearness of our neighbor's life—and fearing for his death. Because the life of the neighbor is *infinitely* dear, our fear for the death of the other person goes so far as to offer up our own life for the sake of another. Such is the basis of *Kiddush HaShem,* the "Sanctification of the Name" that is martyrdom: It is an assertion that life is "very good" in the very midst of a dying for another that transcends death. Unless we are able to thus connect death with the "very good," we remain entrenched in the proposition that there is no higher good than our own survival. Left with nothing but ourselves to live for, we have nothing to die for. And yet in the ghetto there was no dying in order that another may live; at best, there was a dying so that another might live a few more moments—or so that another would not have to die alone, as when Janusz Korczak accompanied the children from his orphanage to the *Umschlagplatz* for deportation to Treblinka. Already one can see that ghetto death is problematic.

There is another problem, however, that must be noted. It is the problem of dying as a human being in a realm where the one dying has been dehumanized. But what does "dying as a human being" mean within Jewish tradition? Quoting Dr. Leo Eitinger, Harry James Cargas explains: "There has been a Jewish religious tradition throughout the centuries, where 'dying as a man' means something quite different from what Western people usually understand by this expression. To die as a man, or as a Jew—for the religious Jew it is the same thing—means to die with the 'Shema' and with the Holy Name of G-d on their lips, without resistance, without 'falling into the abyss of the aggressor, namely to kill just as he did.'"[11] Ultimately, to live as a human being is to die as a human being. And to die as a human being is to affirm even in death that life is very good, speaking even in death the Name of the One who is the origin of the name in a declaration of "Shema Yisrael!" This utterance of "Hear, O Israel" is itself an offering of life to all who hear it. For it is our most fundamental means of answering to our name.

Therefore, even as the tide of death engulfed the world around him, Josef Katz was able to see that, at least in his mother's case, death was not all-encompassing; in his mother's case death itself was encompassed. For soon after he arrived at the camp in Jungfernhof he received a message that read, "My dear Josef, your mother died last night of a stroke in the arms of Chief Rabbi Carlbach. She recited the 'Shema Yisrael.'"[12] What transpires in the Nazis' imposition of death upon all of European Jewry is the opposite of this dying in another's loving arms, with the Shema on the lips; the Nazi seeks not just the end of Jewish life but the end of the Jewish affirmation of life that lies in dying as a human being. For "the Nazi murder machine," Fackenheim points out, "was systematically designed to stifle this *Shema Yisrael* on Jewish lips before it murdered Jews themselves."[13] Public prayer, as we have seen, was forbidden in the ghettos.

Hence there is a connection between the assault on the holy at the core of Jewish life and what might be referred to as "ghetto death." Indeed, *this* death belongs to the singularity of the Holocaust itself: Casting the Jews into a deluge of death calculated to destroy their humanity, the Nazis deprive the Jews of the death—of the "very good"—that forms the foundation of their life and their name as a human being. "We die anonymously," writes Ruth Andreas-Friedrich,[14] who states it: Stifling the Name on the lips of the dying, the Nazis render the Jews themselves not only lifeless but nameless, literally anonymous. They are not laid to rest in a grave, with their names inscribed on a memorial. Rather, they are forced to "live" in a grave that remains unmarked, lest they be murdered, forced to somehow survive in what Hillel Seidman calls the "underground world" of bunkers and hiding places.[15] While Helena Dorembus delighted in the sight of SS men being killed during the Warsaw Ghetto Uprising,[16] in death those German dead retained a certain connection to life, a connection that was denied to the Jews: They retained their names. But the Nazis saw to it that the Jewish dead had no such link to the living. Each Jew was murdered many times over, in body, in soul, in memory, in name, in substance—and in death.

Perhaps that is why Adam Czerniakow, head of the Warsaw Jewish Council, kept a model of a Jewish gravestone on his desk: to remind himself not only of the ubiquitous death that overwhelmed the Jews but also of the calculated obliteration of death that was a distinctive aspect of the Nazis' assault on humanity.[17] It was a memorial and a name for a people who had neither, a sign of their link to life in a realm devoid of all such signs. And as soon as he situates this sign among the signifiers that comprise his diary, the diary itself becomes such a sign. Let us consider, then, the ghetto death laid bare in the ghetto diaries by diarists who sought to recover an affirmation of life when the very *idea* of life was under assault—as was the idea of death. Let us see how, transformed into ghetto death, the death that engulfed Jewish life contributed to the death of the Angel of Death. For ghetto death is precisely the death that is not death, the death that is the murder of death.

Life and Death Torn Asunder

If death has meaning when the totality of death is transcended by dying for the sake of another, life is rendered void of meaning when death becomes the totality. Just such a totality confronts the Romanian teenager Mirjam Korber, when she declares, "Hundreds of people die, and usually it is the best ones who die."[18] The best ones are those who choose life. And yet in choosing life they are chosen for death. Why? Because, in the antiworld's overturning of meaning, the very traits of generosity and loving-kindness that engender life in the world—the traits that give a person a *good name*—are turned against those who possess such traits, until finally the ones who choose life end by succumbing to death. "There are times," writes Korber, "when I might manage to hope for the end of this war and to see once more the beautiful days that used to be. But death is better."[19] Which is to say: Death encompasses the days of life to render them lifeless. When such words are forced into the mouth of a child—when a girl in the flower of life deems death to be better than life—death is indeed all encompassing. It is the ether of the antiworld. No longer a task to be engaged in the course of choosing life, death becomes the stuff of a life transformed into an antilife. Suddenly we realize what the symbol set like a frontlet between the eyes of the SS signifies: The Death's Head Division defines and confines the "life" of the Jew to an all-encompassing death.

Indeed, we saw in the previous chapter that, for the Jew, the encompassing hand of death reaches even into the womb: Pregnancy itself became a capital crime. Without the secure future of the child, the essence of the mother is broken. This assault on the relation that constitutes the mother as mother entails not only dealing out death; it also entails displacing life with death. It entails a *confusion* of life and death, so that where there should be life, there is only death. The womb goes dark. And where it manages to bear life, it bears but only more death in a tearing of life from death. The Angel of Death is left with nothing to do.

The witnesses of this transformation of life into antilife, however, grope for a metaphor from the time when life and death were brethren. They look around, and, seeing nothing but darkness, they invoke the Angel of Death, who no longer puts to them the question concerning their name but is as mute as the very heavens. And so in his Warsaw Ghetto diary Seidman asserts, "The dark wings of the Angel of Death spread over the extinguished sparks of life."[20] In the image of these wings we have the radical antithesis of the image in the *El Molei Rachamim,* where we pray, "O G-d, full of compassion, who dwells on high, grant true rest upon the wings of the Shekhinah...." Where prayers are outlawed, so are the dead.

Soon death itself becomes the temptation, so that many spent the days of their lives seeking death. Soon cyanide capsules are as expensive as bread.

"The number of suicides among the Jews," Czerniakow records in his diary on 10 October 1940, "has been greatly increasing during the last months."[21] Instilling in the Jews a desire for death, the Nazis achieve just what they set out to achieve: Not only would they kill the Jews, but they would force them into a longing for death—that is how they would murder the Angel of Death. And those who do not succumb to suicide succumb nevertheless. "Typhus is raging," says Czerniakow on 4 December 1941. "Friends and acquaintances are dying all around me."[22] Of course the Jews do not "die" only of starvation, typhus, and other diseases. By and large they are simply slaughtered. A sea of blood rises all around them, until death becomes as all-encompassing as a sea is to a drowning man. "Already a lot of Jewish blood has flowed," Dawid Rubinowicz writes from the Bieliny Ghetto. "When will this terrible bloodshed finally end? If this goes on much longer then people will drop like flies out of sheer horror."[23] The horror arises here not just at the spectacle of death and murder but at the sense that death and murder are the only reality.

Indeed, the horror is itself a kind of death that steals over the living before they are dead. Planet Auschwitz, which extends far beyond the confines of the murder camp, has an immense field of gravity that tugs on the soul of every Jew, and its deadly, ashen atmosphere fills every Jewish mouth. Thus the Romanian diarist Emil Dorian cries out, "I try to tear myself out of the vortex that is pulling me down,…but everything has a taste of ashes and sticks in my throat like a foretaste of death."[24] If Dorian has any lifeline at all, it consists of the words that he consigns to the pages of his diary. Returning meaning and life to the word is one means of resisting the overturning of meaning in the realm of antideath. The word is the key. Tearing life and death asunder, the Nazis tear meaning from the word, so that life is not life and death is not death. The foretaste of death that fouls his mouth, then, issues from the mouths of the Nazis and their minions, whose death orders vibrate on their breath and foul the air.

Just so, Herman Kruk comments on an announcement of death made by the notorious Jacob Gens, head of the Jewish Council in the Vilna Ghetto, saying, "A gust of Ponary bursts into the hall, a breath of death, memories of men, women, and children snatched away."[25] Once again, like the atmosphere surrounding Planet Auschwitz, the breath of corruption rises up from Ponary to flood the Vilna Ghetto. "The district Ponar,"

Yitskhok Rudashevski cries out, "is soaked in Jewish blood. Ponar is the same as a nightmare, a nightmare which accompanies the gray strand of our ghetto-days."[26] The nightmare is a daymare, as banal and diurnal as the setting of the sun. But in the Kingdom of Night the sun does not set—it turns to darkness. Instead of living in the light of day, the Jew is turned over to the gray of the ghetto-day, which swallows up any light that may issue from the heavens and any life that may issue from the earth.

Indeed, the antideath that the Nazis spread over the Jews is so pervasive that the earth itself seems to wither at its touch. "Throughout the summer," laments David Kahane, for example, "I have seen no green vegetation or the shape of a flower.... Are there any Jews left in the world?...Do Jews still rise to say Selikhoth somewhere?"[27] Here we see even more clearly the connection between the absence of Jews and the absence of prayer, between the absence of prayer to the absence of life. In the ghetto what becomes commonplace are not the beds of flowers seen in the neighborhoods of humanity, but pools of blood. "Puddles of blood have become a common sight," writes Elik Rivosh from the Riga Ghetto. "We walk past them and step in them."[28] Like death itself, the blood of the dead clings to the living: The Jew who walks these streets leaves behind him a trail of ghetto death, tracking it through the streets and into his home. Thus established as the condition assigned to Jewish existence, this "death" is not only ontologically all-encompassing. It is altogether ordinary.

"We become quite used to the sight of women walking to their death," Josef Katz comments on the situation at Stutthof, "and the chimney, too, no longer bothers us."[29] The clouds bellowing from the chimney are as mundane as the clouds in the sky. To be sure, like the antideath that displaces death, they displace the clouds in the sky, eclipsing those clouds that G-d set in the heavens, eclipsing G-d Himself. For in their assault on the Name the Nazis have set other clouds on high, clouds in the shape of the SS death's head that brings all things low, to the same level of empty indifference, erasing the difference between life and death. "There is a marked, remarkable indifference to death, which no longer impresses," says Emmanuel Ringelblum of the attitude that pervades the Warsaw Ghetto. "One walks past corpses with indifference."[30] The Yiddish word that Ringelblum uses for "indifference" is *gleikhgiltikeit,* which literally means "having the same value."[31] The same value as what? The same value as life: There is no qualitative distinction between life and death. Once again we see that the lines of demarcation between life and death have been erased: Torn asunder, death and life lose their distinction and collapse into a *gleikhgiltikeit.*

No longer, then, is one human being joined to another according to an everyday life shared; their only interhuman link, which is not inter*human* at all, is an antideath endured each day. The most glaring evidence of the erasure of life and death—the obliteration of the difference between life and death—is the erasure of the word, which is the most fundamental link between one human being and another. What makes the living indistinguishable from the dead, and at times indifferent toward the dead, is this deathly silence imposed on both. As the Nazis flood the world with antideath, they deluge the world with silence. It is not, however, the silence of no one speaking; it is the silence of words torn from meaning and of death torn from life. Both opposing this silence and transmitting it, the witness fetches the words from the mouths of the dead and draws them into his testimony, where, perhaps, the difference between life and death may be reestablished, even if for only a moment. And the difference is reestablished by making that difference into a nonindifference.

We cannot assume a stance of nonindifference toward the death of the other human being without being implicated by that death and by the indifference that would collapse the distinction between life and death. In our relation to the other person we see more than he can see: We see his face, on which are inscribed both his sanctity and his mortality. We see his face, because we see the Angel of Death creeping up behind him. With the death of the Angel of Death, then, we become blind to the face of the other human being, which is a blindness to life and death, just as it is a blindness to light and dark. Through the words he sets to the page in an act of nonindifference, the Holocaust diarist sees excessively; that is, he comes to see more than the totality of death that surrounds him. And where does he see the life and death, to which the all-encompassing death threatens to blind him? In the other person.

"Death," says Lévinas, "is *present* only in the Other, and only in him does it summon me urgently to my final essence, to my responsibility."[32] Getting rid of the other, the Nazis get rid of death. Only others lie in the cemeteries. But during the Holocaust even those who lay in their graves in the cemeteries were under attack. For eliminating the "others"—the

Jews—was the Nazis' aim, and this they did, in part, by eliminating the cemeteries. Such was the project that the Nazis undertook in the murder of death: Removing Jewish death from Jewish life, they sought to remove the Jew from life. Let us consider how this process might be understood.

Anti-Death and the Murder of Death

In the foregoing we saw that horror is a form of death that steals over the living before they are dead. Here we realize that if horror is a kind of death, it may well be viewed not as a fear of death but as the obliteration of death. It is antideath. "Horror is nowise an anxiety about death," Lévinas makes this point. "In horror a subject is stripped of his subjectivity, of his power to have a private existence…. It is a participation in the *there is*, in the *there is* which returns in the heart of every negation, in the *there is* that has 'no exits.' It is, if we may say so, the impossibility of death, the universality of existence even in its annihilation."[33] Here both person and world are stripped of all significance. No one calls him by name—and no one answers when he calls out to the Name.

To be a subject who lives and dies—to be a human being with a name—is to take up the project of making sense of a world. Bereft of both world and sense, the human being is not alive—he or she is simply there, a lone pocket of emptiness in the midst of a crowded void. The world has no inherent meaning or value—it too is simply there, a silence in the midst of a deafening noise. The "there is," then, consists of being in the midst of an indifferent being, void of any valuation of life or death and therefore of any distinction between life and death: In the "there is" there is no human *being*. Bodies are not consigned for burial; like trash, they are collected for disposal. Mourners neither prayer nor sit *shivah*—they are not mourners at all. Death is not so much impossible as it is meaningless. In the "there is" that descends upon the concentrationary universe, death is not a rite of passage; neither rite nor passage, it simply is. Which amounts to saying: It simply is *nothing*. Hence death dies.

Or rather, it is murdered. For in Shoah the conditions and contexts that would make death matter are not just absent; they are annihilated. Fackenheim explains: "In Ezekiel's image [of the dry bones], the dead have fallen in battle. The dead of the Holocaust were denied battle, its opportunity and its honours. Denied the peace even of the bones, they were denied also the honour of graves, for they, the others, ground their bones to dust and threw the dust into rivers. To apply Ezekiel's image of Jewish death to the Holocaust, then, is impossible. The new enemy, no mere Haman, not only succeeded where Haman failed, for he murdered the Jewish people. He murdered also Ezekiel's image of Jewish death."[34] In a word, he murdered the Angel of Death, so that there would be no wrestling with the Angel. Taking note of Fackenheim's reference to the prophet Ezekiel, we realize that sacred texts often address the sanctification of death; as G-d breathes life into Adam, for instance, so does He reclaim the breath of life in the kiss that He places on the mouth of Moses, the mouth that uttered the Name from which the soul is made. How is a Jew, then, removed from life? By removing him from the kiss of the Divine that is death.

One indication of this removal from death may be seen in the removal of the Jew from the grave that signifies and sanctifies his or her life. For G-d not only kisses Moses; He lays him in his grave. Thus it is written in the Talmud: As G-d buried the dead, so must we bury the dead (Sotah 14a). Usurping G-d, the Nazis are literally grave robbers: They rob the Jews of their graves. Robbing the Jews of their graves, the Nazis rob them of the Angel who comes to their graves to ask them: What is your name? Therefore it is not surprising to discover that for the Nazis the Jewish dead were not only objects of contempt; they were sources of curiosity and amusement. Michael Zylberberg reports from the Warsaw Ghetto that the Germans "gleefully photographed the dead and the accompanying relatives, and even went as far as taking snapshots of the corpses as they were laid out in the mortuary. The Nazis were particularly active in this respect on Sundays, when they would visit the cemeteries with their girlfriends. This, rather than the cinema, was a place of amusement for them."[35] And so the Sunday routine for many Nazis was church, lunch, and a stroll through the mortuary. Of course, when a mortuary becomes a place of amusement, it is no longer a mortuary, and the dead are no longer the dead. To be sure, once the Jew is robbed of his name and is reduced to an object, he cannot die because he is not alive in any meaningful sense. Thus the Jewish dead become "amusing."

In their desecration of the dead and their murder of death, however, the Nazis went far beyond such amusements, as one can see from the testimony Chaim Kaplan recorded in his Warsaw Ghetto diary. On 6 August 1940, for example, he writes, "Every great man or leader of his people who passes on in these evil times is carried to his grave alone, with his death and burial unknown to anyone."[36] The great men and leaders to whom Kaplan refers are those who engendered life in their communities and died for the sake of those communities. That is what made them great; that is what makes their death death. What makes this devastation *evil,* and not just horrific, is precisely the absence of any recognition of the life that these dead fostered. The absence of such recognition belongs to the erasure of life's sanctity, so that the dead too lose their sanctity. Hence, says Kaplan on 9 October 1941, "the dead have lost their traditional importance and sanctity. The sanctity of the cemetery is also being profaned; it has been turned into a marketplace."[37] Finally, a month later, he notes, "Henceforward people accompanying their dead for burial will be denied permission to enter the cemetery grounds. They will be permitted to come only as far as the gate and then strangers will accompany the departed to their graves."[38] No stones are to be laid on the gravestones, no measures to be taken against the loss of memory and the loss of a name.[39]

Just as the murder of death is linked to the assault on the Holy One, so too is it tied to the destruction of the family in this divorce of the family from the dead. Bodies are desecrated as they are torn from the hands of loved ones and turned over to strangers who have lost their human image. Denied entry into the cemetery, the family members are denied their status as family—as mothers and fathers, as sons and daughters, and, above all, as Jews. Since for a Jew mourning is a form of prayer and prayer was forbidden, the Nazis would brook no Jewish mourners. So great is the *mitzvah* of accompanying the dead to burial, the Talmud tells us that even "the study of Torah may be suspended for escorting a dead body to the burying place" (*Megillah* 29a; also *Ketuvot* 17a). Denied the performance of this *mitzvah* for the dead, the Jews are denied the *mitzvah* of choosing life: A Jew cut off from the *mitzvot* pertaining to death is a Jew cut off from life and from the Source of life.

From chapter 1 it will be recalled that the word *mitzvah,* which means "commandment," is derived from the Aramaic word *tzavta,* which means "connection." Says Rabbi Chayim ben Attar in the *Or HaChayim,* "Every *mitzvah* is meant to close a gap that may exist between man and G-d" (on

Exodus 30:13). Its importance, Rabbi Adin Steinsaltz points out, "lies not in its content or efficacy, be it material or spiritual, but in the fact that it constitutes a point of contact with the Divine."[40] When the Jew is unable to establish that point of contact with the Origin of life at the end of a life, the *mitzvah* that the Jew performs in bearing witness to this horror becomes all the more pressing: In the case of Kaplan, the witness becomes the only remaining mourner to accompany the dead to the graves that they are denied. Hence his diary becomes a form of prayer.

Such are the implications of the notation that Czerniakow makes in his diary about a Jew who committed suicide. "The body of a stoker who hanged himself three days ago," he writes, "is still in the boiler room at Jagiellonska Street. He cannot be buried since the workers in the funeral home cannot obtain the passes. To make things more difficult they have forbidden burials at the Praga cemetery."[41] Here death is slain by refusing the living the means of burying the dead and thereby observing the passage of those who in life had borne the image of the Holy One. This point becomes all the more clear when in Czerniakow's diary we read, "Continuous complaints that there is nothing to bury the dead in. They have to be left naked in holes dug in the ground. There isn't even any paper which could be used as a substitute for linen shrouds."[42] Very often the linen burial shroud for a man was the *tallit* or the *kittel* that he wore in prayer,[43] so that once again we have the connection between the assault on prayer and the murder of death.

Notice also that in this entry, instead of referring to a grave in the cemetery where a loved one is laid to rest, Czerniakow speaks of a hole in the ground where a corpse is left. But a grave is not a hole. Whereas a hole swallows up a life, a grave opens up a life. A grave is a tract of ground made sacred through the ritualistic interment of a human body in the earth and the marking of the site with a memorial stone and flowers. When the grave takes on the status of a hole, this marking too loses its status, as in a perverted inversion to which Czerniakow bears witness. "I looked out my window," he says on 21 May 1942, "and saw a hearse full of flowers which were being taken from the cemetery to the ballroom."[44] What transpires in the ballroom decked out with these flowers is neither the dance of life nor the dance of death. It is the Nazis' dance of antideath danced upon the mass grave of the Jews who do not merit having these flowers on their graves, which have been transformed into black holes that swallow up death itself.

Just as the flowers are among the fixtures that adorn this macabre revelry, so are the bodies of human beings among the fixtures that adorn the Warsaw Ghetto. "Not having the money to bury their dead," Ringelblum relates on 26 August 1941, "the poor often throw the corpses into the street.... On the other hand, the police district chiefs, not wanting to bother with the formalities connected with corpses, simply throw the bodies from one streetcar to the next."[45] And so we have the image of the murdered riding around the ghetto alongside the yet-to-be-murdered: The tram is turned into a hearse bound for every stop except the cemetery. Before long, then, not only would the Jews have no money to bury their dead—they would have no place to bury them. In an entry dated 12 May 1942, Ringelblum writes, "The Praga cemetery, which is more than 150 years old, is being leveled. The devils won't even let the dead rest. They've done the same sort of thing elsewhere in Poland and Germany."[46] Thus the assault on death is taken to the dead themselves in a campaign to destroy Jewish death.

In a similar vein David Kahane comments on "the wanton, barbaric profanation of the Jewish cemetery" in Lvov. "The Nazis," he says, "were not content with tormenting the living Jews; they also vented their spleen upon the dead. A special labor battalion of Jewish workers from the camp was ordered to uproot and smash all the tombstones on the cemetery."[47] Not only, then, do the Nazis undertake the task of desecrating the dead and removing death from Jewish life; they force Jewish hands to engage this task of destroying the graves where they once said the Kaddish over their mothers and fathers. To the Jews who have no cemeteries, the world is itself a cemetery, which is to say, it is not a world at all. Antideath and antiworld are interwoven. For the world is a place in which the living define a realm where people are laid to rest and prayers are said at their graves. When the graves and the prayers over them are obliterated, the world and the life that constitutes it are also obliterated.

And so we see how the word *death* grows meaningless. Even—or especially—in phrases such as "death camp" and "death factory," it soon becomes a euphemism that threatens to veil the truth of the Nazis' project. "Natural death no longer exists," declares Emil Dorian,[48] a point that Yitzhak Katznelson makes more powerfully still in his *Vittel Diary*, when he cries out, "Throughout the era of Hitler, the agent of the whole non-Jewish world, not a single Jew died, they were just murdered, murdered."[49] That is why the Nazis targeted the old and the ailing for murder, as they flooded the earth with death: Refusing to simply wait for them to expire, they were determined to see to it that no Jew would die, that the new Nazi god would eliminate Jewish death itself from the world. For this erasure of Jewish death from existence was a key to the elimination of the significance of Jewish existence itself. How, then, does the Angel of Death "die"? With the death of Jewish death.

Which brings us to still more questions: With the death of Jewish death, how can a Jew die in a *Kiddush HaShem,* that is, in the "Sanctification of the Name" martyrdom? And if the Sanctification of the Name is under assault, is the Name itself not also assailed?

The Problem of Martyrdom

We have seen that in the Jewish tradition what is often referred to as an act of martyrdom is called a *Kiddush HaShem,* or a "Sanctification of the Name." While the Kantian categorical imperative may prohibit murder, in order to preclude others from murdering oneself,[50] it cannot command martyrdom—that is, choosing death over murder, idolatry, or adultery—as the Talmud does (see *Sanhedrin* 74a; *Ketuvot* 19a). For the Kantian imperative is rooted in a being-for-oneself, whereas the Talmudic dictum is grounded in a being-for-the-other, both as G-d and as person.[51] Even Socrates died for no more than an idea, and his example is the highest philosophy can attain.

Why? Because speculative philosophy cannot deduce the teaching we receive from the Talmudic sage Shimon bar Yochai in the *Sifre* on Deuteronomy (33:5): "When you are My witnesses," G-d cries out, "I am G-d; when you are not my witnesses, I am not G-d" (see also *Pesikta de-Rav Kahana* 12:6). To be a martyr is to be G-d's witness, in an affirmation that my life is not my own. Therefore to be G-d's witness is to live and die according to Torah, in a sanctification of His Name. It does not lie in theological or philosophical indulgences. We have seen that, in the concentrationary universe, to be G-d's witness was a capital crime. Therefore the Jews who bore witness to the Nazi assault from the very depths of that assault may in some sense be regarded as martyrs—if not for what they stood up and said, then for what they stood for as a people.

What, then, do we learn from their testimony on the death of the Angel of Death? Written along the edge of annihilation and consigned to oblivion, the diaries of these witnesses are akin to a grave from which the voices of the dead reverberate, as most of these diarists were fated to lie in unmarked trenches or to ascend to the clouds on fading columns of smoke. Much of what went into their diaries is like a prayer said for those who were robbed of prayers, a memorial inscription consecrated to take the place of the desecrated memorials that once marked the lives and the deaths of European Jews. Witnesses of the annihilation of Jewish death, the diarists faced the overwhelming task of transforming the antideath imposed upon the Jews into a moment of witnessing, a moment of remembrance, and a moment of martyrdom.

In one of his most famous statements, Albert Camus opens *The Myth of Sisyphus* by saying, "There is but one truly serious philosophical problem, and that is suicide."[52] To this remark Rabbi Abraham Joshua Heschel replies, "There is only one really serious philosophical problem: and that is martyrdom."[53] Why? Because suicide negates the sanctity of life, whereas martyrdom affirms it. "In martyrdom," Leo Baeck asserts, "death is no longer a mere end of life, a mere fate. It becomes a deed of freedom and of love for G-d"—and, we may add, of love for humanity.[54] For martyrdom is "an ethical affirmation of the soul," as Baeck states it,[55] and ethical affirmation entails both the relation to G-d and the relation to humanity. In the Sanctification of the Name, the Jew's conduct of his life carries him into death and beyond, to the point where life and death intersect in the testimony of martyrdom. "In martyrdom," André Neher maintains, "human history receives a meaning. Martyrdom is the negation of the absurd. Everything receives a meaning through the ultimate testimony of the man who accepts that meaning to the very limit. Everything is oriented in relation to that testimony. Everything becomes *sanctified* through it."[56] Therefore, every Jew who could find a voice, no matter how inarticulate, offers up his testimony to the sanctity of human life. Thus he becomes a messenger who is a witness—a martyr—to Jewish martyrdom. And Jewish martyrdom is precisely the opposite of the Nazi antideath: It is the declaration of one's name before the Angel of Death, in a Sanctification of the Name.

But that is just where the difficulty arises: Obliterating the signs of sanctity surrounding both Jewish life and Jewish death, the Nazis undertook an assault on Jewish martyrdom itself. "In making the teaching of the Jewish book a capital crime," Fackenheim explains, "Hadrian had created the possibility of Jewish martyrdom for Jewish believers. In making Jewish existence a capital crime, Hitler murdered Jewish martyrdom itself."[57] But should the Jews allow the Nazis to determine the status of their own martyrdom? And do they not represent a certain testimony as *Knesset Yisrael,* as the Jewish People? Confronted with these questions, the Jewish witness confronts the task of reestablishing martyrdom in Jewish life and death through an affirmation of the invisible. What underlies the ghetto diary, then, is a desire for the invisible—or for the Invisible One, a metaphysical desire for the metaphysical—that arises precisely where, by all that meets the eye, it should not arise. It is the desire that Lévinas invokes when he says, "The very dimension of height is opened up by metaphysical Desire. That this height is no longer the heavens but the Invisible is the very elevation of height and its nobility. To die for the invisible—that is metaphysics."[58] And that is martyrdom.

Where, moreover, is the Invisible One made visible? Not only in Torah, prayer, and acts of loving-kindness, but also in His emissary, in the Angel of Death. Dying for the invisible—dying in the midst of a living that, from every visible indication, should not be there—is what characterizes the affirmation of life undertaken by the Jewish witness in the midst of this assault on death. That is how the Jew restores Jewish death to its proper, sacred ground. And that is how the Jew clings to life and wrestles with death, both during and after the Holocaust. But what about this *after*? How does memory situate the death of the Angel of Death in the *after*math of the Event? And how does the Jew manage to emerge from the Event?

The Problem of Liberation

In the previous chapter we saw that in the Nazis' desecration of the origin all the Jews of Europe were rendered homeless: Jewish homes and possessions, all the having that goes into having a home, were confiscated before Jewish lives were obliterated. When that center is destroyed—when the family, the very ones who bear us into the world and lay us into the earth, have been reduced to ashes and dust—so is meaning obliterated. When meaning is lost, so is any direction that one might pursue. And when direction is lost, so is freedom.

Liberation from the realm in which even the Angel of Death came under assault comes not only with the breaking down of the prison gates but with the opening up of a path to follow. If that path has been erased, then there can be no liberation. When the gates marked *Arbeit Macht Frei* were unlocked, many did not move, for they had nowhere to go. Having lost a home to which they might return, the Jews were faced with a movement of return that could not even be initiated. Saul Friedländer asks, "Where did this need of a return, a return toward a decimated, humiliated, miserable group, come from?"[59] The answer: It comes from the loss of a center to which memory incessantly returns—incessantly because the one who remembers has been robbed of every avenue of return. The need announces itself not only in the absence of a dwelling place but also in the impossibility of the return; thus it bespeaks the failure of liberation. Yet what is absent assumes a kind of presence precisely in the need for it. This presence-in-the-mode-of-absence (if one may speak thus) fuels the movement of memory in the aftermath of the death of the Angel of Death. Therefore it fuels a renewed encounter with the Angel. But since this presence is manifested as an absence—manifested, that is, in the mode of longing—the movement is never at an end: There is no dying away from the death of the Angel of Death.

Charlotte Delbo, although not a Jew, remembers what overwhelmed every Jew: The longing for a return that they scarcely believed in. "The women who had stopped believing in their return," Delbo relates, "were dead."[60] But this death is an antideath, a death that is not death, a death that is neither an end to life nor a return to the origin of life. It arises not only from the loss of belief in return but also from the loss of all memory of a place to return to; death happens when the memory of the future dies. Near the end of her memoir Delbo makes this point by describing the living death imposed on every woman turned over to the antiworld:

> Her eyes have emptied out
>
> And we have lost our memory.
>
> None of us will return.[61]

The memory lost is the memory of a name. It is signified by the empty-ing of life from the eyes; they cannot return to life because the memory of life, the memory of a name, will not return to them. And, with this loss of memory, it is as if the Angel of Death, the Angel with a thousand eyes, grows blind to them. For, once they have lost the memory of their name, it is as though the Angel has nothing to ask of them.

In the remembrance of the Event, the first thing retrieved is not pre-cisely the memory of a name but memory itself. Memory in this instance not only *seeks* a recovery of life and a liberation from the Kingdom of Death—it *is* that recovery and liberation; or rather, it is a movement *to-ward* a recovery that does not come because the liberation cannot happen. For in one memoir after another what is remembered is the ineluctable fact that "none of us will return." To be liberated from the antiworld would mean leaving it behind, in the past, so that the past, present, and future of life's time might be regained. Emptied of the Angel of Death, Auschwitz will not be left behind, and the passing of the years yield no past. In her memoir, Bertha Ferderber-Salz declares, "Pictures from the past and the images of the people I loved are always with me. It is not natural to live constantly in the past, but I cannot do otherwise."[62] One gets the impres-sion that something other than the survivor speaks in the memoir, that in the memoir lurks a voice with which the voice of memory constantly struggles. Can it be the Angel of Death, who himself struggles to put to us his question: What is your name? Or is it the voice of Mengele, the one who usurped the Angel of Death?

"It's not me who's doing the thinking," Fania Fénelon insists, "'it' thinks *for* me.... I spend every night there—every night!"[63] Liberation would en-tail a liberation from the dominating voice of the *it* of Auschwitz. With the obliteration of the word that we have seen, the word—and with it the name—is left to the nondescript *it*. It is a pronoun without an antecedent. In that deafening silence that allows no sleep, the Angel of Death cannot get a word in edgewise; and so the survivor is left to languish along the edge. Freedom, then, is not possible, as we see in Ferderber-Salz's recollec-tion of the day of her release from the camp. Although the smell of spring is in the air, she writes, "in every limb of my pain-racked body I feel that freedom is not possible for me. I am still totally immersed in the nightmare of yesterday."[64] The images of spring here are not just descriptions of the time of year or of a vernal environment; beyond that, they signify an image of life diametrically opposed to the survivor's own image as one who has lived through her own death. She who has lived through her own death cannot be free because she cannot die; her death is not the last thing but rather lies in a past that she cannot leave behind. It is an antideath. She cannot die because she has no future whose meaning is shaped by a death that is *not yet;* for her time has collapsed, leaving her *outside.*

Were the SS right after all? Was the only way out of the camp through the chimney? If that is so, then a sky transformed into a cemetery is an antisky overflowing with antideath. And yet—or therefore—there are those who clamber to get into that sky, if only to present their death to the Angel of Death. One may now better understand the story that Wiesel tells, for example, in *A Beggar in Jerusalem,* about a survivor who threw himself on top of a mass grave and begged the dead to not reject him: It was his only pathway to liberation, since only then could he confront the Angel of Death.[65] But he cannot crawl into that grave, for it has crawled into him. Because the Nazis set out to destroy not only the body of Israel but its very soul—because their enemy was not only the Jewish people but Jewish *being*—the soul remains a prisoner even when the body is freed.

"I remained stranger," says Livia Bitton-Jackson of her so-called liberation. "Even with the Americans, our liberators. Oh, G-d, what is liberty?"[66] The Americans opened the gates, but they could not show the prisoners the way out. Neither they nor anyone else could offer any understanding or explanation that might place a closure on the Event. Neither they nor anyone else could return the home and its sacred center to the survivors. Neither they nor anyone else could free the survivors from the death that overtook them before their lives were over. Neither they nor anyone else could return to them the who that had been their name. Where indeed, then, is the liberation?

The prisoner released from the prison becomes a fugitive relentlessly pursued by a place and a past. And a fugitive, it is written in the Talmud, "is like a captive" (*Bava Metzia* 39a). In this case she is the captive of silence, of homelessness, and of the death of the Angel of Death. There is no getting the horror "off her chest" because it is curled up in her soul. She speaks, but no one listens, for no one can understand. She returns home but finds nothing. She longs for a life that has death as its closure, but that death has been killed by the premature death manufactured in the "death" factory. "Our motionlessness and our silence betray reality," says Bitton-Jackson. "We are dead. Dead survivors of a long-lost struggle."[67] Dead survivors: When it comes to the Holocaust, this is not a contradiction in terms. It means that with this memory the survivor is turned over to an unending struggle for life and liberation. It means that liberation has failed. It means that the Jew is left to a ferocious silence where her name had been.

The Ferocious Silence of Isolation

"Death is silence," says André Neher, "silence overtaking life."[68] He goes on to assert that "Auschwitz is, above all, silence."[69] Putting the two together may be ontologically accurate, but it is Jewishly problematic. From a Jewish standpoint, as we have seen, to be turned over to death is to be turned over not to silence but to a question put to us by the Angel of Death. If, however, Auschwitz is the death of the Angel of Death, Neher is quite right when he says, "Auschwitz is, above all, silence." It is the "silence" that in Hebrew is *shtikah,* a cognate of the word *shituk,* which means "paralysis." It is the silence of the muted Angel.

When Eugene Heimler was finally freed from the concentrationary universe of silence, the silence followed him into an open field. "I became aware that the silence was within me, too," he writes, "a silence such as there must have been before the days of creation."[70] Why the silence before the days of creation? Because this is a silence imposed by an absolute, metaphysical destruction of life and death. It is the mute silence of an imposed absence, the silence of the word torn from its meaning and of the man torn from a life that inheres in language. It is the silence of the silenced Angel.

"There is the silence which preceded creation," Wiesel has said, "and the one which accompanied the revelation on Mount Sinai. The first contains chaos and solitude, the second suggests presence, fervor, plenitude."[71] The first is the silence of the Name before He uttered a name. The second is the silence of meaning within and beyond the name, the silence of human relation expressive of the relation to the Name. The return to freedom lies in a return to these relations that constitute the substance of life; it lies in having a place, a *Makom,* to return to. Liberation from Auschwitz, therefore, would be liberation from the silence of chaos and isolation and a return to presence and plenitude. For the survivor, this liberation means that when he speaks to a human being, he meets with a human response; it means that when he speaks, someone listens. For this offering and receiving of the word is just what creates a place, a space between two, where presence may enter human life. But this space does not open with the opening of the gates.

The case of Moshe the Beadle in Wiesel's *Night* may be seen as a paradigm for the condition of the one who emerges from the Kingdom of Death. Like Moshe, the survivor returns from the depths of a mass grave to tell the tale of his own death, but he cannot complete his return, for no one listens. "He no longer talked to me of G-d or of the cabbala," Wiesel relates, "but only of what he had seen. People refused not only to believe his stories, but even to listen to them."[72] In *One Generation After,* Wiesel remembers Moshe, saying, "He alone survived. Why? So that he could come back to his town and tell the tale. And that is why he never stopped talking. But his audiences, weary and naive, would not, could not believe.... Finally he understood and fell silent. Only his burning eyes revealed the impotent rage inside him. His muteness bordered on madness."[73] Like Moshe, many other survivors were locked into the ferocious silence of isolation through the silence they encountered in others. Liberated from one prison, they were delivered over to another, to the prison of refusal and disbelief erected by those who were outside the antiworld.

The victims who had been removed from the human world could be liberated only by regaining contact with that world. The most essential element of this contact lies in the word, in a language that would engender the human relation within which freedom lives. But the word lives through the response it invokes. When the response fails, so does the liberation. And the most urgent response—the response that brings a genuine liberation—is the response to the question that the Angel of Death puts to us. One realizes, then, how profound is the urgency underlying the word that comes to us through the testimony and through the eyes of those who saw what took place in that realm. And one realizes what is placed in our care: Shall we, too, refuse to listen and thereby refuse these witnesses their liberation?

The survivors put to us this question precisely in their testimony on the failure of liberation, on their encounters with disbelief and the refusal to listen. It is not a matter of being unable to hear or incapable of belief;

all too often it is a question of being unwilling to believe or afraid to listen. Kitty Hart, for example, recalls that her uncle in England told her not to speak of what she had seen. "I don't want my girls upset," he explained. "And I don't want to know."[74] Everyone in England was telling their war stories, but the Jews who had emerged from the Kingdom of Night were tacitly forbidden to speak of what they had endured. Whenever she was asked about the tattoo on her arm, Hart recalls, she would at first tell the truth. But "the reaction was always an awkward silence, as if I had said something terribly ill mannered."[75] The soldiers are not the only ones faced with the task and the responsibility to liberate the Nazis' victims; we who receive their words also have a part in that liberation. To refuse them an ear is to refuse them their return to life; it is tantamount to refusing the fact of the Event itself. Which is to say: We too must penetrate the silence that is Auschwitz to engage the Angel of Death. Coming before their testimony, I come before the Angel who asks me, "What is your name?" Perhaps that is where the Angel of Death is returned to life.

Among those who would silence the Angel of Death and keep the Jew locked into the ferocious silence of isolation are the historical revisionists, who argue either that the Holocaust did not happen or that it was not as bad as the Jews make out. Others abet this effort to kill the victims yet again and are thus complicit in the death of the Angel of Death, people who would put the blame on the Jews, spouting such lies as: "They went like sheep to the slaughter," "They were rich and naturally aroused the anger of their neighbors," "They could have run away," and "They cooperated with their own murderers." Then there are those who would "put it behind us" because it happened "so long ago," and those who would level it into a sameness with every other human catastrophe. All of this goes into the isolating silence that cuts off the path of liberation for the survivors. Many of us do not want them to be liberated because then we would have to listen to them.[76] We do not want to listen to them because in their testimony lies the Angel's question, resurrected to implicate us in our own responsibility, in our own humanity.

Even within the murder camp itself no sooner did the dream of liberation arise than it turned into the nightmare that Primo Levi describes as "varied in its detail but uniform in its substance: They had returned home and with passion and relief were describing their past sufferings, addressing themselves to a loved one, and were not believed, indeed were not even listened to."[77] In Charlotte Delbo's memoir we find confirmation of what Levi has observed, for there she describes a dream common among the inmates, one in which they return home and tell their tale only to have their loved ones turn away from them like strangers.[78] The fear expressed in these dreams is a fear of the ferocious silence of isolation, the fear that once you are inside Auschwitz there is no getting out, except through the death that is no longer death.

Liberation lies not only in the exit from the camp where these nightmares occurred but in an exit from the nightmares themselves; and this can come about only upon the reentry into the home where loved ones listen. The wall toward which these figures turn is a wall barring the reentry that would make liberation possible. To be sure, the dream of the encounter with the silence becomes reality, as we see when Levi attempts to relate his story to a group of Poles in Katowice: "I felt my sense of freedom...ebb from me.... I had dreamed, we all had dreamed, of something like this, in the nights at Auschwitz: of speaking and not being listened to, of finding liberty and remaining alone."[79] The silence of chaos and isolation once again comes to mind. Freedom ebbs into that chaos; in that isolation liberation fails. For liberty is not to be found when a man finds himself alone. Even after the enemy was defeated, then, he continued to do his evil and to imprison his victims, as Moshe Sandberg indicates. "You spoke," he affirms, "but it was as if you were talking to yourself, and you lived through it all again,...so that even after his defeat the enemy continued doing his evil. Thus not a few of us were prevented from becoming adjusted to new life, from returning to normal existence."[80] And so the one who seeks a return to the world is returned to the antiworld.

If hope is what drives memory, in this case it is the hope that if the survivor cannot enter the world once more, then at least his memory might. Which is to say: The Angel's question might be regained in the memory of the death of the Angel of Death. That is why memory *appears* to offer a liberation that otherwise will not come. But this hope no sooner arises than it is shattered by yet another collision with yet another wall: Even if the survivor can gain a listener, he cannot be understood. Indeed, the prospect of this failure of liberation arises before the gates of the camp are opened. So it came to pass for Livia Bitton-Jackson when she was faced with relating her story to a Russian soldier who had befriended her but could not fathom what she had to say. She writes, "Who can understand this inconceivable futility that is Auschwitz?...I belong to this void."[81] Belonging to the void called Auschwitz, the survivor's search for a home, for the one place where she has a name, is without end. The void to which she belongs *is* this absence of a home, for home is where a person may be understood. But she cannot be understood. Hence she moves from silence to silence; she cannot return home.

The Death of the Angel and the Exile of the Jew

"Isolation negates life," Rabbi Michael Munk has rightly said. It obstructs "man's relationship with his Creator," and not just with his neighbor.[82] The isolation of which we have spoken is the most extreme sort of exile, since it is the exile not only of the Jew but also of the Angel. Why both? Because it is an exile that is an isolation from the Name, that is, from the One in whose Name the Angel poses his question. To use a Hebrew word, the post-Holocaust exile is a condition of being *shamam,* or "desolate." The cognate verb *nasham* means to "be ruined" or to "be devastated"; in its *hitpael* form, *hishtomem,* it means to "be horrified" or to "become desolate." Indeed, the state of desolation that defines this exile is a state of horror, as suggested by the word for "desolation" or "wasteland": It is *shemamah,* and it also means "astonishment" or "horror." The desolate horror that continues to haunt the Jew in the post-Holocaust exile is not that there is so much evil and death in the world. On the contrary: The horror is that with the death of the Angel of Death there is neither evil nor death in the world, that there is nothing but the exile in the midst of a mute being, a being that is no longer a *Who* but an *It.* And if there is no *Who* but merely an *It* pervading and underlying being—if the Angel puts to us no question concerning our name—then there is no authentic *who* about the human being; instead, the human being is mere raw material, an *it* forever lost in the desolation of exile.

One mark of this desolation is the fear of freedom that one sees in survivors such as Paul Trepman. "We are afraid of freedom," he asserts. "Now that I'm free, all I feel is a terrible ache of loneliness."[83] Trepman's ache of loneliness is the ache of homelessness for which there is no balm.

The fear of freedom, then, is not a fear of release but of return. Alexander Donat says it well when he explains that when it was "over" his only wish was to become a watchman in a Jewish cemetery, where he could be alone with the dead. Why was he afraid of going home? He answers, "I was afraid that when I did, my last ties to life would be irrevocably broken. There would be nothing left."[84] Better the cemetery than the home because the cemetery has become home: That is where the Jewish mothers and fathers and children now reside. The only problem is that the cemetery itself has vanished.

This vanishing is what constitutes the exile, if not the death, of the Angel of Death, and it poisons the soul that cannot return. "We felt in our veins the poison of Auschwitz," says Primo Levi. "Where should we find the strength to begin our lives again?"[85] Here we find an important reason for this particular exile of the Jew: The poison of Auschwitz is not behind its victim but within him and before him. The death camp does not follow him like a shadow but rather precedes him, making him into its shadow and every place of return into a desert. Thus Levi declares, "Liberty…had come, but it had not taken us to the Promised Land. It was around us, but in the form of a pitiless deserted plain."[86] This deserted plain is the *shemamah* described above. What distinguishes the desolation of the plain is not the absence of vegetation or of artificial signs of human life; it is the absence of a place to return to.

This exile of the Jew is neither an environmental condition nor an existential circumstance; rather, it is a metaphysical category that belongs to the death of the Angel of Death. It is a category that belongs to the murder of the soul. Suddenly we realize some profound implications of Fackenheim's assertion that "Eichmann sought to destroy souls before he destroyed bodies,"[87] and his insistence that in the murder camp the murderers' target was the image of the divine within the human.[88] For the divine image imprinted upon the soul is precisely what the Angel asks us about. The murder of the soul, therefore, requires the death of the Angel of Death. And, since any genuine liberation has to include the liberation of the soul, the murder of the soul entails the murder of liberation. Gerda Klein illustrates this point: "Perhaps, I thought, we will survive, but what then? I will go home, of course…. And for the first time in all those years, the thought of going home did not ring right."[89] The thought does not ring right because the word has lost its meaning, just as the Jew has lost her name. It has lost its meaning because the home has lost not only the life but also the death that belong to dwelling in the world. "The dwelling is not situated in the objective world," Lévinas states it, "but the objective world is situated by relation to my dwelling."[90] Thus the condition of exile that arises in the antiworld spills over into the world.

Recall Lily Lerner's memory of her return to Hungary. Not only did she find that in her village of Tolcsva her house "was some other house, beyond recognition,"[91] but in Budapest also she asks, "Was this really home? What were we doing here? Why had we returned?"[92] Home, of course, is made of far more than bricks and furniture. Its essence lies in human relation; a human being returned from exile is a human being returned to human relation. In Tolcsva, Lerner encountered people who had known her family, but "they said nothing.... No one saw us. No one met our eyes."[93] No person is free whose liberation is not accompanied by a greeting; the simple saying of hello is the portal through which the return from exile is made possible. And that is just what is withheld from Lily Lerner.

This collapse of human relation essential to human being is also at the core of the failure of liberation that Rudolf Vrba experienced when he and his friend Fred Wetzler went back to Czechoslovakia: "We found ourselves relating everything to Auschwitz.... Just as we thought we were human beings again, a jagged edge came out of the past and scratched us."[94] For Vrba, the past that scratched him and rendered him other than human left a wound on his face; in the face the word finds its tie to meaning and the home its linkage with life. But when Vrba first saw his mother, who had survived the war, she did not recognize him: "I had seen 1,760,000 people die and it had left a mark on my face."[95] Why did that mark render him unrecognizable? Because in this megadeath that he had witnessed, he witnessed the death of the Angel of Death, of the one who puts to us the question by which we are rendered recognizable. And there is no more painful manifestation of the miscarriage of the return home than this loss of recognition from one's own mother, from one's own origin—from the one who first calls us by name.

Rivaling that pain, however, is the return to a completely empty, voiceless home, as it happened to Nathan Shapell. "I...approached the entrance to the building I had once called home," he recalls his appearance in Sosnowiec. "Waiting to be greeted by someone, anyone. No one, not a voice I knew."[96] And not a soul who knew his name. We see that the deserted plain, the *shemamah*, of which Levi speaks extends not only into the streets of a town but into the heart of the dwelling itself. We see why the concentrationary universe is called a universe: It is not another universe, for there is "room" for only one. Rather, it becomes *the* universe, the desert enveloping us, so that ultimately there is no return home. Hence, Bertha Ferderber-Salz remembers, "Once again I was in Cracow. Emptiness emanated from every corner, every street and every house."[97] And: "I wandered like a ghost through the streets of the city where I had grown up and lived most of my life. The streets, the houses and the people all seemed alien."[98] In desperation she goes to her parents' village of Kolbuszowa, but there too Auschwitz precedes her, making that return, too, impossible. "Everything in my village was strange to me!" she writes. "No one came to greet me. Where were the well-loved voices that had chorused words of affection and welcome whenever I visited my parents' home?"[99] Again, the question repeats itself: Can this be liberation?

The terrible motif continues: There was no one to greet me. Why are the Ten Utterances at Sinai, the site signifying Israel's liberation, divided into human-to-the-Divine and human-to-human relations?[100] Because the Place of liberation arises where human presence arises; each requires the other in order to be present, and liberation requires both. When the image of the divine within the human is destroyed, there is no return to the Place of dwelling, which is to say: There is no return of the human to the human. "I need people who need, and I want to give," says Bitton-Jackson, remembering the time when the slaughter came to an end. "I reach out and there is nothing."[101] This reaching out is a gesture not of grabbing but of offering. It is an attempt to take on a name where there is no one to ask, "What is your name?" Thus we see the connection between the death of the Angel and the exile of the Jew. "Suddenly we became shatteringly aware that we meant exactly nothing to anyone," Sim Kessel recalls the opening of the gates of Auschwitz.[102] Which means: There is no one *for* whom they might be in the being-for-the-other essential to the life and to the freedom of a human being. For the survivors the tragedy lies not in the absence of an embrace that they might have received but in the absence of anyone to whom they could offer an embrace.

With this failure of the embrace, the one who was "liberated" went from pain to pain, from exile to exile, as it happened to Primo Levi. "In the very hour," he writes, "in which a hope of a return to life ceased to be crazy, I was overcome by…the pain of exile, of my distant home, of loneliness."[103] The distance from home lies not in the miles that separate the man from Italy but in the void that isolates him from the human beings around him, both living and dead. That void has a name. It is the name of the absence of the Name: It is Auschwitz, which is the name of a metaphysical hunger that can make a human being forget his name. For the Lager *is* hunger, as Levi has said.[104] The satisfaction of physical hunger, moreover, merely intensifies a metaphysical hunger. "The end of our hunger," says Levi, "laid bare and perceptible in us a much deeper hunger. Not only desire for our homes,…but a more immediate and urgent need for human contact."[105] Made of human contact, the home is the place where one is *touched,* where the caress is offered and received. In the caress the physical meets with the metaphysical, with the truth and the holiness of humanity, that is eternally sought but never seized. The caress, Lévinas expresses it, searches for "what slips away as though it *were not yet.*"[106] What does it seek? The divine within the human. Where does it search? In the Place, the *Makom,* where dwelling takes place: in the home.

The man freed from Auschwitz searches for a home. But even if he should find his way home, as Levi did, the time that constitutes the home—that is, the future opened up within the home—is eclipsed by an insistent past that inserts itself into an elusive present, like the jagged edge that marked Vrba's face. For Levi, it comes as an alien word that invades his sleep and stands in the way of his liberation, the alien command to rise to meet the Auschwitz day that will not be left behind: *Wstawàch.*[107] Once again we see that Auschwitz precedes the Jew who struggles to return home. When the Jew is at home, abiding in his native tongue, the word is tied to meaning, so that it is not in time, but rather time is in the word: the Jew is liberated, free to offer his word, his soul, and his name to another, for another. But with the invasion of an alien antiword from the antitime, the antiworld of Auschwitz cuts him off from the world and locks him into his exile.

Thus in *The Reawakening,* Levi speaks of the nightmare to which he has reawakened. It is "a dream full of horror" in which he at first takes himself to be in a familiar and comfortable setting only to have the scene shattered: "I am in the Lager once more, and nothing is true outside the Lager." The sign of his imprisonment? It is the alien command that overwhelms his consciousness again and ever again: *Wstawàch*.[108] Upon this command to rise, the man tumbles again into the void. Again he dies a death that is never over with, a death without the Angel of Death, robbed even of the death that would set him free.

With this we return to where we started.

The Memory of the Death of the Angel of Death

It has been said that Holocaust memoirs are written not by people recounting their lives but by people who have lived through their deaths. Living through one's own death is the most basic evidence of the death of the Angel of Death. What, we now ask, is the nature of the memory of that death?

Far from robbing life of its meaning, death defines the parameters of the yet-to-be, from which life derives its direction and therefore its meaning. In the world of humanity, to cite Lévinas once more, "Time is precisely the fact that the whole of existence of the mortal being—exposed to violence—is not being for death, but the 'not yet' which is a way of being against death."[109] The point of the mortal's "being against death" is not to destroy death but to situate it in relation to life in such a way that it is part of, and not opposed to, life's meaning. Here death is not the thief who steals my life away but the occasion for offering up my life for the sake of others. Thus offering up my life, I make my death into a testimony to the dearness of life; hence the mortal overcomes death by making it part of, and not the end of, life. Thus situating life and death on their proper ground, the family sanctifies life upon every burial and every memory of the dead. Thus the Kaddish, which sanctifies the Name and affirms the dearness of life, is part of every Jewish prayer service.

There is an important teaching from the Midrash in this connection. On each of the first five days of the Creation (except the second day) G-d pronounced His labor to be good; but on the sixth day He declared it to be *tov meod,* that is, "very good" (Genesis 1:31). The word *meod* means "more"; its cognate, the verb *himid,* means to "increase." What could possibly be more than good? How can the Good be increased? The Good that belongs to Creation is increased with the creation of the human being; the human being is *more* than being. What is the sign of his being *more*? It is his death, which, conceived as a task, becomes his infinite offering for the sake of the infinitely dear. Therefore, Rabbi Meir maintains that the *meod* in *tov meod* signifies death, a category belonging to human life alone (see *Bereshit Rabbah* 9:5; see also *Zohar* II, 103a).[110] To choose life is to choose this *tov meod* that distinguishes the animate from the inanimate, the human from the animal, and a living Good from a conceptual good. Choosing the *tov meod* means understanding that the basis of our relation to another human being—underlying the commandment to love our neighbor—is our fear for his death.

In their metaphysical overturning of Jewish being, the Nazis decreed and carried out the murder of this *tov meod* in the murder of the Angel of Death. One example of this crime that rests on the complete confusion of life and death is found in Elie Wiesel's *Night*. There, on his first day in Auschwitz, he, his father, and their comrades were manipulated into reciting the Kaddish not for the dead who have passed away, but for themselves, for the living, who in that setting died before their passing.[111] Thus these men find themselves in a place that is antithetical to the Place; it is a realm from which there is no liberation, not even the liberation of death. For the "living" are dead already, dead before the Angel of Death can find them. And so the once-living gaze upon the dead only to have their own reflection thrown back at themselves: "In every stiffened corpse," says Wiesel, "I saw myself."[112] It is not death, however, that he sees in the mirror image of every stiffened corpse, but the antideath of the antiworld.

We find more evidence of the death of the Angel of Death in one of the most haunting passages in Bitton-Jackson's memoir, where she writes, "The heap of dead bodies, the large pool of blood…is this death?"[113] Her question, of course, is rhetorical. This is not death but the murder of death, the destruction of burial rites, of the Kaddish, of the closure on a life that would be a testimony to the dearness of life and to the holiness of its Creator. It is the annihilation of the Lord's giving and the Lord's taking away, of words spoken over the dead in the presence of the living, of every elegy sung in the name of all that is sacred.

We have seen that part of the process of the soul's liberation from the Nazi horror lies in the ability to put it all behind oneself, to die away from it. And this dying away, this burial of a terrible past, entails the burial of the dead. But such a return to life is just what the antiworld denies its victims; long after the death factories ceased operation, they continued in their assault on the Angel of Death. And so the horror endures. The heart continues to beat when it should have come to a stop. The soul continues to live, and yet it *has* no life, for it has been stripped of the sign, of the category, that would seal the tomb of the past and open up the way to the future. What is the sign that signifies such a closure and brings about a liberation from the horror? It is something we have brought up several times already: the cemetery.

But, as Wiesel has said, "My generation has been robbed of everything, even of our cemeteries."[114] The Nazis made it impossible even to bury the bodies in their bloodied clothing, so as to put the horror in G-d's face, as Jewish law requires (*Kitsur Shulchan Arukh* 197:9). Thus the Jews were robbed of even their outcry. Millions were murdered. But no one was buried. And so their deaths were murdered with them. In the world of humanity we bury the dead, mark their graves, and leave the cemetery; it is burying the dead and marking their graves that enables us to leave the cemetery. But there is no leaving the cemetery of the antiworld, a cemetery without a grave or gravestone. "Even death is too good for a Jew?" asks Isabella Leitner.[115] To this question not only about death but also about death as a part of human life and human being the Nazi answers, "Yes." Again, the Nazi does not want the Jew dead. Or alive. The Nazi wants to erase every predicate from the Jew.

Hence, in the process of murdering Jewish being, the Nazis murdered Jewish death; they erased the sign of Jewish being from the earth by erasing the Jewish grave and gravestone. Nor was this destruction confined to the murder camp; here too the assault on Jewish being extended far beyond the parameters of the electrified fence. Vladka Meed, for example, records her memory of the Jewish cemetery destroyed in Warsaw. "Wherever I turned," she recalls, "there was nothing but overturned tombstones, desecrated graves and scattered skulls.... Yes, the Jews were persecuted even in their graves."[116] Instead of receiving a visit from the Angel of Death, the Jews in these graves were assaulted by the Nazi lords of antideath.

One can now see that Simon Wiesenthal's concern with forgiveness is in fact a concern for the death of the Angel of Death. A dying SS soldier seeks from Wiesenthal the forgiveness that would set him free to die.

Wiesenthal refuses, insisting quite rightly that he cannot offer forgiveness for the suffering and death endured by others. And yet he becomes a prisoner of his refusal; true liberation requires reconciliation, but this he cannot have. For Wiesenthal is the prisoner of the dead whose forgiveness he cannot offer the soldier. Why a prisoner? Because the death of those dead has been murdered in the murder of their names and their souls, in the removal of their every tie with the living through the denial of any grave for them. Refusing to transmit the forgiveness of the dead to one of their murderers, Wiesenthal becomes the signifier of the dead: He becomes their grave and their gravestone, and they will not set him free.

The very title of his book *The Sunflower* establishes this linkage between the murder of death and the failure of liberation, as we see when Wiesenthal gazes upon an SS cemetery. Watching butterflies flitting from sunflower to sunflower on the graves of the SS, it strikes him that from those butterflies "the dead were receiving light and messages. Suddenly I envied the dead soldiers. Each had a sunflower to connect him with the living world, and butterflies to visit his grave."[117] Wiesenthal's envy is steeped in the conviction that he was doomed to an oblivion without a grave, that he was himself already a dead man, even as he continued to breathe. "Each of us," he says, "was carrying around his own death certificate."[118] Thus the question born of the murder of death arises: Why are you still alive?

The memory of this question is found in many of the Holocaust memoirs; indeed, it is a question that shapes the memory of the death of the Angel of Death. Leon Wells, for instance, returned from the concentrationary universe not to be greeted with a liberating welcome or even to be asked about his ordeal. Rather, he recalls, the only thing people wanted to know was why he was alive.[119] This question posed by others is the question that the man fears to confront within himself. He knows he ought to be dead, and this knowledge taints his life and his liberation. For Alexander Donat, in fact, the question comes not from the other but from within himself: "Why was I permitted to live?"[120] And, while Donat is haunted by the question that he must answer for himself, Zivia Lubetkin wonders how she could possibly answer others: "How will I be able to explain how I survived?"[121] Or: How can I explain the death of the Angel of Death?

By now we can see that there is much more than mere guilt underlying the survivor's question. Deeper than guilt, what is at work here is the death of the Angel of Death. Thus the survivor eternally seeks his liberation by seeking the death denied him, the death that would enable him to detach himself from Auschwitz. For death denied is a living death. And, until we can engage the Angel of Death, the recovery from a living death is never complete: We shall never regain the name of Israel. Why? Because, as it is written, the name of the Angel was itself Israel: Jacob wrestled the Angel's name from the Angel of Death (see *Pirke de Rabbi Eliezer* 37).

Engaging the Angel Once Again

In *The Jews of Silence*, Elie Wiesel tells the story of a woman who was shot but only wounded at the mass grave known as Babi Yar. After crawling out of that sea of bodies and blood, he relates, she found shelter with a Ukrainian, only to be handed over to the Germans. Again she was taken to the mass grave; again she was shot and merely wounded. This time she managed to escape the Ukrainians and the Germans. But, says Wiesel, "her mind had snapped. Now she rants aloud, remembering forgotten things, and people say, 'Poor woman, she lives in another world.'"[122] This woman's condition exemplifies the condition of the survivor who must repeatedly engage the Angel of Death and for whom there is no liberation, for whom dying is not the last but continually the last. While it may be true that not every survivor has had his mind snap, every survivor has had his soul wounded. Since every soul of every Jew is tied to every other soul, every Jew has been so wounded. "The people of Israel are compared to a lamb," says the *Mekilta de Rabbi Ishmael*. "What is the nature of the lamb? If it is hurt in one limb, all its limbs feel the pain" (*Bachodesh* 2). And no pain is greater than the pain of namelessness. So the wound refuses closure; refusing closure, it refuses liberation.

"The injury," Primo Levi insists, "cannot be healed: it extends through time,...denying peace to the tormented."[123] We have examined the facets of this torment: the movement from one silence only to collide with another, the return to a home no longer home, the murder of Jewish death and of the death by which the Jew may die away from the Event. And we have seen that there is no dying away from the memory; the survivor leaves the death camp, but the death camp does not leave the survivor. "Bye, Auschwitz," writes Isabella Leitner. "I will never see you again. I will always see you."[124] For she will always be seen, always summoned, by the dead who have no grave, whose cemetery is the sky that arches over all of us. "I belong here," Kitty Hart remembers her return to Auschwitz. "I have never been away."[125] She returns to the site of the antiworld, seeking liberation, just as memory returns in a search of a name. But it does not come; the movement is unending. Why? Because the antiworld has spilled over into our own world. "I still see the features and the routines of Auschwitz everywhere," says Hart, "personal viciousness, greed for power, love of manipulation and humiliation."[126] Primo Levi makes this point in even stronger terms; remembering his passage through Austria after the war, he writes that he and his comrades experienced the "threatening sensation of an irreparable and definitive evil which was present everywhere."[127] And so it continues.

Intellectuals stand by in their postmodern muteness, curl up in the complacent comfort of their endowed chairs, as the blood libel—yes, the blood libel!—is reborn. Where do we see the blood libel? In a column written in April 2001 by Muslim "scholar" Dr. Muhammad bin Saad al-Shweyir for the leading Saudi newspaper *Al-Jazirah.* In the same month *U.S. News and World Report* reported that seventeen Jews were murdered outside Africa's oldest synagogue in Tunisia. Mobs in the Ukraine have vandalized synagogues and cemeteries to chants of "Kill the Jews." A Jewish library in Saskatchewan was torched. The Finsbury Park Synagogue in North London was vandalized in the fifty-second attack on British Jews within a month. Similar incidents regularly take place in Brussels, Amsterdam, Copenhagen, Berlin, and other centers of Western civilization, all to the accompaniment of the age-old silence of the Vatican and the Protestant pulpits. Then, of course, there is France—bastion of *philosophie, beaux-arts,* and *belles-lettres;* birthplace of Voltaire, Clermont-Tonnerre, and the *lumière;* land of *liberté, égalité, fraternité;* home to the Dreyfus Affair; and haven for Jew-haters.

What is in need of liberation is not just a group of Jews who cannot say why they survived the Nazis, but a world in which Jew hatred is still all too fashionable among religious fanatics and liberal intellectuals. What is in need of mending is not just the antiworld's invasion of the world but the world itself, now as much as then. Says Emil Fackenheim, "Jews after Auschwitz represent all humanity when they affirm their Jewishness and deny the Nazi denial,"[128] which has become the Arab Muslim denial: The Angel of Death—or rather the Angel of Murder—now wears a *kaffiyeh*. The recovery of a memory and a name, therefore, is far more than a matter concerning Jews. It is an issue for a humanity continually summoned to a never-ending process of bearing witness. *Our* need for this memory is as great as the need of those who emerged from the death of the Angel of Death at the hands of the Angel of Murder.

Yes: the Angel of Murder... Perhaps that is the one whom the Jew must now engage. Mengele, the one known as the Angel of Death, denied a natural death to the Jews only to die a natural death. Therefore "to return the throne of judgment usurped by Dr. Mengele back to G-d," writes Fackenheim, "has become a Jewish necessity."[129] Perhaps a Jew today can do precisely that, since, thanks to the Jewish state, a Jew today has certain choices that the Jew facing Mengele did not have. If we are to refuse the erasure of Jews and Judaism from the world, as Fackenheim enjoins us to do, then a Jew today must exercise that choice by living and, if necessary, dying on his feet. And he must do so in an affirmation of the Jewish state, which was established not only so that a Jew may have a place to live but also that a Jew may have a place to die *as a Jew*. Without that haven—without that nation and its tie to the millennial testimony of Torah—the light that shines unto the nations through the Jews will be lost.

Notes

1.   Ka-tzetnik 135633, *Kaddish,* trans. Nina De-Nur (New York: Algemeiner Associates, 1998), 37.

2.   Primo Levi, *Survival in Auschwitz: The Nazi Assault on Humanity,* trans. Stuart Woolf (New York: Simon & Schuster, 1996), 90.

3.   Emil L. Fackenheim, *To Mend the World: Foundations of Post-Holocaust Jewish Thought* (Bloomington: Indiana University Press, 1994), 100.

4.   Cf. Levi, *Survival in Auschwitz,* 88.

5.   Fackenheim, *To Mend the World,* 100.

6.   Emil L. Fackenheim, *The Jewish Return into History* (New York: Schocken Books, 1978), 246.

7.   Levi, *Survival in Auschwitz,* 90.

8.   Bachya ibn Paquda, *Duties of the Heart,* vol. 2, trans. Moses Hyamson (New York: Feldheim Publishers, 1970), 389.

9.   It is significant to note that when the visitor to the U. S. Holocaust Memorial Museum emerges from the main exhibit, he comes to an area for reflection. On the walls in that area are three verses from the Torah that the Nazis attempted to destroy. One of those verses is this commandment to choose life by choosing Torah. The other two verses are the commandment to remember what your eyes have seen and pass that memory on to your children (Deuteronomy 4:9) and G-d's outcry to Cain that the blood of Abel has cried out to Him (Genesis 4:10).

10.   See Elie Wiesel, *Somewhere a Master,* trans. Marion Wiesel (New York: Summit Books, 1982), 105.

11.   Harry James Cargas, *Reflections of a Post-Auschwitz Christian* (Detroit: Wayne State University Press, 1989), 25.

12.   Josef Katz, *One Who Came Back: The Diary of a Jewish Survivor,* trans. Hilda Reach (New York: Bergen Belsen Memorial Press, 1973), 37.

13.   Emil L. Fackenheim, *G-d's Presence in History: Jewish Affirmations and Philosophical Reflections* (New York: Harper & Row, 1970), 74.

14.   Ruth Andreas-Friedrich, *Der Schattenmann: Tagebuchaufzeichnungen, 1938–1945* (Berlin: Suhrkamp, 1947), 179.

15.   Hillel Seidman, *Tog-bukh fon Warshever geto* (New York: Avraham Mitlberg, 1947), 221.

16.   Helena Elbaum Dorembus, "Through Helpless Eyes: A Survivor's Diary of the Warsaw Ghetto Uprising," *Moment,* April 1993: 58.

17. Adam Czerniakow, *The Warsaw Ghetto Diary of Adam Czerniakow*, ed. Raul Hilberg, Stanislaw Staron, Joseph Kermisz, trans. Stanislaw Staron et al. (New York: Stein and Day, 1979), 90.

18. Mirjam Korber, *Deportiert: Jüdische Überlebensschicksale aus Rumänien, 1941–1944: Ein Tagebuch*, trans. Andrei Hoisie (Konstanz: Hartung-Garre, 1993), 75.

19. Ibid., 99.

20. Seidman, *Tog-bukh*, 63.

21. Czerniakow, *Warsaw Ghetto Diary*, 205.

22. Ibid., 305.

23. David Rubinowicz, *The Diary of David Rubinowicz*, trans. Derek Bowman (Edmonds, WA: Creative Options, 1982), 55.

24. Emil Dorian, *The Quality of Witness*, ed. Marguerite Dorian, trans. Mara Soceanu Vamos (Philadelphia: Jewish Publication Society, 1982), 167.

25. Kruk: 41.

26. Yitskhok Rudashevski, *The Diary of the Vilna Ghetto*, trans. Percy Matenko (Tel Aviv: Ghetto Fighters' House and Hakibbutz Hameuchad, 1973), 41. Solomon Garbel, a Jew assigned to bury the dead of Ponary before he too was to be shot, managed to escape the killing field. He has this description of the entrance to the murder site: "The grass was red with blood. The entire field was littered with bodies. The trees were splattered with brains. Mutilated children lay beside the tree trunks, many of whom were torn in half, with one leg lying here, another there. There was a whole pile of children's heads." See Abraham Sutskever, "The Vilna Ghetto," trans. David Patterson, in Ilya Ehrenburg and Vasily Grossman, eds., *The Complete Black Book of Russian Jewry* (New Brunswick, NJ: Transaction Publishers, 2002), 248.

27. David Kahane, *Lvov Ghetto Diary*, trans. Jerzy Michalowicz (Amherst: University of Massachusetts Press, 1990), 3.

28. Elik Rivosh, "From the Notebook of the Sculptor Elik Rivosh (Riga)," trans. David Patterson, in Ehrenburg and Grossman, *The Complete Black Book of Russian Jewry*, 407.

29. Katz, *One Who Came Back*, 216.

30. Emmanuel Ringelblum, *Notizn fon Warshever geto* (Warsaw: Yiddish Books, 1952), 194.

31. Ibid., 153.

32. Emmanuel Lévinas, *Totality and Infinity*, trans. Alphonso Lingis (Pittsburgh: Duquesne University Press, 1969), 179.

33. Emmanuel Lévinas, *Existence and Existents,* trans. Alphonso Lingis (The Hague: Martinus Nijhoff, 1978), 61.

34. Emil L. Fackenheim, *The Jewish Bible after the Holocaust* (Bloomington: Indiana University Press, 1990), 67.

35. Michael Zylberberg, *A Warsaw Diary* (London: Valentine, Mitchell & Co., 1969), 31.

36. Chaim A. Kaplan, *Scroll of Agony: The Warsaw Diary of Chaim A. Kaplan,* trans. and ed. Abraham I. Katsh (Bloomington: Indiana University Press, 1999), 176.

37. Ibid., 267.

38. Ibid., 275-76.

39. The reason for the Jewish custom of laying a stone on the gravestone of the one whom we visit in the cemetery is to build up the signifier of the memory of the one who lies in the earth, so that the memory itself will not be worn away by time.

40. Adin Steinsaltz, *Teshuvah: A Guide for the Newly Observant Jew* (New York: Free Press, 1987), 28.

41. Czerniakow, *Warsaw Ghetto Diary,* 218.

42. Ibid., 300.

43. A *tallit* is a prayer shawl. A *kittel* is a white robelike garment worn on Yom Kippur (the Day of Atonement), so that one may resemble the angels.

44. Czerniakow, *Warsaw Ghetto Diary,* 357.

45. Ringelblum, Notizn, 196–97.

46. Ibid., 267.

47. Kahane, *Lvov Ghetto Diary,* 53.

48. Dorian, *Quality of Witness,* 322.

49. Yitzhak Katznelson, *Vittel Diary,* trans. Myer Cohn, 2nd ed. (Tel Aviv: Hakibbutz Hameuchad, 1972), 228.

50. Kant's categorical imperative requires us to always act in such a way as to will a universal maxim from our action (an imperative which, by Kant's own admission, depends on an inherently *good* will).

51. With regard to Kant's imperative to treat all rational beings as an end and never as a means (see Kant, *Grundlegung zur Metaphysik der Sitten,* 433), Abraham Joshua Heschel rightly notes, "If the idea of man being an end is to be taken as a true estimate of his worth, he cannot be expected to sacrifice his life to his interests for the good of someone else or even of a group." See Abraham Joshua Heschel, *Man Is Not Alone* (New York: Farrar, Straus

and Giroux, 1951), 194.

52. Albert Camus, *The Myth of Sisyphus,* trans. Justin O'Brien (New York: Random House, 1955), 3.

53. Abraham Joshua Heschel, *I Asked for Wonder,* ed. Samuel H. Dresner (New York: Crossroad, 1983), 45.

54. Leo Baeck, *The Essence of Judaism,* rev. ed., trans. Victor Grubenwieser and Leonard Pearl (New York: Schocken Books, 1948), 174.

55. Ibid.

56. André Neher, *The Prophetic Existence,* trans. William Wolf (New York: A. S. Barnes, 1969), 338–39.

57. Fackenheim, *Jewish Return into History,* 247.

58. Lévinas, *Totality and Infinity,* 34–35.

59. Saul Friedländer, *When Memory Comes,* trans. Helen R. Lane (New York: Avon, 1980), 139.

60. Charlotte Delbo, *None of Us Will Return,* trans. John Githens (Boston: Beacon Press, 1968), 114.

61. Ibid., 126.

62. Bertha Ferderber-Salz, *And the Sun Kept Shining* (New York: Holocaust Library, 1980), 56.

63. Fania Fénelon, *Playing for Time,* trans. Judith Landry (New York: Atheneum, 1977), ix.

64. Ferderber-Salz, *And the Sun Kept Shining,* 15.

65. Elie Wiesel, *A Beggar in Jerusalem,* trans. Lily Edelman and Elie Wiesel (New York: Random House, 1970), 80.

66. Livia E. Bitton-Jackson, *Elli: Coming of Age in the Holocaust* (New York: Times Books, 1980), 179.

67. Ibid., 166.

68. André Neher, *The Exile of the Word: From the Silence of the Bible To the Silence of Auschwitz,* trans. David Maisel (Philadelphia: Jewish Publication Society, 1981), 37.

69. Ibid., 141.

70. Eugene Heimler, *Night of the Mist,* trans. Andre Ungar (New York: Vanguard, 1959), 188.

71. Elie Wiesel, *One Generation After,* trans. Lily Edelman and Elie Wiesel (New York: Pocket Books, 1970), 108.

72. Elie Wiesel, *Night,* trans. Stella Rodway (New York: Hill and Wang, 1960), 17–18.

73. Wiesel, *One Generation After,* 28–9.

74. Kitty Hart, *Return To Auschwitz* (New York: Atheneum, 1982), 12.

75. Ibid., 13.

76. Here I am reminded of what one survivor said to me after sitting through a session at an annual international conference of scholars of the Holocaust. Realizing what has become of the relation between the scholars and the survivors, as if frightened of her own words, she whispered, "Now I know what they want us do: They want us to die."

77. Primo Levi, *The Drowned and the Saved,* trans. Raymond Rosenthal (New York: Vintage Books, 1988), 12.

78. Delbo, *None of Us Will Return,* 63.

79. Primo Levi, *The Reawakening,* trans. Stuart Wolf (Boston: Little, Brown, 1965), 54.

80. Moshe Sandberg, *My Longest Year,* trans. S. C. Hyman (Jerusalem: Yad Vashem, 1968), 2.

81. Bitton-Jackson, *Elli,* 211.

82. Michael L. Munk, *The Wisdom in the Hebrew Alphabet: The Sacred Letters as a Guide to Jewish Deed and Thought* (Brooklyn: Mesorah, 1983), 79.

83. Paul Trepman, *Among Men and Beasts,* trans. Shoshana Perla and Gertrude Hirschler (New York: Bergen-Belsen Memorial Press, 1978), 222.

84. Alexander Donat, *The Holocaust Kingdom* (New York: Holocaust Library, 1978), 292.

85. Levi, *The Reawakening,* 220.

86. Ibid., 37.

87. Fackenheim, *G-d's Presence in History,* 74.

88. Fackenheim, *Jewish Return into History,* 246.

89. Gerda Weissmann Klein, *All But My Life* (New York: Hill and Wang, 1957), 210.

90. Lévinas, *Totality and Infinity,* 153.

91. Lily Gluck Lerner, *The Silence* (Secaucus, NJ: Lyle Stuart, 1980), 128.

92. Ibid., 121.

93. Ibid., 127–28.

94. Rudolf Vrba and Alan Bestic, *I Cannot Forgive* (New York: Bantam, 1964), 249–50.

95. Ibid., 251.

96. Nathan Shapell, *Witness To the Truth* (New York: David McKay, 1974), 167.

97. Ferderber-Salz, *And the Sun Kept Shining,* 179.

98. Ibid., 189.

99. Ibid., 204.

100. See, for example, *Abraham ibn Ezra: The Secret of the Torah,* trans. H. Norman Strickman (Northvale, NJ: Jason Aronson, 1995), 64–65.

101. Bitton-Jackson, *Elli,* 208.

102. Sim Kessel, *Hanged at Auschwitz,* trans. Melville and Delight Wallace (New York: Stein and Day, 1972), 185.

103. Levi, *The Reawakening,* 15.

104. Levi, *Survival in Auschwitz,* 74.

105. Levi, *The Reawakening,* 165.

106. Lévinas, *Totality and Infinity,* 257–58. Recall also the comments on the caress in the previous chapter.

107. Levi, *The Reawakening,* 5.

108. Ibid., 221–22.

109. Lévinas, *Totality and Infinity,* 224.

110. For a good discussion of this point, see Franz Rosenzweig, *The Star of Redemption,* trans. William W. Hallo (Boston: Beacon, 1972), 155.

111. Wiesel, *Night,* 42.

112. Ibid., 92.

113. Bitton-Jackson, *Elli,* 84.

114. Elie Wiesel, *Legends of Our Time* (New York: Avon, 1968), 25.

115. Isabella Leitner, *Fragments of Isabella,* ed. Irving Leitner (New York: Thomas Crowell, 1978), 23.

116. Vladka Meed, *On Both Sides of the Wall,* trans. Benjamin Meed (Tel Aviv: Hakibbutz Hameuchad, 1973), 334-35.

117. Simon Wiesenthal, *The Sunflower,* trans. H. A. Piehler (New York: Schocken Books, 1976), 20.

118. Ibid., 190.

119. Leon Wells, *The Death Brigade* (New York: Holocaust Library, 1978), 244.

120. Donat, *Holocaust Kingdom*, 293.

121. Zivia Lubetkin, *In the Days of Destruction and Revolt*, trans. I. Tubbin (Tel Aviv: Hakibbutz Hameuchad, 1981), 246.

122. Elie Wiesel, *The Jews of Silence*, trans. Neal Kozodoy (New York: Holt, Rinehart & Winston, 1966), 36.

123. Levi, *The Drowned and the Saved*, 24–25.

124. Leitner, *Fragments of Isabella*, 51.

125. Hart, *Return To Auschwitz*, 163.

126. Ibid., 159.

127. Levi, *The Reawakening*, 215.

128. Fackenheim, *G-d's Presence in History*, 86.

129. Fackenheim, *To Mend the World*, 300.

CHAPTER FIVE

WORD AND MEANING:
A MEMORY AND A NAME

If you have begun to forget, your end will be that you will forget all.
—Rashi, commentary on Deuteronomy 8:19

ॐ

BY NOW WE CAN SEE WHAT IS AT STAKE IN WRESTLING a memory and a name from the Angel of Death—or from the Angel of Murder: More than the name of Israel, it is the very meaning of the humanity of the human being. Indeed, what is at stake is the meaning of the word *human being*. With the assault on the name comes an assault on the word, which in turn is an assault on meaning: When the name is torn from the person, the meaning of *person* is torn from the word. The significance of the name of Israel is that through Israel this teaching is transmitted to the world. It is conveyed, for example, in the archetypal confusion of tongues related in the story of the Tower of Babel in chapter 11 of Genesis. Commenting on the phrase *navlah sham sfatam,* "let us confuse their tongues" (Genesis 11:7), Rabbi Yaakov Culi explains that *navlah* may also be read as *nevelah,* which means "corpse."[1] Read in this way, says Rabbi Culi, the verse means "Let us make their speech produce corpses."[2] Which is to say: In the confusion that tears word from meaning, people lose their memory of what *person* means. And when we forget what a person is, people die, violently and indiscriminately.

Recall in this connection the midrashic teaching that when a man fell to his death during the construction of the Tower of Babel, no one even noticed; but when a brick was dropped and broken, a great lamentation went up and a cry of, "Oh, woe! Where shall we find another like it?" (*Pirke de Rabbi Eliezer* 24). This confusion began when they set out to make themselves a name by creating their own dimension of height, the tower, rather than receive the name the Holy One had named them from on high. When we lose the dimension of height that points toward the Holy One, words lose their meaning, and humans lose their holiness. The mending of the bond between word and meaning is precisely what is attained when the Jew wrestles a blessing and a name—a memory and a name—from the Angel of Death. And it has never been more needful than now, at the onset of the twenty-first century. Why? Because despite all our philosophical concern with language and the word, we have lost the link between word and meaning. The graphic expression of that loss is the Shoah, an event for which philosophy provides a context for its concern with the link between word and meaning, both before and after the Nazi assault on the word.

The Postmodern Concern for the Word

Since the beginning of the twentieth century the link between word and meaning has been a central concern for many thinkers. Indeed, this focus on the interrelations between word and meaning, sign and signifier, truth and discourse, has characterized the shift from modernism to postmodernism. While the former addresses the problematic nature of the connection between word and meaning, the latter exults in the collapse of that connection.

French psychoanalyst Jacques Lacan, for instance, maintains that "the function of Language is not to inform but to invoke. What I seek in the Word is the response of the other. What constitutes me as subject is my question.... I identify myself in Language, but only to lose myself in it like an object."[3] In this case meaning is tied to word not through the response I offer but through the recognition I receive. The difficulty of the word, then, is that it is both necessary and undermining, forever losing the very thing it seeks to pin down, reducing the "I" to an "It"—precisely because it turns the self over to a position outside the self. Here the word has nothing to do with ethical accountability; rather, it is about bringing to light the "language of desire" on the part of the psychoanalytical subject. Therefore the relation between word and "meaning" is forever shifting.

Addressing this shifting relation from another perspective, Jacques Derrida asserts, "As soon as there is meaning, there are only signs,"[4] as if we were trapped in the anxiety-ridden situation of saying, "I see the sign, but where am I?" Here signs merely point to other signs, words to other words, in a process that ultimately looks like little more than psychological or philosophical game-playing and that renders the notion of responsibility meaningless. To be sure, Derrida calls into question the capacity of the word to contain any meaning at all; for Derrida, meaning itself shifts with the shifting of discourse and viewpoint, so that "Being" is always under "erasure."[5] And with that erasure comes the erasure of the Name who summons us to answer to our name. Commenting on Derrida's position, Emmanuel Lévinas correctly points out that "the signified, which is always to come in the signifier, never manages to take shape."[6] Thus I never have to answer for who and what I am, and the world is rendered meaningless: response itself becomes problematic, as does any responsibility that the human being might assume in the declaration of "Here I am."

The most famous and most influential of them all, of course, is the Nazi Martin Heidegger, with his renowned claim that "language is the house of being."[7] It is among the statements that make Heidegger the grandfather of postmodernism. Similar to his postmodern grandchildren and despite the differences among them, Heidegger ties word to being without understanding it to be derived from a higher meaning from beyond Being. As he states it, "Where the word fails there is no thing."[8] To the question of "Who speaks the word?" he answers that it is language itself: "Language *is:* language. Language speaks *[Die Sprache spricht].*"[9] Which amounts to saying: Nothing speaks. Or rather: Nothingness speaks. "Language is the peal of silence," says the Nazi from Freiburg,[10] with the implication that neither word nor silence belongs to anyone. Both amount to nothing but the blank neutrality of being, which, indeed, is the inevitable conclusion of ontological thought: The word is a blank that tries to fill in a blank. The human being, therefore, is basically nameless.

In Heidegger, says Lévinas, the word that issues from "Being" is "the word of no one."[11] The word of no one, it is a nonword, a being that is nonbeing and that summons no one to answer, an empty, unreal, and meaningless being that is justified only by a will to power—that is how "meaning" here is forced into a word that is otherwise merely a sound. It is true that Heidegger states, "The original thanksgiving is the echo of Being's favor, through which the single individual is illuminated.... This echo is the human answer to the word of the silent voice of Being."[12] But this thanks is given to no one and to nothing—to nothingness itself; indeed, "Da-sein," says Heidegger, "means being projected into nothingness."[13] Why? Because Being neither addresses nor can it be addressed. It remains a deaf and indifferent It. The thanksgiving of which Heidegger speaks, then, is empty and vain, the very opposite of the thanks that a Jew offers each morning upon returning to consciousness, saying: *Modeh ani lefaneikha*, "I give thanks before *You*." This *You* is as alien to postmodern thought as it is essential to taking on a name.

While these thinkers are quite varied in their thinking, all of them see the connection between word and meaning in ontological, and not metaphysical, terms. In other words, there are no absolutes. What thus characterizes postmodern thinking about the word is quite unlike the teaching revealed through the Hebrew *davar*. Note, for example, that *davar* means both "word" and "thing," with the implication that the thing is a word: It is the word of the Divine utterance that continually brings it into being. And, like the human being who is created out of his or her name, it has a *divinely determined* meaning. Hence, from the standpoint of the Jewish thought that the Nazis would eliminate with the murder of the Jews, language is not a phenomenon within being; rather, being is a phenomenon within language. This is not to say that language is the Heideggerian house of being, since Heidegger does not take language to have anything like an "origin" in a Divine Utterance from beyond being. For Hebrew thought, the word is a breach of being, the avenue through which being is sanctified and thus made meaningful through the Utterance of the One who contains all of being. It is above all the word of *someone,* who bears the Name and who calls us by name. That Utterance—that Someone—is just what the Nazis would silence by tearing meaning from the word and the name for the person.

Recall in this connection the teaching of the talmudic sage Rabbi Yochanan, who maintained that when G-d created the heavens and the earth, His first utterance broke into seventy sparks, and from those seventy sparks emerged the seventy languages of the world (*Shabbat* 88b): It is this trace of the Divine utterance, and not language games or semiotics, that gives the word meaning. Recall, too, Rabbi Adin Steinsaltz's commentary on the biblical verse "man lives not by bread alone, but by every utterance from the mouth of G-d does man live" (Deuteronomy 8:3). The verse, says the rabbi, means that "man does not live only from the calories provided by bread, but from Divine energy. This is what the Torah calls the *'utterance from the mouth of the Lord.'* It makes the bread 'live' and forms its true essence. In other words, although superficially I am only eating matter, in fact I am ingesting language, because the raw material of bread is the Divine word."[14] Every "item" or "thing," every "tool" or "utensil," is also a "vessel," as these possibilities of meaning for the Hebrew word *kli* suggest. A vessel of what? Of the Divine teaching and commandment, of the Divine word, by which it exists. This is the Jewish view of word and meaning, which is radically different from the views of the philosophers and that was subject to erasure with the Nazis' annihilation of the Jews.

Further, none of the postmodern, ontological thinkers sees the word as a Divine commandment expressive of a Divine covenant. For Heidegger, language may speak; it might even call; but it does not *command.* That is why he is free to be a Nazi. From Heidegger's viewpoint, we may have the word, but we stand in no absolute relation to the Absolute, as only the Divine commandment can determine such a relation. Hence we stand only in an existential relation, and not an ethical relation, to other beings. An avid pagan, Heidegger may invoke "the trace of the fugitive gods" as the object of the poet's attention,[15] and the need for "the gods" to bring us to language, so that the word may take on its "naming power."[16] But this "word" has no ethically commanding power. Therefore it may name, but it does not summon by name.

For the Jew, what is at stake in the relation between word and meaning is a memory and a name. Undertaking an assault on the link between word and meaning, the Nazis opposed the antiword of the antiworld to the Divine utterance that was the name of the Jew. In order to regain that utterance, we return to a consideration of the Jewish word opposite the Nazi antiword.

The Jewish Word Opposite the Nazi Anti-Word

The outcome of the strictly ontological, postmodern interest in language has been precisely an undermining of language, a tearing of word from meaning in an undermining of meaning; this tearing is essential to the Nazis' extermination of the Jewish people. Indeed, in the parlance of the Nazis, not a single Jew was murdered at Auschwitz; rather, "units" were "processed." In the Nazis we see that philosophical curiosity is no mere game playing: The tearing of word from meaning is more than a justification for the annihilation of the Jews—it is a definitive aspect of the Event. It is a tearing of husband from wife, of father from son, of human from human. It shows itself in the assertion from Elie Wiesel's *Night,* when the head of a block tells the young Eliezer, "Here, there are no fathers, no brothers, no friends. Everyone lives and dies for himself alone."[17] Which means: Words like *father* and *brother* signify nothing. The "signified," in the parlance of Derrida, "never manages to take shape," so that the human is no longer human and the "entity" now "lives" and "dies" ferociously alone.

The upshot of this Nazi position—which is perfectly in keeping with the postmodern position, whereby any word can mean anything—is manifested graphically and concretely one night in the Kingdom of Night, when, Sara Nomberg-Przytyk relates, "the stillness was broken by the screaming of children, as if a single scream had been torn out of hundreds of mouths, a single scream of fear and unusual pain, a scream repeated a thousand times in the single word 'Mama,' a scream that increased in intensity every second, enveloping the whole camp and every inmate. Our lips parted without our being conscious of what we were doing, and a scream of despair tore out of our throats, growing louder all the time."[18] What is the word that has its meaning torn from it by the roots, both by Nazi ideology and by the postmodern, Heideggerian thought that plays into its hands? It is the word *Mama,* a word transformed into a wordless scream. That scream is the sound of Auschwitz. It is the antiword that overshadows the postmodern preoccupation with language and discourse, which was already under way with the Nazi Martin Heidegger. It is the outcome of that preoccupation.

From Heidegger onward, the postmodern thinkers transform the word into an antiword by equating the word with being and thus fail to see the word as what Franz Rosenzweig calls "a bridge" between being and what exceeds being, a bridge made of *mitzvot,* of commandments. "The word is not part of the world," he writes, "it is the seal of man."[19] Which means: The word is not reducible to vibrations of air and vocal cords or language games or systems of signs that refer to nothing but each other. Rather, its very manifestation is the manifestation of the transcendent. The word is the seal of man not merely because man speaks; rather, man speaks because he is created in the image of the Holy One and speaks in response to the summons of the Holy One. That speaking is what the Nazis set out to silence.

Because the human being is created in the image of the Holy One, the human being is a breach of being. Hence, says Rabbi Schneur Zalman, "All things are subdivided into four categories—mineral, vegetable, animal, and man [or] 'speaker'—corresponding with the four letters of the blessed Name."[20] To the extent that philosophy equates the word with being and being with thought, as Heidegger does, it cannot get beyond the categories of mineral, vegetable, and animal. In its speculative, ontological form, then, philosophy is dehumanizing; thus philosophy plays unwittingly—or, in the case of Heidegger, altogether wittingly—into the hands of the National Socialist agenda to exterminate the G-d of Abraham in the extermination of the Jews. Here we realize that the ontological thinking of Western philosophy can make no more of the human being than a "highly evolved animal." "But the notion of development," Rosenzweig rightly points out, "deprives him [the human being] of the privilege of being human—a privilege which is also a duty. Evolution takes the place of man."[21] Therefore, both despite and because of its postmodern efforts, philosophy ultimately does not know what to make of language, because it does not know what to make of the human being. For philosophy is deaf to the word that announces the creation of the human being in the image and likeness of the Holy One.

And what is the word that eludes the philosophers of language and discourse? It is the word *atah,* the word "You," the very one swallowed up by the Same, by the counterfeit *I,* which stands at the center of ontological, postmodern thought. That is why philosophy, particularly in its postmodern garb, is dehumanizing. That is why it does not know what to make of the word or of the human being: Unable to see past the "I" that is in truth "nothing," the *ani* that is *ain*, it does not know what to make of *atah*.

"The word *atah*, You," explains Rabbi Schneur Zalman, "indicates all the letters from *Alef* to *Tav*, and the letter *Hey*, the five organs of verbal articulation, the source of the letters."[22] The five organs he refers to are the larynx, the palate, the tongue, the teeth, and the lips. Since the letter *hey* is an abbreviation of the Divine Name, we might also read the addition of the *hey* to the *alef* and the *tav* of *atah* as the addition of the Divine Presence to all the words made of all the letters, from *alef* to *tav*. The word *atah*, then—and not the I of "I think, therefore I am"—would be the seal of the human being, the trace of the Divine manifest in the word. The word *atah* is the word of the beginning that dispels the darkness that lurks over the face of the deep. It is not exactly the opposite of nothingness; rather, it is a category that is beyond the distinctions of being and nothingness. Just so, André Neher describes Abraham as "the inventor of the word," because Abraham is the first figure in the Bible to use the word *you:* Abraham said *at*, the feminine form of *atah*, to Sarah (Genesis 12:11).[23]

If we consider further this feminine form of "you," we find a striking possibility for interpreting the first four words of the Torah: *bereshit bara Elokim at*, "In the beginning G-d created the 'you'" (Genesis 1:1). Or: "In the beginning G-d created the letters from *alef* to *tav*, the stuff of the word, which is *at:* You" (cf. *Zohar* I, 15b). In the beginning G-d created the avenue through which we may enter into a relation to Him. For "in every You," as Martin Buber has said, "we address the eternal You."[24] The trace of the divine in my fellow human being is the You in my fellow human being. That is why "the You knows no system of coordinates."[25] Manifest in the face, to borrow from Lévinas, the You "is signification, and signification without context."[26] To be sure, the face is the origin of the word: The face speaks. It speaks by declaring to us, "I am a You." Thus, through the face the Holy One commands us to treat that human being with loving-kindness. Says Lévinas, "A face *enters* into our world from an absolutely foreign sphere, that is, precisely from an absolute."[27] *That* is the meaning of the Word that issues from the face.

Which is to say: The word *atah* that constitutes the face derives its meaning not from a system of signs or from a being that is under erasure, but from the Divine Presence that abides silently within the word, that abides in the silence of all tongues. The Nazis sought to impose on the

Jews the absence of any word or meaning, of any memory or name. And they did it with a sound and a fury signifying nothingness, with the roar of barking and bellowing, of flames and furnaces. They did it with the *raash* that is not only "noise" but is also an "earthquake," one in which the ground of meaning crumbles with the crumbling of the human being. The Hebrew word *raash* reveals to us the truth that when all we hear is noise, the earth shifts beneath our feet, and we plunge into the despair of word-lessness. This rumbling of the void echoes in the noise we create, as Wiesel suggests: "The world has become increasingly noisy. Society has never used so many means to tell, report, investigate, explain, comment, articulate, reveal, expose, and criticize; no generation has ever been more talkative—and no generation has managed to say less."[28] And no generation has had such trouble remembering names. For the din drowns out both the names and our memory of the names, a memory driven by a capacity for hearing the voices and the names of those who cry out from the ashes.

The opposite of this din is the word that abides in the *kol,* which trans-lates not only as "sound," as in the phrase *kol shofar* or "the sound of the shofar" (for example, Psalms 98:6), but also as "voice": From the stand-point of Jewish thought every sound is a voice because every thing *is* a word. And within every word there is a Voice other than our own, as Meir ibn Gabbai has taught: "There is no uttered word that does not have a 'Voice.'"[29] Laden with meaning and message, the *kol* that is both sound and voice cries out for a word, a thought, and a deed in response to the Di-vine word that speaks in the silence that abides within every word uttered. Abiding within the word, the Voice within the silence—the Voice in the mode of silence—speaks from the depths of the cosmos, as Neher has said: "The silence of the cosmos is simply the most eloquent form of the Divine revelation."[30] Silence, therefore, is not the absence of sound any more than darkness is the absence of light. In the daily prayers we bear witness to G-d who *yotser or uvore choshekh,* who "forms light and creates darkness." This is understood to mean that G-d forms light out of the substance of Himself and creates darkness out of nothing—or perhaps out of nothingness—as a distinct reality. In a parallel manner, G-d forms the word out of the sub-stance of Himself and creates silence out of nothing.

Hence the Talmudic teaching of the sage Rabbi Sheshet: "G-d's appear-ance is announced by a deep silence" (*Berakhot* 58a). That deep silence is what the Nazis would transform into a blank silence by tearing the meaning from the word and the name from the human being. In the post-Holocaust endeavor to restore meaning to the word and the name to the Jew, what is needed is a word that would oppose the Nazi-imposed silence.

The Word Opposed To Silence

"If language and silence were not in conflict," Elie Wiesel has said, "language would not be poetic, literary, or truthful."[31] The poetry of language unfolds whenever we strive to impart extraordinary meaning to ordinary words. It is about releasing the divine sparks of meaning from words. It is about attending to the voice of silence.[32] It is about the relation between word and silence, between word and meaning, when words overflow with meaning. Meaning is not in the word—it is in the silence that is curled up in the word, the silence that summons another word and another silence. More than the word can contain, meaning arises from a realm of "speech before speech," as Rosenzweig states it, "the speech of the unspoken, the unspeakable."[33] Hence meaning belongs to silence: The word is uttered and defined while the silence that belongs to the word opens up its mystical dimension of meaning, which is inexhaustible.

Does this mean that one should refrain from speaking? Not at all. But it does mean that we must be extremely careful with words.[34] For the same reason that the Lubavitcher Rebbe, Rabbi Menachem Mendel Schneerson, teaches that our aim in life is to transform darkness into light[35]—that is, to release the light from darkness—so is it our aim to transform silence into utterance, not to hide or fill the silence, however, but to transmit it, so that we "somehow charge words with silence," as Wiesel puts it.[36] "If I use words," he says, "it is not to change silence but to complete it."[37] For similar reasons Rosenzweig asserts that he who has not written poetry is not human.[38] Here, as everywhere, the conflict between word and silence is one in which each needs the other in order to be what it is, as the white fire needs the black fire, as man needs G-d and G-d needs man—as the soul needs its name. If the word should utterly overwhelm the silence, we would have nothing but noise, nothing but the sound of the ground crumbling from under our feet; if silence should completely swallow up the word, we would be turned over to sheer nothingness.

Truth lies in a tension, in an embrace, between the word and silence; it is made of the conflict Wiesel refers to above. It lies in the silence of all tongues. Because the assault on the Name in the Holocaust Kingdom entailed the forced imposition of a radical silence, the tension of truth was lost, so that the two denizens of that realm, the Nazi and the Jew, stood in a relation that negated truth. For the Nazi, nothing was true and everything was permitted; for the Jew, everything was true and nothing was permitted. One undertook an assault on the Name, and the other was rendered nameless. The silence of the concentrationary universe, therefore, is marked by a namelessness that characterizes an absolute isolation from the word. Hence it is a condition of having no name, of hearing no one calling your name, and having trouble remembering your name. The Hebrew verb *nadam* applies: It means "to be silenced" or "rendered mute" as well as "to be destroyed." The soul cannot abide in silence, because the soul cannot live without a name.

To be rendered nameless, moreover, is to be rendered mute, as one can see upon consideration of another Hebrew word: It is *ilem,* which means both "silent" and "mute." In this word we find a silence that is the opposite of the eloquence of the Divine silence. It appears, for instance, in the psalms of King David, where he gives voice to this very silence, crying, *neelamti dumiyah,* "I was mute, silent" or "I was struck dumb with silence" (Psalms 39:3).[39] In his account of the Nazi assault on the Name and the soul of Israel written in the Warsaw Ghetto, Rabbi Kalonymos Kalmish Shapira explains the meaning of *ilem* by describing it as a silence that overcomes a person "so broken and crushed that he has nothing to say; who does not appreciate or understand what is happening to him; who does not possess the faculties with which to assess or assimilate his experiences; who no longer has the mind or the heart with which to incorporate the experience. For him, silence is not a choice; his is the muteness of one incapable of speech."[40] Because this muteness is the muteness of a human being, however, within it lies hidden an outcry. Indeed, the muteness itself "stands erect," as Rabbi Shapira says,[41] like Joseph's "sheaf," which, in a play on *ilem,* is *alumah.* The muteness of *ilem* is more than deafening; it is defiant and accusing. It announces a certain dialectic between word and silence.

One finds an illustration of this dialectic in the Hebrew language: While *sheket* means "silence," "hush," "quiet," or "calm" and implies a certain peacefulness, *shatkan* is more like an imposed "silence." The latter's cognate *shitek,* for instance, means "to silence," as well as "to paralyze." One implication of what is revealed in this word becomes clear in an example from a novel by Elie Wiesel, in which his main character, the Russian Jewish poet Paltiel Kossover, collides with a paralyzing silence. Listen to Paltiel, as he speaks from the solitary confinement of a Soviet prison cell:

> As an adolescent in Liyanov, I yearned for silence…. I begged G-d to find me a mute master who would impart his truth—and his words—to me wordlessly. I spent hours with a disciple of the Hasidic school of Worke, whose rebbe had turned silence into a method…. Later, with Rebbe Mendel-the-Taciturn, we tried to transcend language. At midnight, our eyes closed, our faces turned toward Jerusalem and its fiery sanctuary, we listened to the song of its silence—a celestial silence and yet terrible silence in which both voices and moments attain immortality. No master had ever warned me that silence could be nefarious, evil…. No master had ever told me that silence could become a prison.[42]

Here we recall the insights from Lévinas, in his discussions of the "there is." With the appearance of the "there is," he writes, "the absence of everything returns to us as a presence, as the place where the bottom has dropped out of everything, an atmospheric density, a plenitude of the void, or the murmur of silence."[43] That "murmur" of silence is a death sentence—or worse, as Paltiel discovered: It is a being sentenced to languish under the gaze of Dumah, the angel who silently presides over the dead, for whom death is not the last but is continually the last. Like the horror of the "there is," silence means: There is no getting it over with, a point emphasized in the previous chapter.

A slogan associated with a famous horror film comes to mind; it speaks to what is truly horrifying to any human being. It is: "In space no one can hear you scream." To ponder this line is to feel the horror grow: In space not only does no one hear you scream—in space you hear no one scream. Not even yourself. In space the silence that overwhelms you is the silence not only of the cosmos and your muteness, but also of your being *charash,* that is, "silent" as in "deaf." Here, to recall the words of Paltiel Kossover, silence "acts on the imagination and sets it on fire. It acts on the soul and fills it with night and death."[44] Thus we are reminded once more that just as darkness is not the absence of light, silence is not the absence of sound. And we are reminded once more that death is not the absence of life. A passage from Josef Bor's *Terezín Requiem,* a novel about the camp at Theresienstadt, drives this point home:

> The silence had penetrated here, Schächter realized, from outside, from above, from everywhere, and now it spread throughout the room, strident and imperative; it overwhelmed everything, froze the walls into dumbness, maimed the people; not even a quiver of air moved here now. The murmur is silenced, the hum of everyday life, which at other times flows everywhere, in the streets, in the house, even in yourself, though you are solitary. The walls receive it and return an echo, the air is tremulous and warm with it, there is so much of it everywhere, and yet you never notice it. As you never feel the air you breathe. And suddenly the hum has ceased. At first you don't even realize that something has happened. There is only a chill somewhere in the marrow of your bones, as though the coldness of the dark night had touched you. As though the breath of death itself had wafted over you.... Then suddenly you are aware of the silence.[45]

Like darkness and death, silence is a veil that hides the light, the life, and the word of G-d. In order to make manifest the holiness of the Holy One, we must transform silence into word—not by "filling" the silence with words, words, words, but by making the silence itself speak. But how?

Lévinas suggests one way. "In *giving,*" he says, "silence speaks,"[46] and in Hebrew "giving," *hav,* is the root of "love" or *ahavah.* Love leads us to write poetry because love improves our hearing; like prayer, poetry is every bit as much about listening as it is about speaking. To "get" the poem is to hear the eloquence of the silence that it calls forth through its manifestation of love. It is not for nothing that when we pray aloud the *kriat Shema*—the "recitation" or "calling out" of the "Hear, O Israel" prayer in the morning service—the Shema is both preceded and followed by forms of the word for *love:* having chosen us with love, G-d cries out to us that if we love, we shall hear, and if we hear, we shall love. For love is the giving, the *hav,* that makes silence speak. Once again we find an illustration of this insight in Wiesel's *The Testament,* where Paltiel's son Grisha gives himself over to a muteness that cries out louder than any word. For his father, silence was a prison. For Grisha, silence was a living sanctuary, a sanctuary over which he kept a most stern vigil: In order to protect his father at a moment when his father was threatened—when the KGB wanted him to "talk"—Grisha bit off his own tongue.[47] For Grisha, silence was the language of prayer and the substance of language.[48]

Before we stand to pray in silence, we utter the words that King David cried out: *Adonai sfatai tiftach ufi yagid tehilatekha,* "Lord open my lips, and my mouth shall declare Your praise" (Psalms 51:17). This prayer that precedes the prayer calls upon G-d to do more than open our lips: We ask G-d to open up our "languages," for the word *safah* also means "language." Which "language"? Both the language of our own utterance and the language of the Divine silence, our two "lips," so to speak. The one in prayer asks G-d to help him make heard the "silent Voice" that Rabbi Eleazar describes as "the supernal Voice from which all other voices proceed" (*Zohar* I, 210a). What is the silent Voice from which all other voices proceed? It is the Voice that utters our name in the creation of our soul. It is the Voice that the Nazis set out to silence.

When in gematria, or numerological interpretation, we sometimes calculate the numerical value of a word and then add the *kollel* or one more, it is not simply one for the word itself, as some suppose; no, it is one for the silence, within the word. It indicates, as Matityahu Glazerson points out, that the root of the word is still in the upper realms, in the silent realms.[49] And the upper realms, according to Chayyim Vital, are the inner realms (see *Shaarei Kedushah,* Part 3, Gate 1). The silence, therefore, resides in every word, indeed, in every letter. It is the silence that makes possible the word as *utterance.* And it is the word that makes possible a world in which words are tied to meaning and a memory is tied to a name. In order to attain that world, however, there must be a mending of the world after the Nazi destruction of the world: a *teshuvah* and *tikkun olam.*

Teshuvah, which is "return" and not "repentance," is a return to the Name effected through a return to my name. And the return to my name—to the name about which the Angel of Death questions me—is a return to the Torah of which I am made. Only then can a Jew bring about the *tikkun olam* that will return to the world a place for the Name as well as a place for the Angel of Death. For the Angel of Death is the emissary of the Name who asks me about a fundamental relation between my memory and my name: Do you remember your name? Which is to ask: Do you remember the Torah that was placed in your care and to which you must answer by name? *Tikkun olam,* then, entails a return to one's name and to the Divine Name, which is a return to Torah. It is not merely a matter of being ethical or of being nice. It entails a return to the *mitsvot* commanded by *HaShem,* in an affirmation of the absolute sanction underlying the Divine commandment. For our mission is precisely to mend the world through Torah—or, what amounts to the same thing—through a return of meaning to the word, which is a return of G-d's presence—of G-d's Name—to the world.

The Name That Summons a Name

In his book on the Chasidim, Milton Aron relates a story about Levi Yitzhak of Berditchev and what transpired upon his return home after studying with Rabbi Dov Ber, the renowned Maggid of Mezeritch. On the day of his homecoming he was seated at the table for the evening meal, when his father-in-law said to him, "So tell me: Did you learn anything special from the Great Maggid?"

"I have learned," replied the young Levi Yitzhak, "that G-d is in the world."

"But everyone knows that," retorted his father-in-law, who then called over their maid and asked her whether G-d is in the world.

"Yes," she answered without hesitation.

"You see," the father-in-law said triumphantly.

"She says," the inspired Levi Yitzhak shot back, "but I know."[50]

From a Jewish standpoint, to know that G-d is in the world is to know that we must engage in a constant examination of our soul in a *cheshbon hanefesh,* a taking stock of the soul, through which we may wrestle our name from the Angel of Death. Indeed, if he knows nothing else, the Jew knows that, unless he engages in some kind of self-examination, not only is his life without meaning, but it is impossible to live in search of any meaning. For the post-Holocaust Jew, returning meaning to the word becomes as essential to life as is eating or breathing. In the post-Holocaust era many Jews sense the risk of incurring grave dangers in wrestling with the Angel; that may be why we are so reluctant to do so. Yet Jews also sense something of great import at stake in a response to the summons. The Jews' stake in their testimony goes beyond anything so shallow as "self-esteem" or "self-affirmation"; it concerns a communal salvation. Which is to say: The drive to return meaning to the word is a drive to recover the memory and the name of the human being within a human community.

The standard for this *tikkun olam* after the Event is set from within the Event, when Holocaust diarists struggled to return meaning to the word in the midst of the assault on word and meaning. We see, for example, that the very language used by the Holocaust diarists in their diaries harbors a summons to respond to a holiness and a humanity that cries out to their souls and through their souls. Their testimonies constitute an address that attests to this being addressed. Because the word lives within and imparts meaning to a community, the Jews who pursue the word do so in a response to a community, either implicitly or explicitly. And for a people that understands the world to be sustained by the word of G-d, their testimony strives to become part of that sustaining utterance. As we speak, so is the Holy One either muted or made heard, and human life is either wounded or made whole.

According to Jewish tradition, words decide not only truth but also life and death. "For everything is in the word," Elie Wiesel expresses this mystical teaching. "It is enough to arrange certain syllables, to form certain sentences, speak certain words according to a defined rhythm, to be able to lay claim to celestial powers and master them."[51] Equally important to the Jewish diarist writing at the risk of his or her life is the process of engaging human life and meaning that transpires in the moment of their testimony. Engaging life and meaning is precisely what it means to sustain Creation. For the authors of the Holocaust testimonies, this means that by engaging the word they may engage the life of the soul that was threatened at every turn. Like the workers who, according to the Talmud, would occasionally descend into the Holy of Holies in *tevot,* or boxes, to make repairs (see *Midot* 37a), these authors also descend in *tevot,* which also means "words," not just into death but into the holy, where they struggle to retrieve meaning in the word and a memory of the name. If the summons to write comes from within, its voice is heard from beyond. Who calls? It is the very word, the very Name, under assault. And it calls the witness by name.

In an entry dated 28 February 1941, Emmanuel Ringelblum notes, "The drive to write down one's memoirs is powerful: Even young people in labor camps do it."[52] That this writing issues from a *drive* to write may suggest that the impetus arises from some innate aspect of human nature. Having noted this internal aspect of bearing witness to the event from the midst of the event, however, we must not psychologize the phenomenon of writing and jump to the conclusion that it is reducible to a natural drive to meet a natural need. To be sure, if the drive for survival is "natural," bearing this witness is "unnatural," as it is done at the risk of the witness's life. Upon further examination of the diarist's assessment of what drives him to write, we find that it is rooted more in moral obligation than in natural need. This is what makes the writing of the diary a response to the summons of the *Name:* Unlike the satisfaction of a personal need, meeting a moral obligation lies in a certain relation to others in answer to the One who commands that relation, whether the witness acknowledges the source of the summons or not.

The Westerbork inmate Philip Mechanicus, for example, realizes that he must "record the daily happenings for those who in time to come will want to get an idea of what went on here. So I have a duty to go on with my writing."[53] I have a *duty:* Writing the Holocaust diary, the one summoned by the Name is summoned not as a historian or a journalist or even as a victim, but as a human being who stands in a moral relation to other human beings and who, through that relation, must answer to his own name. Which is to say: Meeting that moral obligation under such circumstances, he wrestles a name from the Angel. If the diarist is not free to refrain from writing, this is not due to some inner psychological necessity but to a moral imperative that the writer encounters both outside himself and within himself, despite himself: It is inscribed by the Name within his name. "All my inwardness," in the words of Lévinas, "is invested in the form of a despite-me, for-another,"[54] and this inwardness is the soul, which is "the other in me," the name uttered by the Name.[55] Far from being the manifestation of a natural drive, a psychological need, or a cultural phenomenon, this testimony is the manifestation of a soul that seeks its life through a response to another soul, in the light of a higher responsibility for what there is to hold dear.

"Remember the yoke of responsibility that rests upon you," said Rabbi Shapira. "All the worlds, even the fate of G-d's holiness in this world, depend on you."[56] The summons of the Name is the summons of the Good Name, which is the summons of the Good. It lays claim to the witness as a human being whose humanity lies in being for the other, in answering to the other, both as a person and as the One who is the Good. If the witness has no choice in his or her testimony, it is because the Good, in the words of Lévinas, "is not the object of a choice, for it has taken possession of the subject before the subject had the time—that is, the distance—necessary for choice. There is indeed no subjection more complete than this possession by the Good, this election."[57] Hence, answering the summons of the Name, the Jewish witness discovers what it means to be one who is chosen by name: It means engaging the Angel of Death.

Diary writers such as Emil Dorian[58] and Yitzhak Katznelson[59] point out that the Nazis had made writing diaries and other Jewish testimonies illegal. And now we see why: The Nazis sought to destroy not only the body of Israel but also the soul of the Jew, not only the memory and the name of the Jew but also the memory and the Name. In order to destroy the name of which the soul is made, they had to destroy the Good; and in order to destroy the Good, they had to destroy the response to the summons of the Name. For it is precisely in the midst of this response that the voice of the *HaShem* is heard. "The glory of the Infinite," as Lévinas has said, "reveals itself through what it is capable of doing in the witness."[60] And this is just what the Nazis do not want revealed.

The assault on the testimony, then, is part of a metaphysical assault on the Good, on the Holy, and on the Truth; in a word, it is part of the assault on G-d. As Emil Fackenheim states it, the Nazi, like Amalek of old, "singles out Israel for attack *because* Israel is singled out by G-d for a covenant, his aim being to destroy the covenant as he destroys Israel."[61] Therefore, in the case of the *Jewish* witness to the mass murder, the sense of ethical obligation has a metaphysical aspect; written in an ethical response to others, it harbors a metaphysical response to G-d, an implicit affirmation of the covenant with the Divine through the response to the human. Indeed, from a Jewish standpoint, the path to the Divine always leads through the human. What this means for the Jewish writer and his writing Lévinas makes clear when he explains that the other human being

> is situated in a dimension of height, in the ideal, the Divine, and through my relation to the Other, I am in touch with G-d. The moral relation therefore reunites both self-consciousness and consciousness of G-d. Ethics is not the corollary of the vision of G-d, it is that very vision. Ethics is an optic, such that everything I know of G-d and everything I can hear of His word and reasonably say to Him must find an ethical expression. In the Holy Ark from which the voice of G-d is heard by Moses, there are only the tablets of the Law…. The attributes of G-d are given not in the indicative, but in the imperative. The knowledge of G-d comes to us like a commandment, like a *Mitzvah*. To know G-d is to know what must be done.[62]

This aspect of the moral obligation underlying the witness's sense of duty takes us beyond what we may have thought we understood in Ringelblum's mention of the drive to write or Mechanicus's invocation of the duty to write. More than a matter of feeling a need or even sensing a duty, the writing of the diary arises from a condition of being commanded to write. If Zelig Kalmanovitch, a diarist of the Vilna Ghetto, declares, "Verily, each day should be recorded,"[63] it is because the day itself is constituted by the commandment; the day itself is inscribed with the Name. G-d enters the day through the commandment, and through the day He enters into history. Thus the obligation to answer the commandment by answering others situates the Jew in a position of answerability to history.

"It is difficult to hold a pen," says Chaim Kaplan, "to concentrate one's thoughts. But a strange idea has stuck in my head since the war broke out—that it is a duty I must perform."[64] In war we are forced to determine why we live, why we die, and why we kill; in war we are forced to attest to what transcends life and therefore to what makes life meaningful. War not only makes history—it unmakes it, and so it constitutes a breach or a fracture in the fabric of Being. But, as Lévinas argues, the human being is also a "fracture in Being which produces the act of giving with hands which are full, in place of fighting and pillaging. This is where the idea of being chosen comes from."[65] In Kaplan's case, a hand has taken hold of him, and so his hand takes hold of a pen; he has been given a task, and so he engages in an act of giving, which is an act of writing, that opposes the outbreak of war. Indeed, his writing is the only thing he has left to give. And if he has a sense of anything, he has a sense of being chosen.

Chosen for what? For a response to this rupture in history before the G-d of history. Hence on 16 January 1940 he writes, "Anyone who keeps such a record [as this] endangers his life, but this does not frighten me. I sense within me the magnitude of this hour, and my responsibility toward it, and I have an inner awareness that I am fulfilling a national obligation, a historic obligation that I am not free to relinquish."[66] And this responsibility rules the writer and his writing to the very end. On 26 July 1942, just a week before his final entry, he notes:

> Some of my friends and acquaintances who know the secret of my diary urge me, in their despair, to stop writing. "Why? For what purpose? Will you live to see it published? Will these words of yours reach the ears of future generations? How?" …And yet in spite of it all I refuse to listen to them. I feel that continuing this diary to the very end of my physical and spiritual strength is a historical mission which must not be abandoned. My mind is still clear, my need to record unstilled, though it is now five days since any real food has passed my lips. Therefore I will not silence my diary![67]

To silence the diary would be to succumb to the silence that, in the words of André Neher, becomes "a spokesman for the invincible Nothingness."[68] The diarist, on the other hand, becomes the spokesman for the Presence that opposes nothingness. Though it is written in silence, the diary is opposed to silence, opposed to the indifference that underlies death in war and despair in the human being.

Notice further that the issue of whether the testimony of the witness will see the light of day or will reach an ear is irrelevant. Why? Because this testimony is summoned by the Name that names and implicates the diarist from on high, in the mode of commandment: There is One who looks over the shoulder of the diarists even in the dead of night as they pen their precarious lines, despite themselves. Thus many diarists speak if only to note that they cannot speak. On 22 September 1942, for example, Kalmanovitch writes, "A peculiar thing: All my thoughts have vanished. I forgot what I wanted to record."[69] It is not, however, merely a matter of forgetfulness, as a statement from Menahem Kon's diary indicates: "No pen can write down what the eye saw, no phantasy can picture it. Still in a nightmare, we find it very hard to write at all.... But I shall try."[70] The difficulty in recording what was seen lies not just in the horror of the spectacle or in the limits of the imagination but in the divorce between word and meaning. This is what makes it a response not only to suffering but also to the word that seeks a return to meaning in the return of meaning to life.

This writing to record an incapacity to write is a recurring motif in the Romanian diary of Emil Dorian. On 20 December 1940, for example, he writes, "For weeks I haven't touched this notebook.... A psychological paralysis when faced with events; fear of misinterpretation, or at least of misconstruction of my notes; the feeling that any kind of writing is useless; the moral and intellectual hibernation into which I have sunk—all this kept me from these pages."[71] And on 31 March 1944: "Again, after several weeks' pause, I am returning to these pages, with some feeling of weariness and uselessness."[72] What is most striking in this testimony is not why he stopped but why he did *not* stop. In the face of such paralysis, weariness, and uselessness, the answer can only be that writing the diary is the key to sustaining a life that would otherwise succumb to the void of the antiworld. Even if it appears to be useless, answering the summons of the Name is the only thing that can overcome the writer's sense of uselessness, because it is the one thing that enables him to hear the summons to write. Paralysis sets in where the answering leaves off. And only the summons of the Name can penetrate the *rigor mortis* of paralysis.

For the summons of the Name is the summons of life, a summons to return meaning to the word and memory to the man that arises in opposition to death. This point becomes graphically clear when we read the entry dated 21 July 1942 in the Warsaw Ghetto diary of Janusz Korczak: "Ten o'clock. Shots: two, several, two, one, several. Perhaps it is my own badly blacked out window. But I do not stop writing. On the contrary: It sharpens (a single shot) the thought."[73] The shot that takes a life fuels the writing that would recover a life. As the rifle fires its bullets, the pen inscribes its words; the one metes out death, while the other seeks out life. Even when he has nothing to say, for the diarist the word is a refuge. As in the Tent of Testimony, in the word of testimony the witness finds meaning.

Entering the Word, Assuming a Name

To say that for the witness caught in the midst of the maelstrom the word is a refuge is not to say that it is merely a realm into which he flees from death and despair; rather, as we have suggested, it is a realm in which he seeks life and meaning, a memory and a name. In a word, he seeks a voice. For the word *memory,* or *zikaron,* Rabbi Yitzchak Ginsburgh reminds us, means "a source of speech."[74] Unlike witnesses who testify after the fact in the contexts of a world, the diarist makes an *entry* in the midst of the antiworld and thereby *enters into* a place and there seeks to give voice to word and meaning. Which is to say: The soul seeks its name.

Elie Wiesel voices this seeking in his novel *Twilight,* where his character Abraham says, "Please try to understand: The Word is everything. Through the Word we elevate ourselves or debase ourselves. It is refuge for the man in exile, and exile for the righteous. How would we pray without it? How would we live without it?"[75] Wiesel's question concerning prayer suggests that the process of returning meaning to the word is rather like restoring to the word the characteristics of prayer. Recall in this connection the point made about prayer in chapter 2: The Hebrew word for "prayer," *tefillah,* is a cognate of *naftulim,* which means "struggles" or "wrestlings," so that here prayer is not a request submitted for oneself but an encounter between a memory and the Name, as when Jacob wrestled with the Angel. In the diary written along the edge of annihilation, the Jew struggles to restore meaning to the word by himself becoming a sign of the depth and the dearness of another and thereby take on significance—a memory and a name.

A teaching from the Chasidic master Rabbi Nachman of Breslov may help here: "However low you fall, you still have the faculty of speech. You should use it! Speak words of truth: words of Torah, words of prayer and the fear of Heaven. You should speak to G-d. Speak also to your friend, and especially to your teacher. The power of speech is such that at all times it enables you to remind yourself of the closeness to G-d, and so to bring strength to yourself, even in the places which seem furthest from holiness."[76] For the People of the Book, the medium is indeed the message: Writing their book, they seek the life summoned through the Book. It may be that Rabbi Nachman did not realize how far a place can be from the place of holiness. But he did articulate what sort of refuge the word may have provided for these witnesses.

As it assumes some of the characteristics of prayer, the word of testimony becomes not only the means of address but also a presence to be addressed. Here we see a deeper sense in which the process of writing is also a hearing: The word itself listens and responds to the witness, lending an ear in a world grown deaf. How does the word accomplish this? By positing an attentive presence opposite the voice of the diarist. Suddenly, as the witness puts her hand to the page, the indifferent silence of the blank piece of paper becomes the responsive silence of a listener: It becomes a *you.* "How I need you, my dear diary," writes the Romanian teenager Mirjam Korber. "But it is so hard to release the words, not only orally, but also when forcing the hand to write."[77] And Chaim Kaplan declares, "This journal is my life, my friend and ally. I would be lost without it. I pour my innermost thoughts and feelings into it, and this brings relief."[78] In Kaplan's entries we see quite clearly that the process of writing the diary is an integral part of the process of entering into a relation that may sustain a presence in a world dominated by absence. The diary is not just an outlet—it is his life; the diary is not just a document—it is his friend. Which is to say: It calls him by name.

Therefore, if the diary is written in order to meet a responsibility to the human community, the diarist incurs a responsibility to the diary itself. Once he views the diary as the presence of another, the diarist incurs a debt to that presence. Consider, for example, this entry from the first pages of Anne Frank's diary: "Now I come to the root of the matter, the reason for my starting a diary: It is that I have no such real friend.... I want this diary to be my friend, and I shall call my friend Kitty."[79] And: "In the end I always come back to my diary. That is where I start and finish, because

Kitty is always patient. I'll promise her that I shall persevere."[80] Presenting itself as an interlocutor, the diary represents a center, a place from which to start and finish, and that center is made of the word. The word can constitute such a center for two reasons: First, it implies the presence of another to whom it is addressed; second, it is the site where meaning becomes an issue. As the witness enters into the word of testimony, the refuge of the word lies in the meaning created in a world where meaning is undergoing a constant collapse. In these entries from Anne Frank's diary, meaning comes to bear through the promise to persevere. Why? Because the promise opens up the horizon of a future and defines a direction from which meaning may itself be defined. It is a *going forth*.

This prospect of going forth is an entry into the word in such a way as to make the word itself both the object and the subject of the movement. In this spirit Emil Dorian, for instance, not only writes in his diary but in his diary writes about writing. There the word presents itself not only as a responsive presence but also as a subject to be addressed and pursued. "All is not lost," he asserts, "while the hope of writing a poem is still alive."[81] As when Betsalel fashioned the Ark of Testimony in the wilderness (Exodus 37:1), so Dorian and other witnesses introduce the word to their wilderness. In keeping with a tradition that goes back to Betsalel,[82] Dorian is an imitator of the Creator: Like the Creator, he combines the letters and invokes a word that may introduce some order to a world returned to the *tohu vavohu* of chaos and darkness, even if he goes no further than to declare that the word comes hard. As hard as it may come, it comes nevertheless. For Dorian, as for many other diarists, this *nevertheless* constitutes the entry into the word of testimony. It makes the word of testimony into the subject matter of the testimony itself. And that is how the word regains its link to meaning and thus becomes a means of resisting death and affirming life, a means that opens up when all such means have been eliminated.

Thus, like the bullet that sharpened Korczak's thought, the oppression of Jewish life sharpens Dorian's resolve to preserve that life through the preservation of the Jewish word. This effort also becomes part of his diary, as we see when on 20 October 1941 he writes, "In the last two months I managed to do something I would not have thought possible: I worked on, and almost completed, the anthology of Yiddish poets.... The harder the blows rained on Jews, the more passionately I plunged into work reaffirming the permanence of Jewish contributions to art."[83] Thus the diary creates a place where the witness may affirm the importance of this reaffirmation of Jewish life and of this responsibility to Jewish life. The word of testimony, then, includes a commentary not only on death and destruction but also on the means of resisting death and destruction. Here we realize that the *you* addressed in the diary is not a "projection of the psyche" or some other psychological phenomenon—it is life itself. "The spirit must be kept alive if you are to write, and you must write if the spirit is to stay alive," says Dorian.[84] And within his voice we hear the voice of the Name that calls us by name.

As the voice of one who struggles to answer to the Name, the diary is a manifestation of the soul's refusal to be silenced, in spite of itself. If there is an inner depth from which a refusal to go on arises, there is a deeper depth, one that comes not just from within but from beyond, that impels the writer to write. The depth that extends beyond is called word or spirit: The spirit that moved over the face of the deep moves through the word. And the darkness that is the deep itself? According to the Rabbi Berekhyah, it is "the Angel of Death, who darkened the face of Creation" (*Tanchuma Yashev* 4). And so the death that was obliterated, as we saw in the previous chapter, is reestablished as the Name calls us by name. This calling finds its voice in the utterance of the soul; when this utterance fails, so does the sense of reality of self and world, as we see when Dorian writes, "Days of an eerie sensation, like floating above the ground. My whole life, it seems, belongs to someone else. I write as if in a dream. I am not absent from reality, but remote, and this tints all levels of existence with a strange hue of unreality."[85] This disconnectedness from the ground, this distance from the real, is the result of a breach in the man's name. And it distinguishes the endeavor to return meaning to the word and the man to the world.

To be sure, the effort to assume a name exists precisely because this breach exists. "I feel nothing," says Elik Rivosh from the depths of the Riga Ghetto, "neither in my body nor in my soul—I am like a piece of wood."[86] If he is to find a way to return himself to the name that is his body and soul, then he must find a way to articulate the breach. Writing his diary as Elik Rivosh, he answers to a summons that would return meaning to the word and a name to the soul. For the writer of the Holocaust diary, then, the process of writing is a process of answering in which the soul that finds a voice also finds a place. For the One who calls is called *HaMakom,* the Place. Far more than a commentary on the day or a record of events, the diarist's process of writing is a remembering of the elements of life that make dwelling possible. Thus Hanna Levy-Hass notes in her Bergen-Belsen diary that composing the texts of songs brings her closer to the memory of home, closer to the dwelling place that opposes Bergen-Belsen.[87] Here one will note the link between text and home, or the appearance of a text that may for a time replace the home. And the Holocaust diary is just such a text, for it is a text that reconnects word with meaning, and a name with the Name. "Is it possible to consecrate G-d's name in a manner divorced from life itself?" asks Hannah Senesh during her time away from her Hungarian home. "Is there anything more holy than life itself?"[88] Her question is, of course, rhetorical. And it is altogether Jewish.

If the diary is the form of resistance to death that we have claimed it to be, it is much like the resistance that Fackenheim describes when he notes, "German resistance, such as it was, had to discover a true self to be respected. The Jewish resistance had to *recreate* Jewish selfhood and self-respect.... Once again the categories 'willpower' and 'internal desire' seem inadequate. Once again we have touched an Ultimate."[89] Willpower and internal desire are adequate to human endeavor only when the human being has a dwelling place within which and from which he may proceed, and the German resistors had such a place: They were not removed from their homes, where mothers, fathers, and children were still mothers, fathers, and children. Despite their removal from a place in the world, on the other hand, the Jews found ways to recreate a place and with it a relation to the Place, or the *Makom,* that is the Name. And a primary means of creating such a place lay in answering by name to the Name.

In this answering to the Name the witness encounters spirit or *ruach.* "The dimension of *ruach,*" André Neher elaborates on this notion, "goes beyond that of physical bodies, so that it does not seize them in their localization or individualization but in their communication. In possessing the *ruach,* man has not acquired *one* life, but life itself. The *ruach* is the very spirit of life. As soon as that spirit encounters another life, it communicates with it."[90] And in that communication, meaning is returned to the word. The diarist's communication with life is a manifestation of his encounter with spirit, so that the inwardness of the diarist engaged in his testimony is not his alone: It is an inwardness for another that arises in a response to Another. The diary, then, is no mere system of signs but is rather a sign of the Name sought in the midst of the assault on the Name.

It is not just Hillel Seidman, then, who cries out in the diary but the very presence of the Name that cuts through the diary, through its very writing process, that cries, "Jews! Don't allow yourselves to be broken and scattered! Don't succumb to the darkness of despair! Drink deeply to life. To life! Jews, to life!"[91] We can see, moreover, how deep runs the identity of the writer with his writing when we recall Seidman's comment on the suicide of Adam Czerniakow, head of the Warsaw Ghetto Jewish Council: "He left behind no last will or testament. No farewell letter. Only his notebook lying open on his writing table."[92] In his introduction to the English edition of Czerniakow's diary, Israel Gutman notes, "It has been reported that after Czerniakow made the last entry in his diary on July 23, 1942, he left a note to the effect that the SS wanted him to kill the children with his own hands."[93] Signing his name to this last utterance, Czerniakow answered by name to the Name.

How is Czerniakow's suicide related to Seidman's summons for Jews to live? In this way: Both are grounded in the affirmation of life that constitutes the substance of their diaries. Seidman calls upon Jews not only to survive the death and destruction around them but also to embrace the dearness of life *despite* that death and in a refusal to participate in that destruction. Similarly, Czerniakow's suicide is not a rejection of life; it is a refusal to take part in the extermination of life. Where does the word find meaning and the memory a name in this suicide? In Czerniakow's joining his life and his soul to the lives of the children, and thereby to the Jewish future—or to the obliteration of it. The last act of his life, then, makes his life into a commentary on his diary, not the other way around. And so his diary becomes not merely a private record of an individual's soul but a part of life's answering to life. It lies open on his desk—*open* to the people whose name is Israel.

Beyond the sum of individuals, the Jewish people embody the spirit of G-d; the Zohar, we recall, refers to the Community of Israel as the *Shekhinah,* or the Indwelling Presence of the Holy One (see *Zohar* II, 98a). Among the diarists in whom this consciousness of the people as an embodiment of the Name is most pronounced is Yitzhak Katznelson. In his entry for 14 September 1943, for example, he writes, "The blood of the seven million cries out from within me. Where are they? The cry of the whole of my murdered people cries out into the void of this empty, wicked world."[94] Here we come to a startling realization: The life, *the very Name,* is in the blood. Just so, the Name speaks through the Jewish blood that calls out from the earth and pours into the pages of Avraham Tory's diary from the Kovno Ghetto. Commenting on a list of the victims of an *Aktion,* he writes, "From each line, and from each name…the spilled Jewish blood cries for revenge; the memory of Amalek shall be blotted out from under G-d's sky. The people of Israel shall live forever, until the end of all generations."[95] Tory's mention of Amalek is a paraphrase of Exodus 17:14, and in this allusion to Israel's biblical past he makes a point about Israel's future. Both are gathered into the entry dated 6 April 1943. This gathering of the time and the eternity of Israel into the written utterance of the word is what distinguishes this writing as an answering to the Name.

"Write, write, children," a family in the Vilna Ghetto urges Yitskhok Rudashevski and his friends. "It is good this way."[96] And so Rudashevski answers to this calling of the community by bearing witness through his diary, with an eye both toward a tradition and toward a future joined together in this writing. "The ghetto folklore," he says, "which is amazingly cultivated in blood and which is scattered over the little streets, must be collected and cherished as a treasure for the future."[97] That future would come—indeed, has come—in the twilight of memory, in an effusion of memory, among the Holocaust survivors. They are to die, yet even as they die, they remember. And yet, even as their memory constitutes their own name, it is tied to another name: Auschwitz.

The Twilight of Memory, the Affirmation of a Name

Many passages in the Torah begin by declaring, "These are the words that G-d spoke." The Book of Deuteronomy, however, opens by saying, "These are the words that Moses spoke." According to the rabbis, Moses, rather than G-d, addressed the people of Israel on the eve of their entry into the Promised Land in order to transmit to them the memory of how they got there. If they were to emerge from exile, that memory was as important to bear as were the tablets of Torah and the bones of Joseph. Like the vessels that held the commandments of G-d and the remains of the dead, memory itself is a kind of *aron kodesh,* a holy ark, that makes it possible to find a dwelling place in the world. For in the ark of memory abides the Name that summons us to remember.

What is so striking about the last of the Five Books of Moses is that it is both Torah and the tale of Torah. Which means: If Torah and the Name are of a piece, then the Name is also the tale of the Name, even—or especially—when it is the tale of the assault on the Name. As the Israelites were about to enter the Land and there create a place to dwell, Moses transmitted to a new generation a tale of enslavement and liberation, of wandering and revelation (the generation that came out of Egypt, it will be recalled, had passed away). Why? Because a capacity to dwell in the Land rests upon a capacity for this memory of their origin and destiny, of what is at once most fragile and most dear. The memory of the Torah contained in the Torah is not the memory of good times—it is the memory of the *Good;* it is not the memory of suffering—it is the memory of why suffering *matters.* That is what makes it a memory of the Name.

One soon understands the reasoning behind the Baal Shem Tov's statement that just as oblivion is tied to exile, so is memory tied to redemption.[98] Tied to redemption, memory is tied to meaning and direction, to past and future, and above all to humanity; tied to redemption, memory is tied to everything that goes into a name; tied to redemption, memory *is* the Name.[99] And the most fundamental affirmation of a name lies in the movement of return to *HaShem* that is a response to one's name. Thus we have the three basic meanings of the Hebrew word *teshuvah:* redemption, return, and response. One function of memory in the Holocaust memoir is to undertake a movement of return through an act of response—not a return to the camp but a return to the world, to a place where dwelling is possible. If the Nazis set out to murder Jewish souls before destroying Jewish bodies, then they set out to destroy this movement of return that is a response to one's name.

If the Shoah is characterized by an assault on *teshuvah*—on redemption, return, and response—then it is defined by an assault on a memory and a name.[100] One expression of the Nazis' war against memory can be found in a scene from Steven Spielberg's production of *Schindler's List.* In the scene Amon Göth addresses his troops immediately prior to the liquidation of the Krakow Ghetto, proclaiming, "Jews have lived in Krakow for 600 years. By the end of the afternoon those six hundred years will be a rumor."[101] The writers of the memoirs also confront the war on memory, sometimes in even more direct ways. "The weakening of my memory tormented me," writes Alexander Donat.[102] And Olga Lengyel recalls that her fellow inmates in Auschwitz "lost their memory and the ability to concentrate."[103] Writing *this* memoir, the Holocaust memoir, therefore, entails far more than recording the reminiscences of a life; it is an act of remembrance made in response to an assault on memory and the Name, regardless of whether this survivor or that voices any acknowledgment of the Name. Why regardless? Because the act of remembrance is a response to one's name, and it harbors an affirmation of the sanctity of human life that comes only from the Name. Without this act of remembrance there is no returning to life.

Yet relatively few made this response in the years immediately following the war. While there are some, such as Primo Levi and Gisella Perl, who wrote memoirs before 1950, the wave of the survivors' response to the Shoah was slow to rise. But rise it did. In the last decade of the twentieth century it rose to unprecedented heights, even as the number of living survivors dwindled—perhaps, in part, *because* the number of living survivors was dwindling. There are other reasons, both obvious and obscure, for the proliferation of Holocaust memoirs in those years. For good or for ill, the subject found its way into popular culture through film and television; since more of us appeared to be willing to listen, more survivors were willing to speak. Also, since more of us were either ignoring or denying the Event, more survivors sensed the urgency to speak. Perhaps most significantly, many survivors now had grown children who asked them to write their memoirs. Some saw their lives drawing to a close and wanted to speak before they died; others finally took up the struggle in the war against memory to once again engage the Angel of Death.

One of the first signs of the gravity of the issue surrounding late-life remembrance came in 1992 with the publication of Elie Wiesel's novel *The Forgotten*. It is the tale of Elhanan, a survivor who, facing Alzheimer's disease, faces the problem of transmitting his memory to his son. Early in the novel we hear Elhanan's prayer: "G-d of Auschwitz, know that I must remember Auschwitz. And that I must remind You of it.... Remember that only memory leads man back to the source of his longing for You,"[104] which is a longing for the Name. Later his son Malkiel, who becomes the vessel of his father's memory, elaborates: "For a Jew, nothing is more important than memory. He is bound to his origins by memory. It is memory that connects him to Abraham, Moses, and Rabbi Akiba."[105] Although not all survivors are victims of Alzheimer's disease, they are all the victims of time and the fading of memory that comes with time. And they are all faced with transmitting a fading memory. Whereas they once faced the problem of either fear or denial among those to whom they offer their memories, they now face the problem of retrieving that memory. And so, like children of Israel passing their struggle on to their children, they wrestle with the Angel of Forgetfulness.

Memoirs written during the first generation after the Holocaust were written for readers who were alive during the event, readers for whom the event was part of their own world history, part of their own realm of possibility, and therefore part of their own realm of responsibility. In almost every instance the writers of the earlier memoirs were not writing for their families or their children; their families had been slaughtered and their children were as yet unborn. The ones who insisted that they speak were not their grown children, as has often been the case in recent years, but their dead parents, brothers, sisters, aunts, and uncles. They were writing not to leave a legacy, but to pay a debt and to deliver a message in the transmission of a memory. In these earlier memoirs the link to a past filled with destruction and despair is usually much stronger than the link to a future filled with renewal and hope. Therefore the earlier memoirs are often characterized by a struggle not so much to transmit as to recover a memory and a name, a center for what is sacred in life and thereby a return to life.

In the last chapter we saw the problem of liberation that faced those who, like Moshe the Beadle in Wiesel's *Night,* emerged from a mass grave to tell the story of their own death and to warn us about the death that threatens us. Often they recorded their memories in a foreign place and in a foreign tongue. Often they met with indifference and disbelief. While later memoirs are also written in languages and lands other than those of the survivor's birth, they are generally written in places where the survivor has recovered a sense of home, family, and community. Solomon Gisser, for example, had been a cantor for a synagogue in Montreal for forty years by the time he wrote his memoir *The Cantor's Voice* in 1999 (published in 2000). As for Moshe's difficulty in transmitting his testimony, an important part of the earlier memoirs is the memory of being disbelieved, not only by strangers but also by loved ones.

The contexts for the Holocaust memoir have also changed dramatically. Unlike the writers of earlier memoirs, the survivors who have written their memoirs later in life have an audience not only ready to listen but eager to respond. There are scholars and teachers, artists and agents, ready to write books and articles about them, teach courses on them, make movies about them, and arrange speaking engagements for them. Those who have written down their memories in the twilight of memory have as their contexts a Holocaust Remembrance Day and the memorial museums dedicated to the message they are trying to transmit. There are workshops and conferences, professional appointments and professional organizations, devoted to the Holocaust studies; indeed, it is now possible to earn a Ph.D. in Holocaust studies. We have encyclopedias and CDs. We are awash in it. Whenever the word *Auschwitz* was mentioned thirty years ago, many did not know what it was; now most are quick—indeed, too quick—to answer, "Oh, yes, I know all about that."

While this presumed knowledge is a serious problem, it is a separate problem. Nevertheless, it must be asked: What does the later memoir writer face when his audience knows "all about that?" And what does such an audience face when faced with the Holocaust memoir? The survivor no longer comes, like Moshe the Beadle, to warn us of the murder that rages all around us, to cry out to us to beware of what may befall us, as if we knew nothing about it. He does not tell us the story of his death—or rather, he usually does not leave it at that but will include something about his return to life, his getting married and having children. In short, he relates the tale of how he regained a name.

As for those of us who come to the late-life memoir, we feel more comfortable—indeed, too comfortable—with the "happy" ending, or at least with something that does not end with a corpse staring at us from the depths of a mirror, as in Wiesel's *Night.* Those events, moreover, took place before most of us were born: They are alien to us, outside the horizons of our world consciousness, such as it is. But are we in fact so safe? Do the authors of the memoirs written in the twilight of memory indeed speak from a dwelling place in the world, and not from an exile in the antiworld? What do the survivors now seek in this remembrance? What do we now seek? And do we indeed know our name?

Toward a Future of the Name, for the Name

Although the answers to these questions will vary from one testimony to the next, the variation is not so great as to preclude any reflection on the questions. Yes, the memoirs written thirty to forty years ago were written for a different audience, under different circumstances, and with different motives. But the event remembered is the same. The survivor responds to the same assault on the soul, on the Name, on the very idea and identity of humanity; she engages in the same struggle to restore a center of truth, meaning, and sanctity; she writes from the same position of witness and messenger. In a word, memoirs written early on, later on, and in between share the same endeavor to recover a memory and a name. Yes, the earlier memoirs generally despair of the future more than the later ones; but the fact that they are uttered *by* someone *to* someone orients them toward the future. For in that utterance the survivor recovers a name by addressing us by name, so that a future opens up in the response we have *yet* to make.

It seems, in fact, that the later in life the memoir—precisely as less and less of life remains for the author—the greater the orientation toward the future. Seeing this pattern of development, we come to a striking realization: Memory in the Holocaust memoir is memory of the future, for the future. The future of what? The future of our engagement with the Angel. For the future is not a *what;* the future is a *who.* Which means: The future has a *name.* The future is *the other human being*—a point made much more powerfully by the authors of late-life memoirs, who see the face of the future in the eyes of their children, who bear the names of the dead in remembrance of the dead.

Thus the writers of the Holocaust memoir—the late-life writers even more so—do more than retrace a past; they recover a future that exceeds the horizons of their time in this world. To remember is to have time, time for what is infinitely precious, for what there is to love. For the writer of the late-life memoir this remembrance includes both the dead parents and the living children. If Moshe the Beadle is the paradigm for the writer of the early memoir, the author of the late-life memoir finds himself more in the position of one who has come the end of his life, as that end is described in the Jewish teaching referred to in the introduction to this volume. According to this tradition, when we die and lie in the grave, the Angel of Death comes to us to take us into the Presence of the Holy One. In order to enter into the Divine Presence, however, we must pass a test. The test consists of just one question; while the question is the same for everyone, each of us must give a different answer. The question is: What is your name?

Writing her memoir, the survivor asserts her name, as well as the Name that came under assault during the event remembered, by answering to her name. For in nearly every instance of the late-life memoir, she has been asked by someone who loves her to write the memoir. She answers the first question put to the first human being, the question put to every human being—Where are you?—by declaring, "Here I am—for you." This "Here I am" means: "Here is my memory. Here is my name. In it is your name." And she puts to us a question: "What will you do with it?"

If we are to oppose the Nazi view of the human being, then we must embrace the view that they opposed, namely that we are *essentially* connected to every human being as family members are essentially connected to each other—by name. Which means: The writers of late-life memoirs are our mothers and fathers. We are the children to whom they respond when they take up the overwhelming task of this remembrance. And we are the ones who must answer to their response—by name.

If the survival of the memoir's author is a miracle, the memoir itself is an even greater miracle. For in the memoir the author attests to the infinite dearness of the human being after emerging from a realm in which the human being was less than nothing. Contrary to the abuser who abuses because he was abused, these are people who transform unspeakable suffering into ineffable blessing—not so they can feel better about themselves but, especially in the case of late-life memoirs, for the sake of their children. I once heard a survivor asked how he could believe in G-d after what he had been through. He replied that he did not know whether or not he believed in G-d. "But I have children," he explained. "What am I supposed to tell them? That we live in a void and their lives are meaningless? No."

In the late-life Holocaust memoir, then, one often discovers a fulfillment of what Emil Fackenheim describes as the 614th Commandment, namely the injunction to bear Jewish life into the world, even if the world may be hostile to that life—not just to deny the Nazis a posthumous victory but to take up the millennial testimony to the dearness of life that Jews are chosen to bear. And they bear that witness by wrestling the name of Israel from the Angel of Death. Whereas most of the writers of the early memoirs collide with the terrifying silence of Auschwitz, the late-life memoirs often imply the presence of what Fackenheim calls the commanding Voice of Auschwitz.[106] Simply stated, it is the commandment to have Jewish children and to transmit to them the Name that makes them Jews—not just for the sake of survival but for the sake of the Divine presence in the human image.

That presence can be seen in the writer's account of a lifetime that exceeds the deathtime of the antiworld, a life that includes children and grandchildren, as well as the memory of a mother and father whose love and teaching are passed on to the next generation. Solomon Gisser's memoir *The Cantor's Voice* again comes to mind. It begins and ends with the memory of his murdered mother and father. And in between is the tale not only of their murder and his death but of his subsequent pursuit of life. Gisser emerged from the mass grave of European Jewry not to shout curses but to chant prayers he learned as a child for the sake of his children. Indeed, his memoir is itself a kind of prayer. If we are to respond to that memoir—as we must if we are to remain human—then we must answer that prayer with our own prayer, if not in word then in deed, in the prayer that assumes the form of a deed. How does a prayer take the form of a deed, or a deed the form of a prayer? Through the act of loving-kindness that affirms the holy within the human. That is the message that transforms us into messengers.

Which means: These memoirs written late in life are not just eyewitness accounts offered to the world—they are *bequeathed* to us by the mothers and fathers of a generation. That is the difference between a report and a memory: A report we file away, memory we *inherit*. And because they are written late in life, these memoirs come to a generation of children who have grown up to become parents and have transmitted names. What, then, shall we tell our children, not only about the Holocaust but about those who survived it? That their lives were empty, the world is a void, and life is meaningless—just look at the Holocaust? But they do not just look at the Holocaust. They live it, relive it, and go on living—*as Jews*—in spite of it, to bring to the world a truth and a teaching concerning what is most precious and most dear.

Because this memory comes to us not only as the recollection of horror but as an affirmation of humanity, it is presented to us as a testimony both to what happened and to what *must* happen. The survivors' recall harbors a calling and a commandment. Therefore the authors of Holocaust memoirs place in our care what was placed in their care—and more: They place in our care both the cry of the murdered that haunts them and the call of a future that summons them. As their children, we receive their legacy; receiving their legacy, we are made into witnesses and messengers who in turn must answer the question: What is your name? Not only do we receive the tale of a life, but now we must live in a certain manner, in an embrace of the Torah that is the Name. As more and more of these survivors pass on, more and more we are in the position of the one who says Kaddish for his deceased parent and adds, "*Hareyni kaparat mishkavo*—May I be an atonement for his rest." How do we do that? By listening to these memories and by living according to the teaching of Torah that defines them, the teaching that the other human being is a holy being.

All too soon the last remnant of living memory passes. When that living memory passes, it does not pass away; it passes *on*—to us. What will it be a memory of? The shriek of silence or the cantor's voice? This is not an either-or proposition; to be sure, the Holocaust memoir contains both the voice of the survivor and the silence he survived. The question is: How do we attend to the voice without being swallowed up by the silence? The answer: by transmitting the message from our mothers and fathers as mothers and fathers. The assault on the Jews was not just an assault on mothers, fathers, and children. As an assault on the idea of a human being, it was an assault on the very notion of mother, father, and child. That is what makes it an assault on the Name that is the origin of every name.

To honor the memory of our mothers and fathers—both the memory we have and the memory they offer—is to heed their message. We heed their message by living lives worthy of their lives, by attesting to the value of their lives through a testimony to the infinite dearness of the lives around us. And by becoming who we are in the aftermath of a massive struggle with the Angel of Death: *Am Yisrael.*

Notes

1. The word *nevelah* is from the verb *naval*, which means "to wither," "to perish," or "to be destroyed"; the noun *naval* refers to one who is base and vile; it can also refer to one who is godless, an "unbeliever."

2. Yaakov Culi, *The Torah Anthology: MeAm Lo'ez,* vol. 1, trans. Aryeh Kaplan (New York: Maznaim, 1977), 420.

3. Jacques Lacan, *The Language of the Self: The Function of Language in Psychoanalysis,* trans. with commentary by Anthony Wilder (Baltimore: Johns Hopkins University Press, 1968), 299–300.

4. Jacques Derrida, *Of Grammatology,* trans. Gayatri Chakravorty Spivak (Baltimore: Johns Hopkins University Press, 1976), 50.

5. See ibid., xvii.

6. Emmanuel Lévinas, *Of G-d Who Comes To Mind,* trans. Bettina Bergo (Stanford, CA: Stanford University Press, 1998), 116–17.

7. See, for example, Martin Heidegger, *Unterwegs zur Sprache* (Tübingen: Neske, 1959), 166.

8. Ibid., 163.

9. Ibid., 13.

10. Ibid., 30.

11. Emmanuel Lévinas, *Totality and Infinity,* trans. Alphonso Lingis (Pittsburgh: Duquesne University Press, 1969), 299. For the same reason Martin Buber asserts that Heidegger's "existence" is monological, a talking to oneself and a languishing of the soul; see Martin Buber, *Between Man and Man,* trans. Ronald Gregor Smith (New York: Macmillan, 1965), 168.

12. Martin Heidegger, *Wegmarken* (Frankfurt am Main: Vittorio Klostermann, 1967), 105.

13. Ibid., 12.

14. Adin Steinsaltz and Josy Eisenberg, *The Seven Lights: On the Major Jewish Festivals* (Northvale, NJ: Jason Aronson, 2000), 147.

15. Martin Heidegger, *Poetry, Language, Thought,* trans. Albert Hofstadter (New York: Harper & Row, 1971), 94.

16. Martin Heidegger, *Erläuterungen zu Hölderlins Dichtung,* 2nd ed. (Frankfurt am Main: Vittorio Klostermann, 1951), 42.

17. Elie Wiesel, *Night,* trans. Stella Rodway (New York: Bantam, 1982), 105.

18. Sara Nomberg-Przytyk, *Auschwitz: True Tales from a Grotesque Land,* trans.

Roslyn Hirsch (Chapel Hill: University of North Carolina Press, 1985), 83–84.

19. Franz Rosenzweig, *Understanding the Sick and the Healthy,* trans. Nahum Glatzer (Cambridge: Harvard University Press, 1999), 71. Recall in this connection Maimonides' teaching from the *Moreh Nevuchim (The Guide for the Perplexed):* "The words 'speaking animal' include the true essence of man, and there is no third element besides life and speech in the definition of man; when he, therefore, is described by the attributes of life and speech, these are nothing but an explanation of the name 'man,' that is to say, that the thing which is called man consists of life and speech" (1:51).

20. Schneur Zalman, *Likutei Amarim Tanya,* trans. Nissan Mindel et al. (Brooklyn: Kehot, 1981), 183; see also Chayyim Vital's Shaarei Kedushah Part I, Gate 2.

21. Rosenzweig, *Understanding the Sick,* 89.

22. Zalman, *Likutei Amarim Tanya,* 291.

23. See André Neher, *The Exile of the Word: From the Silence of the Bible To the Silence of Auschwitz,* trans. David Maisel (Philadelphia: Jewish Publication Society, 1981), 111–13.

24. Martin Buber, *I and Thou,* trans. Walter Kaufmann (New York: Scribner's, 1970), 57. See also Emmanuel Lévinas, *Outside the Subject,* trans. Michael B. Smith (Stanford, CA: Stanford University Press, 1994), 34.

25. Buber, *I and Thou,* 81.

26. Emmanuel Lévinas, *Ethics and Infinity,* trans. Richard A. Cohen (Pittsburgh: Duquesne University Press, 1985), 86. Elsewhere Lévinas elaborates: "A face has meaning not by virtue of the relationships in which it is found, but out of itself; that is what *expression* is. A face is the presentation of an entity as an entity, its personal presentation. A face does not expose, nor does it conceal an entity. Over and beyond the disclosure and dissimulation which characterizes forms, a face is an expression, the existence of a substance, a thing in itself." See Emmanuel Lévinas, *Collected Philosophical Papers,* trans. Alphonso Lingis (Dordrecht: Martinus Nijhoff, 1987), 20.

27. Lévinas, *Collected Philosophical Papers,* 96.

28. Elie Wiesel, *Somewhere a Master,* trans. Marion Wiesel (New York: Summit Books, 1982), 179.

29. Meir ibn Gabbai, *Sod ha-Shabbat,* trans. Elliot K. Ginsburg (Albany: SUNY Press, 1989), 55.

30. Neher, *Exile of the Word,* 10

31. Elie Wiesel, *Against Silence: The Voice and Vision of Elie Wiesel,* vol. 3, ed. Irving Abrahamson (New York: Holocaust Library, 1985), 109.

32. In highly specialized philosophical terms, Lévinas expresses this idea by say-ing, "Language would exceed the limits of what is thought, by suggesting, letting be understood without ever making understandable, an implication of meaning distinct from that which comes to signs from the simultane-ity of systems or the logical definition of concepts. This possibility is laid bare in the poetic said, and the interpretation it calls for ad infinitum. It is shown in the prophetic said." See Emmanuel Lévinas, *Otherwise Than Being or Beyond Essence,* trans. Alphonso Lingis (The Hague: Martinus Nijhoff, 1981), 169–70.

33. Franz Rosenzweig, *The Star of Redemption,* trans. William W. Hallo (Bos-ton: Beacon Press, 1972), 80.

34. One will recall here Shimon ben Gamaliel's assertion that he found noth-ing better for a person than silence (*Pirke Avot* 1:17) and Rabbi Yitschak's teaching that a man should pursue silence throughout his life (*Chullin* 89a).

35. Menachem Mendel Schneerson, *Torah Studies,* adapted by Jonathan Sacks, 2nd ed. (London: Lubavitch Foundation, 1986), 4.

36. Wiesel, *Against Silence,* vol. 2, 119.

37. Ibid., vol. 3, 267.

38. See Rosenzweig, *Star of Redemption,* 245–46.

39. In a commentary on this verse the Zohar explains that the tearing of word from meaning, or the silence that has descended upon the world, is the re-sult of the tearing of the *vav* from the *hey* of the four-letter Holy Name; for the *hey* represents the *sefirah* of *Malkhut,* which is also called Speech. The separation dries up the source of speech, so that the Voice of *Zeir Anpin* is not present. This separation of the Voice from Speech, of word from mean-ing, is what characterizes the exile of the *Shekhinah* (see *Zohar* I, 116b).

40. Kalonymos Kalmish Shapira, *Sacred Fire: Torah from the Years of Fury, 1939–1942,* trans. J. Hershy Worch, ed. Deborah Miller (Northvale, NJ: Jason Aronson, 2000), 22.

41. Ibid., 23.

42. Elie Wiesel, *The Testament,* trans. Marion Wiesel (New York: Summit Books, 1981), 207.

43. Emmanuel Lévinas, *Time and the Other,* trans. Richard A. Cohen (Pitts-burgh: Duquesne University Press, 1987), 46.

44. Wiesel, *The Testament,* 209.

45. Josef Bor, *The Terezín Requiem,* trans. Edith Pargeter (New York: Avon, 1963), 41–42.

46. Emmanuel Lévinas, *Of G-d Who Comes To Mind,* trans. Bettina Bergo (Stanford, CA: Stanford University Press, 1998), 74.

47. Wiesel, *The Testament,* 304–5.

48. Cf. Elie Wiesel, *Paroles d'étranger* (Paris: Éditions du Seuil, 1982), 171–72.

49. Matityahu Glazerson, *Building Blocks of the Soul: Studies on the Letters and Words of the Hebrew Language* (Northvale, NJ: Jason Aronson, 1997), 68.

50. See Milton Aron, *Ideas and Ideals of the Hasidim* (Secaucus, NJ: Citadel, 1969), 168.

51. Elie Wiesel, *The Golem* (New York: Summit Books, 1983), 44.

52. Emmanuel Ringelblum, *Notes from the Warsaw Ghetto,* trans. and ed. Jacob Sloan (New York: Schocken Books, 1974), 133.

53. Philip Mechanicus, *Year of Fear: A Jewish Prisoner Waits for Auschwitz,* trans. Irene S. Gibbons (New York: Hawthorne, 1964), 181–82.

54. Lévinas, *Otherwise Than Being,* 11.

55. Ibid., 191.

56. Kalonymos Kalmish Shapira, *A Student's Obligation,* trans. Micha Odenheimer (Northvale, NJ: Aronson, 1991), 121.

57. Lévinas, *Collected Philosophical Papers,* 134–35.

58. Emil Dorian, *The Quality of Witness,* ed. Marguerite Dorian, trans. Mara Soceanu Vamos (Philadelphia: Jewish Publication Society, 1982), 126.

59. Yitzhak Katznelson, *Vittel Diary,* trans. Myer Cohn, 2nd ed. (Tel Aviv: Hakibbutz Hameuchad, 1972), 187.

60. Lévinas, *Ethics and Infinity,* 109.

61. Emil L. Fackenheim, *What Is Judaism?* (New York: Macmillan, 1987), 178.

62. Emmanuel Lévinas, *Difficult Freedom: Essays on Judaism,* trans. Sean Hand (Baltimore: Johns Hopkins University Press, 1990), 17.

63. Zelig Kalmanovitch, "A Diary of the Nazi Ghetto in Vilna," trans. and ed. Koppel S. Pinson, *YIVO Annual of Jewish Social Studies* 8 (1953): 50.

64. Chaim A. Kaplan, *Scroll of Agony: The Warsaw Diary of Chaim A. Kaplan,* trans. and ed. Abraham I. Katsh (Bloomington: Indiana University Press, 1999), 144.

65. Emmanuel Lévinas, "Revelation in the Jewish Tradition," in *The Levinas Reader,* trans. Sarah Richmond, ed. Sean Hand (Oxford: Basil Blackwell, 1989), 202.

66. Kaplan, *Scroll of Agony*, 104.

67. Ibid., 383–84.

68. Neher, *Exile of the Word*, 63.

69. Kalmanovitch, *Diary*, 28.

70. Menahem Kon, "Fragments of a Diary (August 6, 1942–October 1, 1942)," trans. M. Z. Prives, in *To Live with Honor and Die with Honor: Selected Documents from the Warsaw Ghetto Underground Archives* "O.S.," ed. Joseph Kermish (Jerusalem: Yad Vashem, 1986,), 84.

71. Dorian, *Quality of Witness*, 129.

72. Ibid., 304.

73. Janusz Korczak, *Ghetto Diary*, trans. Jerzy Bachrach and Barbara Krzywicka (New York: Holocaust Library, 1978), 175.

74. Yitzchak Ginsburgh, *The Alef-Beit: Jewish Thought Revealed through the Hebrew Letters* (Northvale, NJ: Jason Aronson, 1991), 4.

75. Elie Wiesel, *Twilight*, trans. Marion Wiesel (New York: Summit Books, 1998), 98.

76. Nachman of Breslov, *Restore My Soul (Meshivat Nefesh)*, trans. Avraham Greenbaum (Jerusalem: Chasidei Breslov, 1980), 24.

77. Mirjam Korber, *Deportiert: Jüdische Überlebensschicksale aus Rumänien, 1941–1944: Ein Tagebuch*, trans. Andrei Hoisie (Konstanz: Hartung-Garre, 1993), 109.

78. Kaplan, *Scroll of Agony*, 278.

79. Anne Frank, *The Diary of a Young Girl*, trans. B. M. Mooyaart-Doubleday (New York: Modern Library, 1952), 12-13.

80. Ibid., 57.

81. Dorian, *Quality of Witness*, 33.

82. See Nachmanides, *Commentary on the Torah*, Vol. 2, trans Charles B. Chavel (New York: Shilo, 1971), 543.

83. Dorian, *Quality of Witness*, 170.

84. Ibid., 203.

85. Ibid., 91.

86. Elik Rivosh, "From the Notebook of the Sculptor Elik Rivosh (Riga)," trans. David Patterson, in Ilya Ehrenburg and Vasily Grossman, eds., *The Complete Black Book of Russian Jewry* (New Brunswick, NJ: Transaction Publishers, 2002), 409.

87. Hanna Levy-Hass, *Vielleicht war das alles erst der Anfang: Tagebuch aus dem KZ Bergen Belsen, 1944–1945,* ed. Eike Geisel (Berlin: Rotbuch, 1969), 39.

88. Hannah Senesh, *Hannah Senesh: Her Life and Diary,* trans. Marta Cohn (New York: Schocken Books, 1972), 103.

89. Emil L. Fackenheim, *To Mend the World: Foundations of Post-Holocaust Jewish Thought* (New York: Schocken Books, 1989), 222.

90. André Neher, *The Prophetic Existence,* trans. William Wolf (New York: A. S. Barnes, 1969), 94–95.

91. Hillel Seidman, *Tog-bukh fon Warshever geto* (New York: Avraham Mitlberg, 1947), 77.

92. Ibid., 45.

93. Israel Gutman, *Introduction To Adam Czerniakow: The Warsaw Ghetto Diary of Adam Czerniakow,* ed. Raul Hilberg, Stanislaw Staron, Joseph Kermisz, trans. Stanislaw Staron et al. (New York: Stein and Day, 1979), 70.

94. Katznelson, *Vittel Diary,* 220.

95. Avraham Tory, *Surviving the Holocaust: The Kovno Ghetto Diary, ed. Martin Gilbert,* trans. Jerzy Michalowicz (Cambridge: Harvard University Press, 1990), 280.

96. Yitskhok Rudashevski, *The Diary of the Vilna Ghetto,* trans. Percy Matenko (Tel Aviv: Ghetto Fighters' House and Hakibbutz Hameuchad, 1973), 102.

97. Ibid., 80–81.

98. See Elie Wiesel, *Souls on Fire: Portraits and Legends of Hasidic Masters,* trans. Marion Wiesel (New York: Vintage, 1973), 227.

99. Therefore, it is written in the Zohar, "the Supreme King is hinted at in the word Zakhor (remember)" (*Zohar* I, 5b).

100. Recall comments on this point in chapter 1.

101. It is worth noting that Jews had actually been in Krakow for eight hundred years.

102. Alexander Donat, *The Holocaust Kingdom* (New York: Holocaust Library, 1978), 239.

103. Olga Lengyel, *Five Chimneys* (London: Granada, 1972), 96. See also Miklos Nyiszli, *Auschwitz: A Doctor's Eyewitness Account,* trans. Tibere Kremer and Richard Seaver (New York: Fawcett Crest, 1960), 114, and Germaine Tillion, *Ravensbrück,* trans. Gerald Satterwhite (Garden City: Doubleday, 1975), 16.

104. Elie Wiesel, *The Forgotten,* trans. Marion Wiesel (New York: Summit Books,

1992), 11–12.

105. Ibid., 71.

106. See Emil L. Fackenheim, *The Jewish Return into History: Reflections in the Age of Auschwitz and a New Jerusalem* (New York: Schocken Books, 1978), 19ff.

A CLOSING WORD

WHAT IS YOUR NAME?

☙

T HE CHASIDIC MASTER KNOWN AS THE OSTROVITZER Rebbe once commented on "And Jacob was left alone" (Genesis 32:25), by saying, "With the blessing *HaShem* gave Jacob, 'And your name will be Israel,' Israel will be mentioned when Jews gather for prayer or learning as a people. When Jews gather to pray or participate in learning as a people, they reach the much higher standard of 'Israel,' the standard of unity and brotherly love."[1] In this unity and brotherly love lies the identity of the Jew and the answer to the most fundamental question that can be put to a human being, the question that the Angel of Death puts to each of us.

And so the Jew is left with a question: What is your name? Left with this question, the Jew is returned to Peniel, where he or she must decide: Who am I, as a Jew? The holy tongue that the Nazis attempted to silence in their assault on the Name tells us that a Jew is a *Yehudi*. The root of this word is *yadah*, which means "to offer praise" or "to give thanks." Who is the Jew? He is the one chosen to be a light of gratitude unto the nations—*in spite of everything*. Beginning our prayers each morning with *hodu l'HaShem*— "thanks and praise to the Name"—we begin our daily prayers, our daily wrestling, with a declaration of what it means to be a Jew: To be a Jew is to give thanks, especially when we have forgotten what there is to be thankful for. That is the one way, the only way, to regain our memory of who we are and for what we have been chosen. If this book has been a reminder of the horror that characterizes the Nazi assault on the Name, it has also been a

225

reminder of what there is to be grateful for. After all, Jacob wrestled from the Angel not only a name but also a blessing.

What? The Holocaust a blessing? Absolutely not. But the fact that it is an evil, that it is a horror, and that therefore it *matters* is a blessing. The fact that we must answer, that we must care, and that we must therefore affirm the sanctity of life is a blessing. What Torah can provide that is undreamt of in postmodern thought is a sense of this blessing that comes with the name and a sense of this gratitude that comes with the blessing. What the Torah can provide is not only the memory of the Name but also a reason to remember our own name, and therefore a reason to remember the Shoah: It is not merely to prevent a repetition of history but to become the ones we are chosen to become, both as individuals and as a people: to become Israel. The stake in this remembrance is not just the survival of Israel but the very *sense* of humanity that came under the Nazi assault. Therefore we have no choice in the matter of this wrestling: We are already in the ring.

Recall here Emmanuel Lévinas's argument that our connection to the Good is prior to any choosing of the Good. "The Good," he maintains, "is good precisely because it chooses you and grips you before you have had the time to raise your eyes to it."[2] In its Jewish form, the Good is just that sacred tradition that consists of memory and summons all memory. Like the Good, the tradition chooses us before we can contemplate any other choice; we engage in our contemplation *because* the tradition has chosen us. To be sure, that is what makes the past a *tradition:* The past becomes tradition not through the repetition of customs or habits but through the insertion of an immemorial past into a Jewish present. What is immemorial for the Jew? It is wrestling with the Angel—that is what constitutes Jewish tradition and what decides a Jewish future. Where, then, does this wrestling unfold? According to Lévinas, it is in our engagement with the Talmud: "Talmud," he says, "is the struggle with the Angel."[3] Talmud, then, is the key to wrestling an identity from the Angel of Shoah. For without any memory of this tradition that defines us, we shall surely forget our name.

The Hebrew word for "tradition" is *masoret;* its cognate *mesirut* means "devotion" or "dedication." The remembrance that characterizes the devotion to tradition is a forgetfulness of the self, as the expression *mesirat nefesh* suggests. Translated as "self-sacrificing," it is not merely *laying* down a life but *handing* down a life. Self-sacrifice in this sense is a giving that is teaching and testimony, and there is no tradition, no *masoret,* without *mesirat nefesh.* For the meaning of the root verb *masar* is to "transmit" or "hand down." The tradition handed down from generation to generation is not only the link that connects each of us to the other but is also the substance that holds each one together. And what is handed down through tradition, through the *masoret,* is a *meser,* or a "message." It is the message couched in the name Israel, which can be transmitted only by wrestling with the Angel.

The removal of the Jew from the world requires not only the removal of the name from the Jew; it also entails the removal of the Jew from this engagement with the Angel. That is why the very people who would love to see a repeat of the Holocaust deny that it ever happened: If it did not happen, then there is no wrestling. Then the Jew can just slip into a nebulous namelessness and disappear. Then there need be no Jewish state, no Judaism, no Jewish memory. Then the Jew can become part of the anonymity that levels humanity into a faceless mass. And then the fondest wish of the anti-Semite and the postmodernist will have been realized: a world free of the Jewish Question: What is your name?

The Final Solution to the Jewish Question that both modernists and postmoderns would have lies not in answering the question. No, for the modernists and postmodernists the Final Solution to the Jewish Question lies in the erasure of the Question. For, in truth, the Jewish Question can have only one answer: *Am Yisrael Chai.*

Notes

1. See Dovid Kirschenbaum, *Fun di Chasidishe Otsros* (New York: Pardes Publishers, 1948), 115; see also Victor Cohen, ed., *The Soul of the Torah: Insights of the Chasidic Masters on the Weekly Torah Portions* (Northvale, NJ: Jason Aronson, 2000), 54.

2. Emmanuel Lévinas, *Nine Talmudic Readings,* trans. Annette Aronowicz (Bloomington: Indiana University Press, 1990), 135.

3. Emmanuel Lévinas, "The Pact," trans. Sarah Richmond, in Sean Hand, ed., *The Levinas Reader* (Oxford: Basil Blackwell, 1989), 220.

BIBLIOGRAPHY

Abraham ibn Ezra. *The Secret of the Torah.* Trans. H. Norman Strickman. Northvale, NJ: Jason Aronson, 1995.

Alter, Michael J. *Why the Torah Begins with the Letter Beit.* Northvale, NJ: Jason Aronson, 1998.

Améry, Jean. *At the Mind's Limits.* Trans. Sidney Rosenfeld and Stella P. Rosenfeld. Bloomington: Indiana University Press, 1980.

Andreas-Friedrich, Ruth. *Der Schattenmann: Tagebuchaufzeichnungen, 1938–1945.* Berlin: Suhrkamp, 1947.

Arad, Yitzhak, Yisrael Gutman, and Abraham Margolit, eds. *Documents on the Holocaust.* Jerusalem: Yad Vashem, 1981.

Arieti, Silvano. *The Parnas.* Philadelphia: Paul Dry Books, 2000.

Aron, Milton. *Ideas and Ideals of the Hasidim.* Secaucus, NJ: Citadel, 1969.

Bachya ibn Paquda. *Chovot Halevavot: Duties of the Heart.* 2 vols. Trans. Moses Hyamson. New York: Feldheim, 1970.

Baeck, Leo. *The Essence of Judaism.* Revised edition. Trans. Victor Grubenwieser and Leonard Pearl. New York: Schocken Books, 1948.

The Bahir. Trans. with commentary by Aryeh Kaplan. York Beach, ME: Samuel Weiser, 1979.

Bartov, Omer, and Phyllis Macks, eds. *Genocide and Religion in the 20th Century.* New York: Berghahn Books, 2001.

Bauer, Yehuda. "Is the Holocaust Explicable?" In Joseph R. Mitchell and Helen Buss Mitchell, eds. *The Holocaust: Readings and Interpretations.* New York: McGraw-Hill, 2001, pp. 18–30.

Beiser, Frederick C. "Kant's Intellectual Development, 1746–1781." In Paul Guyer, ed. *The Cambridge Companion To Kant.* Cambridge: Cambridge University Press, 1992, pp. 2–61.

Berg, Mary. *The Warsaw Ghetto: A Diary.* Trans. Norbert and Sylvia Glass, ed. S. L. Schneiderman. New York: L. B. Fischer, 1945.

Bernasconi, Robert, and David Wood, eds. *The Provocation of Levinas: Rethinking the Other.* London: Routledge, 1988.

Bezwinska, Jadwiga, ed. *Amidst a Nightmare of Crime: Manuscripts of Members of Sonderkommando.* Oswiecim: State Museum, 1973.

Bitton-Jackson, *Livia E. Elli: Coming of Age in the Holocaust.* New York: Times Books, 1980.

Bor, Josef. *The Terezín Requiem.* Trans. Edith Pargeter. New York: Avon, 1963.

Buber, Martin. *Between Man and Man.* Trans. Ronald Gregor Smith. New York: Macmillan, 1965.

———. *The Eclipse of God: Studies in the Relation of Religion to Philosophy.* Trans. Maurice Friedman et al. New York: Harper, 1957.

———. *I and Thou.* Trans. Walter Kaufmann. New York: Scribner's, 1970.

———. *The Legend of the Baal Shem.* Trans. Maurice Friedman. New York: Schocken Books, 1969.

———. *The Prophetic Faith.* Trans. Carlyle Witton-Davies. New York: Harper and Brothers, 1960.

Camus, Albert. *The Myth of Sisyphus.* Trans. Justin O'Brien. New York: Random House, 1955.

Caputo, John D. "Heidegger's Scandal: Thinking and the Essence of the Victim." In Tom Rockmore and Joseph Margolis, eds., *The Heidegger Case: On Philosophy and Politics.* Philadelphia: Temple University Press, 1992, pp. 265-81.

Cargas, Harry James. *Reflections of a Post-Auschwitz Christian.* Detroit: Wayne State University Press, 1989.

———. *Shadows of Auschwitz: A Christian Response To the Holocaust.* New York: Crossroad, 1990.

Cassirer, Ernst. *Kant's Life and Thought.* Trans. James Haden. New Haven: Yale University Press, 1981.

Chayim ben Attar. *Or Hachayim.* 5 vols. Trans. Eliyahu Munk. Jerusalem: Munk, 1995.

Cohen, Victor, ed. *The Soul of the Torah: Insights of the Chasidic Masters on the Weekly Torah Portions.* Northvale, NJ: Jason Aronson, 2000.

Cordovero, Moses. *The Palm Tree of Devorah.* Trans. Moshe Miller. Southfield, MI: Targum, 1993.

———. *Pardes Rimmonim.* Jerusalem, 1961.

Crétella, Henri. "Self-Destruction." In Alan Milchman and Alan Rosenberg, eds., *Martin Heidegger and the Holocaust.* Atlantic Highlands, NJ: Humanities Press, 1996, pp. 150–66.

Culi, Yaakov. *The Torah Anthology: MeAm Lo'ez.* Vol. 1. Trans. Aryeh Kaplan. New York: Moznaim, 1977.

Czerniakow, Adam. *The Warsaw Ghetto Diary of Adam Czerniakow.* Ed. Raul Hilberg, Stanislaw Staron, Joseph Kermisz. Trans. Stanislaw Staron et al. New York: Stein and Day, 1979.

Delbo, Charlotte. *None of Us Will Return.* Trans. John Githens. Boston: Beacon Press, 1968.

Derrida, Jacques. *De l'esprit.* Paris: Éditions Galilee, 1987.

———. *Of Grammatology.* Trans. Gayatri Chakravorty Spivak. Baltimore: Johns Hopkins University Press, 1976.

Descartes, René. *Meditations on First Philosophy.* Trans. Donald A. Cress. 3rd Ed. Indianapolis: Hackett, 1993.

Donat, Alexander. *The Holocaust Kingdom.* New York: Holocaust Library, 1978.

Dorembus, Helena Elbaum. "Through Helpless Eyes: A Survivor's Diary of the Warsaw Ghetto Uprising," *Moment,* April 1993: 56–61.

Dorian, Emil. *The Quality of Witness.* Ed. Marguerite Dorian. Trans. Mara Soceanu Vamos. Philadelphia: Jewish Publication Society, 1982.

Dribben, Judith. *And Some Shall Live.* Jerusalem: Keter, 1969.

Ellis, Marc H. *Unholy Alliance: Religion and Atrocity in Our Time.* Minneapolis: Fortress Press, 1997.

Fackenheim, Emil L. *Encounters between Judaism and Modern Philosophy.* New York: Basic Books, 1993.

———. *G-d's Presence in History: Jewish Affirmations and Philosophical Reflections.* New York: Harper & Row, 1970.

———. "The Holocaust and the State of Israel." In Michael L. Morgan, ed. *A Holocaust Reader: Responses To the Nazi Extermination.* New York: Oxford University Press, 2001, pp. 131–38.

———. *The Jewish Bible after the Holocaust.* Bloomington: Indiana University Press, 1990.

———. *Jewish Philosophers and Jewish Philosophy.* Ed. Michael L. Morgan. Bloomington: Indiana University Press, 1996.

———. *The Jewish Return into History.* New York: Schocken Books, 1978.

———. *Quest for Past and Future: Essays in Jewish Theology.* Bloomington: Indiana University Press, 1968.

———. *To Mend the World: Foundations of Post-Holocaust Jewish Thought.* New York: Schocken Books, 1989.

————. *What Is Judaism?* New York: Macmillan, 1987.

Farías, Victor. *Heidegger and Nazism.* Trans. Paul Burrell. Philadelphia: Temple University Press, 1989.

Fénelon, Fania. *Playing for Time.* Trans. Judith Landry. New York: Atheneum, 1977.

Ferderber-Salz, Bertha. *And the Sun Kept Shining.* New York: Holocaust Library, 1980.

Feuerbach, Ludwig. *The Essence of Christianity.* Trans. George Eliot. New York: Harper & Row, 1957.

Fichte, Johann Gottlieb. *Addresses To the German Nation.* Ed. George Armstrong Kelly. New York: Harper & Row, 1968.

Finkel, Avraham Yaakov. *Kabbalah: Selections from Classic Kabbalistic Works from Raziel HaMalach To the Present Day.* Southfield, MI: Targum Press, 2002.

Finkelstein, Louis. *Akiba: Scholar, Saint, and Martyr.* New York: Atheneum, 1981.

Flinker, Moshe. *Young Moshe's Diary.* Trans. Shaul Esh and Geoffrey Wigoder. Jerusalem: Yad Vashem and Board of Jewish Education, 1971.

Frank, Anne. *The Diary of a Young Girl.* Trans. B. M. Mooyaart-Doubleday. New York: Modern Library, 1952.

Fridman, Lea Wernick. *Words and Witness: Narrative and Aesthetic Strategies in the Representation of the Holocaust.* Albany: State University of New York Press, 2000.

Friedländer, Saul. *When Memory Comes.* Trans. Helen R. Lane. New York: Avon, 1980.

Geve, Thomas. *Youth in Chains.* Jerusalem: Rubin Mass, 1981.

Gikatilla, Joseph. *Sha'are Orah: Gates of Light.* Trans. Avi Weinstein. San Francisco: Harper, 1994.

Ginsburgh, Yitzchak. *The Alef-Beit: Jewish Thought Revealed through the Hebrew Letters.* Northvale, NJ: Jason Aronson, 1991.

Gisser, Solomon. *The Cantor's Voice.* Ed. David Patterson. Memphis: Serviceberry Press, 2000.

Glazerson, Matityahu. *Building Blocks of the Soul: Studies on the Letters and Words of the Hebrew Language.* Northvale, NJ: Jason Aronson, 1997.

Guyer, Paul, ed. *The Cambridge Companion To Kant.* Cambridge: Cambridge University Press, 1992.

Hand, Sean, ed. *The Lévinas Reader.* Oxford: Basil Blackwell, 1989.

Hart, Kitty. *Return To Auschwitz.* New York: Atheneum, 1982.

HeChasid, Yehuda. *Sefer Chasidim.* Trans. Avraham Yaakov Finkel. Northvale, NJ: Jason Aronson, 1997.

Hegel, G. W. F. *Early Theological Writings.* Trans. T. M. Knox. Chicago: University of Chicago Press, 1948.

Heidegger, Martin. *Erläuterungen zu Hölderlins Dichtung.* 2nd Ed. Frankfurt am Main: Vittorio Klostermann, 1951.

———. *Introduction To Metaphysics.* Trans. Ralph Mannheim. New York: Doubleday, 1961.

———. *Kant and the Problem of Metaphysics.* Trans. J. S. Churchill. Bloomington: Indiana University Press, 1962.

———. "Martin Heidegger: A Philosopher and Politics: A Conversation." In Guenther Neske and Emil Kettering, eds. *Martin Heidegger and National Socialism.* Trans. Lisa Harries. New York: Paragon, 1990, pp. 175–95.

———. *Nietzsche.* 2 vols. Trans. D. Krell. San Francisco: Harper & Row, 1979.

———. *Sein und Zeit.* Tübingen: Max Niemeyer, 1963.

———. *Unterwegs zur Sprache.* Tübingen: Neske, 1959.

———. *Vom Wesen des Grundes.* 5th ed. Frankfurt am Main: Klostermann, 1965.

———. *Wegmarken.* Frankfurt am Main: Vittorio Klostermann, 1967.

Heimler, Eugene. *Night of the Mist.* Trans. Andre Ungar. New York: Vanguard, 1959.

Heine, Heinrich. *Words of Prose.* Trans. E. B. Ashton. New York: L. B. Fischer, 1943.

Heschel, Abraham Joshua. *I Asked for Wonder.* Ed. Samuel H. Dresner. New York: Crossroad, 1983.

———. *Man's Quest for G-d: Studies in Prayer and Symbolism.* New York: Charles Scribner's Sons, 1954.

———. *Man Is Not Alone.* New York: Farrar, Straus and Giroux, 1951.

———. *The Sabbath: Its Meaning for Modern Man.* New York: Farrar, Straus and Giroux, 1981.

Huberband, Shimon. *Kiddush Hashem: Jewish Religious and Cultural Life in Poland during the Holocaust.* Trans. David E. Fishman. Ed. Jeffrey S. Gurock and Robert S. Hirt. Hoboken, NJ: Ktav and Yeshiva University Press, 1987.

Jonas, Hans. "Heidegger's Resoluteness and Resolve." In Guenther Neske and Emil Kettering, eds. *Martin Heidegger and National Socialism.* Trans. Lisa Harries. New York: Paragon, 1990, pp. 197–203.

Kahane, David. *Lvov Ghetto Diary*. Trans. Jerzy Michalowicz. Amherst: University of   Massachusetts Press, 1990.

Kalmanovitch, Zelig. "A Diary of the Nazi Ghetto in Vilna." Trans. and ed. Koppel S. Pinson, *YIVO Annual of Jewish Social Studies* 8 (1953): 9–81.

Kant, Immanuel. *Anthropology from a Pragmatic Point of View*. Trans. Victor Lyle Dowdell and ed. Hans H. Rudnick. Carbondale: Southern Illinois University Press, 1978.

———. *The Conflict of the Faculties*. Trans. Mary J. Gregor. New York: Abaris, 1979.

———. *The Critique of Practical Reason*. Trans. Lewis White Beck. New York: Macmillan, 1985.

———. *Grounding for the Metaphysics of Morals*. Trans. James W. Ellington. 3rd Ed. Indianapolis: Hackett, 1993.

Kaplan, Chaim A. *Scroll of Agony: The Warsaw Diary of Chaim A. Kaplan*. Trans. and ed. Abraham I. Katsh. Bloomington: Indiana University Press, 1999.

Katz, Josef. *One Who Came Back: The Diary of a Jewish Survivor*. Trans. Herzl Reach. New York: Herzl Press and Bergen-Belsen Memorial Press, 1973.

Katz, Steven T., ed. *Interpretations of Judaism in the Late Twentieth Century*. Washington, DC: B'nai B'rith Books, 1991.

———. *Post-Holocaust Dialogues: Critical Studies in Modern Jewish Thought*. New York: NYU Press, 1983.

Ka-tzetnik 135633. *Atrocity*. Trans. Nina De-Nur. New York: Kensington, 1977.

———. *House of Dolls*. Trans. Moshe M. Kohn. New York: Pyramid, 1958.

———. *Kaddish*. Trans. Nina De-Nur. New York: Algemeiner Associates, 1998.

———. *Phoenix over the Galilee*. Trans. Nina De-Nur. New York: Harper & Row, 1969.

———. *Shivitti: A Vision*. Trans. Eliyah De-Nur and Lisa Herman. New York: Harper & Row, 1989.

———. *Star of Ashes*. Trans. Nina De-Nur. Tel Aviv: Hamenora, 1971.

———. *Sunrise over Hell*. Trans. Nina De-Nur. London: W. H. Allen, 1977.

Katznelson, Yitzhak. *Vittel Diary*. Trans. Myer Cohn. 2nd ed. Tel Aviv: Hakibbutz Hameuchad, 1972.

Kessel, Sim. *Hanged at Auschwitz*. Trans. Melville and Delight Wallace. New York: Stein and Day, 1972.

Kielar, Wieslaw. *Anus Mundi: 1,500 Days in Auschwitz/Birkenau*. Trans. Susanne Flatauer. New York: Times Books, 1980.

Kirschenbaum, Dovid, ed. *Fun di Chasidishe Ostros*. New York: Pardes Publishers, 1948.

Kisiel, Theodore. "Heidegger's Apology: Biography and Philosophy and Ideology." In Tom Rockmore and Joseph Margolis, eds. *The Heidegger Case: On Philosophy and Politics*. Philadelphia: Temple University Press, 1992, pp. 11–54.

Kitov, Eliyahu. *The Book of Our Heritage*. 3 vols. Trans. Nathan Bluman. New York: Feldheim Publishers, 1973.

Kitsur Shulchan Arukh—Code of Jewish Law. 4 Vols. Compiled by R. Solomon Ganzfried, trans. Hyman E. Goldin. Rev. ed. New York: Hebrew Publishing Co., 1961.

Klein, Gerda Weissmann. *All But My Life*. New York: Hill and Wang, 1957.

Klonicki-Klonymus, Aryeh. *The Diary of Adam's Father*. Trans. Avner Tomaschiff. Tel Aviv: Hakibbutz Hameuchad, 1973.

Kon, Menahem. "Fragments of a Diary (August 6, 1942–October 1, 1942)," trans. M. Z. Prives, in *To Live with Honor and Die with Honor: Selected Documents from the Warsaw Ghetto Underground Archives* "O.S." Ed. Joseph Kermish. Jerusalem: Yad Vashem, 1986, pp. 80–86.

Korber, Mirjam. *Deportiert: Jüdische Überlebensschicksale aus Rumänien, 1941–1944: Ein Tagebuch*. Trans. Andrei Hoisie. Konstanz: Hartung-Garre, 1993.

Korczak, Janusz. *Ghetto Diary*. Trans. Jerzy Bachrach and Barbara Krzywicka. New York: Holocaust Library, 1978.

Kruk, Herman. "Diary of the Vilna Ghetto." Trans. Shlomo Noble. *YIVO Annual of Jewish Social Science* 13 (1965): 9–78.

———. *The Last Days of the Jerusalem of Lithuania: Chronicles from the Vilna Ghetto and the Camps, 1939–1944*. Ed. Benjamin Harshav. Trans. Barbara Harshav. New Haven, Yale University Press, 2002.

Kuper, Leo. "Theological Warrants for Genocide: Judaism, Islam and Christianity." *Terrorism and Political Violence* 2 (1990): 351–379.

Lacan, Jacques. *The Language of the Self: The Function of Language in Psychoanalysis*. Trans. with commentary by Anthony Wilder. Baltimore: Johns Hopkins University Press, 1968.

LaCapra, Dominick. *Writing History, Writing Trauma*. Baltimore: Johns Hopkins University Press, 2001.

Lang, Berel. *Act and Idea in the Nazi Genocide*. Syracuse: Syracuse University Press, 2003.

Langer, Jiří. *Nine Gates To the Chassidic Mysteries*. Trans. Stephen Jolly. New York: Behrman House, 1976.

Leitner, Isabella. *Fragments of Isabella.* Ed. Irving Leitner. New York: Thomas Crowell, 1978.

Lengyel, Olga. *Five Chimneys.* London: Granada, 1972.

Lerner, Lily Gluck. *The Silence.* Secaucus, NJ: Lyle Stuart, 1980.

Levi, Primo. *The Drowned and the Saved.* Trans. Raymond Rosenthal. New York: Vintage Books, 1988.

———. *The Reawakening.* Trans. Stuart Wolf. Boston: Little, Brown, 1965.

———. *Survival in Auschwitz: The Nazi Assault on Humanity.* Trans. Stuart Woolf. New York: Simon & Schuster, 1996.

Levin, Abraham. "Extract from the Diary of Abraham Levin." *Yad Vashem Studies* 6 (1967): 315–30.

Lévinas, Emmanuel. *Collected Philosophical Papers.* Trans. Alphonso Lingis. Dordrecht: Martinus Nijhoff, 1987.

———. *Difficult Freedom: Essays on Judaism.* Trans. Sean Hand. Baltimore: Johns Hopkins University Press, 1990.

———. *Ethics and Infinity.* Trans. Richard A. Cohen. Pittsburgh: Duquesne University Press, 1985.

———. "Ethics as First Philosophy." Trans. Sean Hand and Michael Temple. In Sean Hand, ed. *The Levinas Reader.* Oxford: Basil Blackwell, 1989, pp. 75–87.

———. *Existence and Existents.* Trans. Alphonso Lingis. The Hague: Martinus Nijhoff, 1978.

———. *The Levinas Reader.* Ed. Sean Hand. Oxford: Basil Blackwell, 1989.

———. *Nine Talmudic Readings.* Trans. Annette Aronowicz. Bloomington: Indiana University Press, 1990.

———. *Of G-d Who Comes To Mind.* Trans. Bettina Bergo. Stanford, CA: Stanford University Press, 1998.

———. *Otherwise than Being or Beyond Essence.* Trans. Alphonso Lingis. The Hague: Nijhoff, 1981.

———. *Outside the Subject.* Trans. Michael B. Smith. Stanford, CA: Stanford University Press, 1994.

———. "The Pact." Trans. Sarah Richmond. *In Sean Hand,* ed. *The Levinas Reader.* Oxford: Basil Blackwell, 1989, pp. 211–26.

———. "Revelation in the Jewish Tradition." Trans. Sarah Richmond. In *Sean Hand,* ed. *The Levinas Reader.* Oxford: Basil Blackwell, 1989, pp. 190–210.

———. *Time and the Other.* Trans. Richard A. Cohen. Pittsburgh: Duquesne University Press, 1987.

———. *Totality and Infinity.* Trans. Alphonso Lingis. Pittsburgh: Duquesne University Press, 1969.

———. "Useless Suffering." Trans. Richard A. Cohen. In Robert Bernasconi and David Wood, eds., *The Provocation of Levinas: Rethinking the Other.* London: Routledge and Kegan Paul, 1988, pp. 156–67.

Levy-Hass, Hanna. *Vielleicht war das alles erst der Anfang: Tagebuch aus dem KZ Bergen Belsen, 1944–1945.* Ed. Eike Geisel. Berlin: Rotbuch, 1969.

Loeve, Yehuda. *Nesivos Olam: Nesiv Hatorah.* Trans. Eliakim Willner. Brooklyn: Mesorah, 1994.

Löwith, Karl. "Last Meeting with Heidegger." In Guenther Neske and Emil Kettering, eds. *Martin Heidegger and National Socialism.* Trans. Lisa Harries. New York: Paragon, 1990, pp. 157–59.

Lubetkin, Zivia. *In the Days of Destruction and Revolt.* Trans. I. Tubbin. Tel Aviv: Hakibbutz Hameuchad, 1981.

Lustig, Arnošt. *A Prayer for Katerina Horovitzova.* Trans. Jeanne Nemcova. New York: Harper & Row, 1973.

Lyotard, Jean-François. *Heidegger and "the jews."* Trans. Andreas Michael and Mark S. Roberts. Minneapolis: University of Minnesota Press, 1990.

Maimonides. *The Commandments.* 2 vols. Trans. Charles B. Chavel. New York: Soncino, 1967.

———. *The Guide for the Perplexed.* Trans. M. Friedlaender. New York: Dover, 1956.

Maybaum, Ignaz. *The Face of G-d after Auschwitz.* Amsterdam: Polak and Van Genep, 1965.

Mechanicus, Philip. *Year of Fear: A Jewish Prisoner Waits for Auschwitz.* Trans. Irene S. Gibbons. New York: Hawthorne, 1964.

Meed, Vladka. *On Both Sides of the Wall.* Trans. Benjamin Meed. Tel Aviv: Hakibbutz Hameuchad, 1973.

Meir ibn Gabbai. *Sod ha-Shabbat.* Trans. Elliot K. Ginsburg. Albany: SUNY Press, 1989.

Mekilta de-Rabbi Ishmael. 3 vols. Trans. Jacob Z. Lauterbach. Philadelphia: Jewish Publication Society, 1961.

Midrash on Psalms. 2 vols. Trans. William G. Braude. New Haven, CT: Yale University Press, 1959.

Midrash Rabbah. 10 vols. Trans. and ed. H. Friedman, Maurice Simon et al. London: Soncino, 1961.

Midrash Tanchuma. 2 vols. Jerusalem: Eshkol, 1935.

Milchman, Alan, and Alan Rosenberg, eds. *Martin Heidegger and the Holocaust.* Atlantic Highlands, NJ: Humanities Press, 1996.

Mitchell, Joseph R., and Helen Buss Mitchell, eds. *The Holocaust: Readings and Interpretations.* New York: McGraw-Hill, 2001.

Mordechai Yosef of Isbitza. *Mei HaShiloach.* Trans and ed. Betsalel Philip Edwards. Northvale, NJ: Jason Aronson, 2001.

Morgan, Michael L., ed. *A Holocaust Reader: Responses To the Nazi Extermination.* New York: Oxford University Press, 2001.

Mosse, George L. *Nazi Culture.* New York: Grosset & Dunlap, 1966.

Müller, Filip. *Auschwitz Inferno: The Testimony of a Sonderkommando.* Trans. Susanne Flatauer. London: Routledge and Kegan Paul, 1979.

Munk, Michael L. *The Wisdom in the Hebrew Alphabet: The Sacred Letters as a Guide to Jewish Deed and Thought.* Brooklyn: Mesorah, 1983.

Nachman of Breslov. *Advice.* Trans. Avraham Greenbaum. Brooklyn: Breslov Research Institute, 1983.

———. *Restore My Soul (Meshivat Nefesh).* Trans. Avraham Greenbaum. Jerusalem: Chasidei Breslov, 1980.

———. *Tikkun.* Trans. Avraham Greenbaum. Jerusalem: Breslov Research Institute, 1984.

Nachmanides. *Commentary on the Torah.* 2 vols. Trans. Charles B. Chavel. New York: Shilo, 1971.

———. *Writings and Discourses.* 2 vols. Trans. Charles B. Chavel. New York: Shilo, 1978.

Nathan of Nemirov. *Rabbi Nachman's Wisdom: Shevachay HaRan and Sichos HaRan.* Trans. Aryeh Kaplan. Ed. Aryeh Rosenfeld. New York: A. Kaplan, 1973.

Neher, André. *The Exile of the Word: From the Silence of the Bible To the Silence of Auschwitz.* Trans. David Maisel. Philadelphia: Jewish Publication Society, 1981.

———. *The Prophetic Existence.* Trans. William Wolf. New York: A. S. Barnes, 1969.

Neske, Guenther, and Emil Kettering, eds. *Martin Heidegger and National Socialism.* Trans. Lisa Harries. New York: Paragon, 1990.

Newman, Louis I., ed. *The Hasidic Anthology.* New York: Schocken Books, 1963.

Nietzsche, Friedrich. *Beyond Good and Evil.* Trans. Walter Kaufmann. New York: Vintage Books, 1966.

———. *The Gay Science.* Trans. Walter Kaufmann. New York: Vintage Books, 1974.

Nomberg-Przytyk, Sara. *Auschwitz: True Tales from a Grotesque Land.* Trans. Roslyn Hirsch. Chapel Hill: University of North Carolina Press, 1985.

Nyiszli, Miklos. *Auschwitz: A Doctor's Eyewitness Account.* Trans. Tibere Kremer and Richard Seaver. New York: Fawcett Crest, 1960.

Pascal, Blaise. *Pensées.* Paris: Club des Libraires de France, 1961.

Patterson, David. *In Dialogue and Dilemma with Elie Wiesel.* Wakefield, NH: Longwood Academic, 1991.

Peli, Pinhas H. *The Jewish Sabbath: A Renewed Encounter.* New York: Schocken Books, 1988.

Perl, Gisella. *I Was a Doctor in Auschwitz.* New York: International University Press, 1948.

Pesikta de-Rab Kahana. Trans. William G. Braude and Israel J. Kapstein. Philadelphia: Jewish Publication Society, 1975.

Pirke de Rabbi Eliezer. Trans. Gerald Friedlander. New York: Hermon Press, 1970.

Pisar, Samuel. *Of Blood and Hope.* Boston: Little, Brown, 1979.

Polen, Nehemia. *The Holy Fire: The Teachings of Rabbi Kalonymus Kalman Shapira.* Northvale, NJ: Jason Aronson, 1999.

Rabinowicz, Harry M. *Hasidism: The Movement and Its Masters.* Northvale, NJ: Jason Aronson, 1988.

Rashi, *Commentary on the Torah.* 2 vols. Trans. M. Rosenbaum and N. M. Silbermann. Jerusalem: The Silbermann Family, 1972.

Ringelblum, Emmanuel. *Notes from the Warsaw Ghetto.* Trans. and ed. Jacob Sloan. New York: Schocken Books, 1974.

———. *Notizn fon Warshever geto.* Warsaw: Yiddish Books, 1952.

Rivosh, Elik. "From the Notebook of the Sculptor Elik Rivosh (Riga)." Trans. David Patterson, in *The Complete Black Book of Russian Jewry,* ed. Ilya Ehrenburg and Vasily Grossman. New Brunswick, NJ: Transaction Publishers, 2002, pp. 396–411.

Rockmore, Tom, and Joseph Margolis, eds. *The Heidegger Case: On Philosophy and Politics.* Philadelphia: Temple University Press, 1992.

Rose, Paul Lawrence. *German Question/Jewish Question.* Princeton: Princeton University Press, 1990.

Rosenberg, Alfred. *Race and Race History and Other Essays.* Ed. Robert Pais. New York: Harper & Row, 1974.

Rosenfeld, Alvin. *A Double Dying: Reflections on Holocaust Literature.* Bloomington: Indiana University Press, 1980.

Rosenfeld, Oskar. *In the Beginning Was the Ghetto: 890 Days in Łódź.* Ed. Hanno Loewy. Trans. Brigitte Goldstein. Evanston: Northwestern University Press, 2002.

Rosenzweig, Franz. *Franz Rosenzweig's "The New Thinking."* Trans and ed. Alan Udoff and Barbara Galli. Syracuse: Syracuse University Press, 1999.

———. *The Star of Redemption.* Trans. William W. Hallo. Boston: Beacon, 1972.

———. *Understanding the Sick and the Healthy.* Trans. Nahum Glatzer. Cambridge: Harvard University Press, 1999.

Roth, John K., and David Patterson, eds. *Fire in the Ashes: God, Evil, and the Holocaust.* Seattle: University of Washington Press, 2005.

Rubinowicz, David. *The Diary of David Rubinowicz.* Trans. Derek Bowman. Edmonds, WA: Creative Options, 1982.

Rubinstein, Donna. *I Am the Only Survivor of Krasnostav.* New York: Shengold, 1982.

Rudashevski, Yitskhok. *The Diary of the Vilna Ghetto.* Trans. Percy Matenko. Tel Aviv: Ghetto Fighters' House and Hakibbutz Hameuchad, 1973.

Rummel, R. J. *Death by Government.* New Brunswick: Transaction Publishers, 1994.

Saadia Gaon. *The Book of Belief and Opinions.* Trans. Samuel Rosenblatt. New Haven: Yale University Press, 1976.

Sacks, Jonathan. *Crisis and Covenant: Jewish Thought after the Holocaust.* Manchester, England: Manchester University Press, 1992.

Salton, George Lucius. *The 23rd Psalm: A Holocaust Memoir.* Madison: University of Wisconsin Press, 2002.

Sandberg, Moshe. *My Longest Year.* Trans. S. C. Hyman. Jerusalem: Yad Vashem, 1968.

Sassoon, Agnes. *Agnes: How My Spirit Survived.* Edgeware, England: Lawrence Cohen, 1983.

Schneerson, Menachem M. *Torah Studies.* Adapted by Jonathan Sacks. 2nd ed. London: Lubavitch Foundation, 1986.

Scholem, Gershom. *Kabbalah.* New York: New American Library, 1974.

Sefer Yetzirah: The Book of Creation. Trans. with commentary by Aryeh Kaplan. York Beach, ME: Samuel Weiser, 1990.

Seidman, Hillel. *Tog-bukh fon Warshever geto.* New York: Avraham Mitlberg, 1947.

Senesh, Hannah. *Hannah Senesh: Her Life and Diary.* Trans. Marta Cohn. New York: Schocken Books, 1972.

Sforno. *Commentary on the Torah.* 2 vols. Trans. Raphael Pelcovitz. Brooklyn: Mesorah, 1987–1989.

Shapell, Nathan. *Witness To the Truth.* New York: David McKay, 1974.

Shapira, Kalonymos Kalmish. *Sacred Fire: Torah from the Years of Fury, 1939–1942.* Trans. J. Hershy Worch. Ed. Deborah Miller. Northvale, NJ: Jason Aronson, 2000.

———. *A Student's Obligation.* Trans. Micha Odenheimer. Northvale, NJ: Jason Aronson, 1991.

Sifre on Deuteronomy. New York: Jewish Theological Seminary, 1993.

Sluga, Hans. *Heidegger's Crisis: Philosophy and Politics in Nazi Germany.* Cambridge: Harvard University Press, 1993.

Steinsaltz, Adin. *The Seven Lights: On the Major Jewish Festivals.* Northvale, NJ: Jason Aronson, 2000.

———. *The Sustaining Utterance: Discourses on Chasidic Thought.* Trans. and ed. Yehuda Hanegbi. Northvale, NJ: Jason Aronson, 1989.

———. *Teshuvah: A Guide for the Newly Observant Jew.* New York: Free Press, 1987.

Sutskever, Abraham. "The Vilna Ghetto." Trans. David Patterson, in *The Complete Black Book of Russian Jewry,* ed. Ilya Ehrenburg and Vasily Grossman. New Brunswick, NJ: Transaction Publishers, 2002, pp. 241–67.

Taminiaux, Jacques. *Heidegger and the Project of Fundamental Ontology.* Trans. and ed. Michael Gendre. Albany: SUNY Press, 1991.

Tillion, Germaine. *Ravensbrück.* Trans. Gerald Satterwhite. Garden City: Doubleday, 1975.

Tory, Avraham. *Surviving the Holocaust: The Kovno Ghetto Diary.* Ed. Martin Gilbert. Trans. Jerzy Michalowicz. Cambridge: Harvard University Press, 1990.

Tosefta. Jerusalem: Wahrmann, 1970.

Trepman, Paul. *Among Men and Beasts.* Trans. Shoshana Perla and Gertrude Hirschler. New York: Bergen-Belsen Memorial Press, 1978.

Vinocur, Ana. *A Book without a Title.* Trans. Valentine Isaac and Ricardo Iglesia. New York: Vantage, 1976.

Vital, Chayyim. *Shaarei Kedushah.* Jerusalem: Eshkol, 2000.

Vrba, Rudolf, and Alan Bestic. *I Cannot Forgive*. New York: Bantam, 1964.

Wasser, Hersh. "Daily Entries of Hersh Wasser." Trans. Joseph Kermish. *Yad Vashem Studies* 15 (1983): 201–82.

Weinreich, Max. *Hitler's Professors: The Part of Scholarship in Germany's Crimes against the Jewish People*. New Haven: Yale University Press, 1999.

Wells, Leon. *The Death Brigade*. New York: Holocaust Library, 1978.

Wiesel, Elie. *Against Silence: The Voice and Vision of Elie Wiesel*. 3 vols. Ed. Irving Abrahamson. New York: Holocaust Library, 1985.

———. *Ani Maamin: A Song Lost and Found Again*. Trans. Marion Wiesel. New York: Random House, 1973.

———. *A Beggar in Jerusalem*. Trans. Lily Edelman and Elie Wiesel. New York: Random House, 1970.

———. *Evil and Exile*. Trans. Jon Rothschild. Notre Dame: University of Notre Dame Press, 1990.

———. *The Forgotten*. Trans. Marion Wiesel. New York: Summit Books, 1992.

———. *From the Kingdom of Memory: Reminiscences*. New York: Summit Books, 1990.

———. *The Gates of the Forest*. Trans. Frances Frenaye. New York: Holt, 1966.

———. *The Golem*. New York: Summit Books, 1983.

———. *A Jew Today*. Trans. Marion Wiesel. New York: Random House, 1978.

———. *The Jews of Silence*. Trans. Neal Kozodoy. New York: Holt, Rinehart & Winston, 1966.

———. *Legends of Our Time*. New York: Avon, 1968.

———. *Messengers of God*. Trans. Marion Wiesel. New York: Random House, 1976.

———. *Night*. Trans. Stella Rodway. New York: Hill and Wang, 1960.

———. *One Generation After*. Trans. Lily Edelman and Elie Wiesel. New York: Pocket Books, 1970.

———. *Paroles d'étranger*. Paris: Éditions du Seuil, 1982.

———. *Somewhere a Master*. Trans. Marion Wiesel. New York: Summit Books, 1982.

———. *Souls on Fire: Portraits and Legends of Hasidic Masters*. Trans. Marion Wiesel. New York: Vintage, 1973.

———. *The Testament*. Trans. Marion Wiesel. New York: Summit Books, 1981.

———. *Twilight*. Trans. Marion Wiesel. New York: Summit Books, 1998.

Wiesenthal, Simon. *The Sunflower.* Trans. H. A. Piehler. New York: Schocken Books, 1976.

Wood, Allen W. "Rational Theology, Moral Faith, and Religion." In Paul Guyer, ed., *The Cambridge Companion To Kant.* Cambridge: Cambridge University Press, 1992, pp. 394–416.

Wundt, Max. *Deutsche Weltanschauung.* Munich: J. F. Lehmans, 1928.

Wyschogrod, Edith. *Spirit in Ashes: Hegel, Heidegger, and Man-Made Death.* New Haven: Yale University Press, 1985.

Yaakov Yosef of Polnoe. *Toledot Yaakov Yosef al HaTorah.* Jerusalem: Agudat Beit-Vialipoly, 1944.

Zalman, Schneur. *Likutei Amarim Tanya.* Trans. Nissan Mindel et al. Brooklyn: Kehot, 1981.

The Zohar. 5 vols. Trans. Harry Sperling and Maurice Simon. London: Soncino, 1984.

Zylberberg, Michael. *A Warsaw Diary.* London: Valentine, Mitchell & Co., 1969.

Zyskind, Sara. *Stolen Years.* Trans. Margarit Inbar. Minneapolis: Lerner, 1981.

INDEX